WILLIAM JENNINGS BRYAN

Orations—Volume twenty-five

ORATIONS

FROM HOMER TO
WILLIAM McKINLEY

EDITED BY

MAYO W. HAZELTINE, A.M.

ILLUSTRATED

IN TWENTY-FIVE VOLUMES

VOL. XXV

NEW YORK
P. F. COLLIER AND SON
MCMII

CONTENTS

VOLUME TWENTY-FIVE

CONTENTS

STUBBS

CHARLES WILLIAM STUBBS, an eminent English author and preacher, was born in Liverpool, September 3, 1845, and received his education at the Royal Institution School in that town and at Sidney Sussex College, Cambridge, where he graduated with high honors. In 1868 he became senior curate of St. Mary's, Sheffield, and from there he was transferred to Granboro', Buckinghamshire, where he was vicar for thirteen years. From 1884 till 1888 he was vicar of Stokenham, South Devon, and from 1888 to 1894 rector of Wavertree, Liverpool. In the latter year he was made Dean of Ely. From 1881 till 1895 he was select preacher at Cambridge, and in 1883 he filled a similar post at Oxford. He served for two years as president of the Liverpool Royal Institution. Among his publications are " Village Politics," addresses and sermons on the labor question (1878); "Christ and Democracy" (1883); "The Conscience, and Other Poems " (1884); "God's Englishmen," sermons on the prophets and kings of England (1887); "The Land and the Laborers" (1890); "Christ and Economics " (1893); "Christus Imperator " (1894); "A Creed for Christian Socialists " (1896); "Pro Patria " (1901). In 1900 he visited the United States, preaching at Harvard University and elsewhere.

INTERNATIONAL PEACE

"A YOUNG MAN'S VISION"

[A sermon preached at the Hague in connection with the Peace Congress, Whit-Sunday, 1899.]

" And it shall come to pass afterward that I will pour out my spirit upon all flesh, and your sons and your daughters shall prophesy, and your old men shall dream dreams, and your young men shall see visions."—Joel ii, 28.

THESE words of the prophet Joel had their fullest accomplishment, as you all know, in that new revelation of God to the world symbolized in the rushing wind and the fiery tongues of Pentecost, which we to-day are commemorating on this Whit-Sunday, on this great Church festival of the Holy Ghost. But the prophetic words have also had a special fulfilment—have been fulfilled from epoch to epoch in the history of the Church of God.

In the ancient Church they found an immediate realization. For almost within the generation in which Joel lived we see the simultaneous rise of prophets of all degrees of cultivation and from every station in life. Amos, the sheep-master of Tekoa, the gatherer of figs, the prophet of simple style and rustic imagery; Zechariah, the cultured priest and gentle, courtly seer; Micah, the wild village anchorite, pouring out his terrible warnings on the drunkenness, the folly, the oppression of his country, and yet telling also of a reign of universal peace when men shall " beat their swords into ploughshares, and their spears into pruning-hooks "; and, greatest of all, Isaiah, the statesman-prophet of Israel, of great and faithful vision, " very bold," as St. Paul says of him, in extending and enlarging the boundaries of the Church, looking beyond the dark and stormy present to the onward destiny of the human race, when God " shall be found of them that seek him not, and made manifest unto them that ask not of him."

These are but a few. There are many prophets of that period whose very names are lost. Some, no doubt, were wild enthusiasts only, whose ravings did perhaps as much harm as good. Some were hypocrites, who " affected the black prophetic dress without any portion of the prophetic spirit." But all were characteristic of one of those great revivals of religion, one of those spiritual flood-tides in the history of humanity, which have, alas! their baser as well as their nobler aspect.

But Joel did more than utter a special prediction for his own time. He declared one of those great principles which, as I have said, are fulfilled over and over again, and play so large a part in human history.

The principle is this: that ever and anon, in a nation's or a Church's history, after some great national calamity, after some long-continued ecclesiastical torpor, there comes a sudden and mighty out-flood of the Spirit, stirring a nation or a people to its depths, vivifying an almost dead Church, rousing dull spirits into energetic life, exalting common men and women above their ordinary selves.

On every side at such periods in the world's history there arise prophets and heroes, warriors and preachers, holy and devoted souls.

Five centuries after Joel, when Israel was a conquered and tributary people, its kings no more, its national and church life crushed down, there came such a flood-tide of the Holy Spirit of God, which is the spirit of holy valor, and patriotism, and national righteousness.

You may read the whole grand story in the Book of Maccabees. It was a time when the tameness and commonness went out of life for all men. New hopes and aims, new daring and strength seemed to pass into every heart. Men and women, in their daily task, lived not only for that, but for their country and their God. Old men dreamed dreams, and young men saw visions, and upon the servants and the handmaids was poured out the new spirit of faithfulness and truth.

Two centuries later the principle was at work again on a vaster scale. The old world was waiting for a new birth. Old religions, old philosophies, old political systems, all seemed to have reached a stage of decrepitude. The power of imperial Rome, the traditional wisdom of Greece, the narrow national cult of the Hebrew,—all seemed to be worn out.

The last element of good seemed to have gone, for hope was dead. The world seemed to have reached—

> " That last drear mood
> Of envious sloth and proud decrepitude:
> No faith, no ark, no king, no priest, no God,
> While round the freezing founts of life in snarling ring
> Crouched on the bare worn sod,
> Babbling about the unreturning spring,
> And whining for dead gods that cannot save,
> The toothless systems shiver to their grave."

But when the hour was darkest there came the new birth, the founding of the Christian Church, the preaching of the Apostles, the fervor of the Martyrs, the wonders of the first Christian age. St. Peter saw the fulfilment of the prophet Joel's words in their fullest sense on the first Whit-Sunday. The chill and gloom of the Crucifixion Day had passed. The little Church of the first Believers had awakened to a sense of its mighty mission, and every member of it felt the glow of inspiration in his earnest heart.

And ever since that time, nearly two thousand years ago now, men have been living under what is called a new dispensation, a new order of things. Ever since that time when the last great crowning revelation of God was made to man there has been in the world a society of men who looked out upon life in a new way.

They looked out upon this matter-of-fact world of ours, and somehow they came to see that it was not only what it appeared to be from outside; they came to see that life, human life, had not only to do with outward things; that they, as men, had not only to obey certain laws of conduct and living, under penalty of punishment from the governor, or the king, or the emperor, whose subjects they were; but they came to see that they were members also of a great invisible kingdom, ruled over by a Lord whose throne was not

upon earth, governed by laws whose sanction rested not in outward things, in penalty or punishment, but lay in a divine compulsion which they felt in their own hearts, in their own inmost spirit, in a conscience, they called it, not a mere outward authority saying to them at every turn. " Thou shalt," and " Thou shalt not," but an inner voice of the soul ever whispering " I ought," and " I ought not."

And this new way of regarding life these men came to think was the most important thing in all the world. They gave up everything, they left their secular callings, their business in life, to go abroad everywhere telling people of this new, wonderful way of regarding things. They could not help it. A mysterious divine compulsion was laid upon them. It burned in their hearts as a divine energy, it touched their tongues with a divine fire.

If we could have asked them what it all meant, they would have said, " It is the baptism of the Holy Ghost and of fire,— it is that enthusiasm, that influence, that energy, which our ascended King promised he would send down upon us, his own Spirit, the Paraclete, the Comforter, the Spirit of Truth who should guide us into all truth."

And, full of this divine compulsion, and because of it, they were able to touch the hearts of other men; they got them to see life as they saw it, to obey the invisible King, as they obeyed him, from love and loyalty of heart; they drew men into their brotherhood, into this society of the Holy Ghost, this spiritual kingdom, this Church of the new believers, of the men who thought about life in a new way.

And now nearly two thousand years, as I said, have passed away, and to-day that little society of earnest believers in that far-distant land has become a mighty corporation, having branches in all parts of the world, with a long history behind

it, a record of heroes, and saints and martyrs, and doctors and
teachers, the holiest and the noblest of our race, and with a
long future before it of beneficence and salvation for the
world.

And in that long history, over and over again as the ages
went on, the words of the prophet Joel have been fulfilled.
For although, alas! it is true that over and over again also
the vision has faded and the prophecy has disappointed; that
at times even the Church itself has only seemed to be
Christian to its own shame and to its Master's dishonor—
"Christiana ad contumeliam Christi"; that the new heavens
and the new earth have never yet fully come; still, still,
thank God, there has been progress—who can deny it?—
progress by periodic movements, flood-tides of the Spirit of
God, on which the ark of humanity and civilization and social
order, the ark of the Church, has ridden nearer and nearer
to the haven where it would be.

> " For while the tired waves, vainly breaking,
>   Seem here no painful inch to gain,
> Far back, through creeks and inlets making,
>   Comes silent, flooding in, the main.
> And not by eastern windows only,
>   When daylight comes, comes in the light,
> In front, the sun climbs slow, how slowly!
>   But westward, look, the land is bright."

For " when Christ ascended up on high, he led captivity
captive and gave gifts unto men ": for the individual the
gift of true life, for society the gift of prophecy and vision
and of dreams.   " I will pour out of my spirit upon all flesh;
and your sons and your daughters shall prophesy, and your
young men shall see visions, and your old men shall dream
dreams."

The gift of Prophecy: the power to recognize new truth
from God and to speak it forth, to interpret it to mankind in
words of fire or deeds of light.

The gift of Vision: the strong, clear grasp of master-ideas, the keen, living sense which a young and generous mind feels for great principles struggling perhaps for life in some mean age of scrambling and selfishness and greed; setting the heart strong and resolute to uphold the cause of righteousness and peace and joy in the Holy Ghost through the coming years.

And the gift of Dreams: no longer the fantastic vision of minds half-dazed with new light, but the conviction of the old man's dearly bought experience, that what perhaps he may be unworthy to see or bring to pass shall yet surely come, shall yet be a common thing full of blessing for the world, and while his own hopes depart of seeing it, yet suffers not his heart to harden, but passes solemnly in spirit into another age, and sees God surely bringing life to its perfect end at last.

It would be impossible, of course, in a single sermon to characterize fully any one of those great epochal movements in the history of Christian civilization which has made modern Christendom what it is to-day. And even if I ask you to think only of one aspect of that civilization,—the origin and growth of sentiments of international morality and law,—a subject which must be in all our minds at this time, in this place, on this historic soil,—it is impossible to do more now than place a cursory finger from point to point on that marvellously diversified chart which shows the onward progress of humanity toward higher and nobler and more Christ-like conceptions of statecraft and government.

It has been said that when Charles the Great knelt by the high altar of St. Peter's, at Rome, and received from the hand of Pope Leo III the crown of the Cæsars, and the shout of the people rang out through the church,—"*Karolo*

Augusto, a Deo coronato, magno et pacifico imperatori, vita et victoria."[1]—modern history began.

Certainly with him began a new vision of power in Europe, new in reality, new in its relations to society. For the first time since the fall of the Roman Empire in the West a great king had arisen among the new nations to rule with strength and glory, a founder of social order, a restorer of religion, a patron of education, a statesman, a legislator, an emperor, as the popular acclaim had entitled him, truly "great and peace-giving," because his aim was not only to conquer and overthrow and selfishly to enjoy, but to labor long and resolutely, and with deliberate purpose, to bring order out of chaos, government out of confusion, for the benefit of man and the good of the peoples.

It is true that his romantic reign of nearly fifty years was but an episode of political order and statesmanship in a wild and tumultuous age, but the work of Charles—a genius preeminently creative—was not lost in the anarchy which followed, for he had laid the foundations upon which, for many generations, men continued to build.

His policy and deeds were gradually wreathed round with a gorgeous mist of legend and romance, but at least he left behind a memory and a tradition of a settled government and of a noble and extensive scheme of polity, an ideal of imperial duty and obligation, to which his successors in a later age could look back with a devout admiration. For so wisdom is justified of all her children, and God fulfils himself in many ways.

And again, in that later time of turbulence and political confusion, through all the disasters of private war and public

---

[1] "To Charles Augustus, crowned of God, the great and peace-giving Emperor, life and victory."

feud which characterized the peoples of Europe from the tenth to the thirteenth centuries, who shall say that the old prophecy of Joel, the newer promises of Pentecost, had no fulfilment? Into "that wilderness of the peoples" the Church of Christ had gone forth, and had proved herself "not only a herald of spiritual blessings and of glorious hopes in another life, but a tamer of cruel natures, the civilizer of the rude, the cultivator of the waste places, the educator, the guide, and the protector" of the weak and oppressed. When little else could be done, was it nothing, do you think, that the Church organized "the Truce of God"?

"From Thursday evening among all Christians"—so ran the words of an ordinance of the Council of Limoges in 1031 —"friends or enemies, neighbors or distant, peace must reign till Monday at sunrise: and during these four days and four nights there ought to exist a complete security, so that every one can go about his own affairs in safety from all fear of his enemies, and under protection of this truce and this peace. Let those who observe this peace be absolved by the Father, All-powerful, by Jesus Christ his Son, and by the Holy Ghost. Let those who have promised truce and have voluntarily broken it be excommunicated by God."

There are many sad chapters, it is true, in the history of Christendom, humiliating to the disciple of Christ, but surely that chapter in the "Gesta Christi" of the Middle Ages is at least a touching one, which, although it tells, first, of desolated towns, depopulated villages, wasted fields, plundered peasants, widows and orphans weeping under the curse of war, yet goes on to speak of that "Crusade of Peace" preached by the Church for two centuries and more, made the subject of conciliar and synodical and episcopal enactment, quieting, if only for a time, the waves of strife, inspiring men with a new spirit of good will and concord and brotherhood, under which, it might be for months, or weeks only, or days, the bloody sword was suffered to rest in its sheath, the homes of the poor to go unplundered, and the unwonted " Peace of God " to fall upon a land drenched with tears and blood.

It was not, however, until the fifteenth century was passed, and the various communities of Europe, each retaining characteristics of its original source, but each also taking to itself, with the assertion of individual freedom, new characteristics, had finally separated by definite national signs into free and liberal States, that the foundation was laid of the modern system of International Policy.

The adoption of standing armies, although they may seem to have created new dangers for our modern industrialism, it must never be forgotten, disarmed war of half its terror. But the need of some recognized code of law to regulate the intercourse of the new nations became pressing. In 1625 the groundwork of such a code was laid by Grotius, Advocate-General of the Treasury of Holland and Pensionary of Rotterdam, in his treatise, " De Jure Belli et Pacis," a work which has been said by jurists to have contributed more than any other uninspired book to the commonwealth of nations.

And indeed, in memory of the Pentecostal promise, ought we to speak of the book as uninspired?

It is true that such a code as that of Grotius could not have arisen in any country where the jurisprudence of ancient Rome had not been the fountain of all legal ideas and the groundwork of all positive codes, nor could it have been written by any man who was not a learned student of that ancient system.

But Hugo Grotius was not only a student of Roman jurisprudence; he was something higher and better. He had been a great Christian poet before he became a great Christian publicist. I venture, therefore, to say that it was because in his youth he had seen poetic visions of the ideal truths of Christianity that in his old age he dreamed wise dreams of the true relations which should bind together the nations of Christendom, and saw clearly how necessary to the maintenance of the social State is the recognition of the sphere of spiritual as well as of temporal government. Certainly his immortal work is permeated, every line of it, in every chapter and in every section, with the Christian spirit. In the first words of his preface he touches the keynote of all Christian progress through comradeship and association when he says:

" The Sacred History doth not a little provoke us to mutual love, by teaching that we are all of us born of the same first parents."

And in the last chapter of his book he strikes once again the true chord of Christian fellowship as he recalls to the memory the parting benediction of the great Master in the memorable words with which he closes:

" A safe and honored peace is not too dearly bought if it may be had by foregoing as well the offending as the charges and damages of war, especially to us Christians, to whom our great Lord and Master hath bequeathed peace as his last legacy. . . . God, who alone can do it, instil these things into the hearts of those who manage the affairs of Christendom ! "

Once more, and lastly, for I must hurry to a conclusion, can we doubt that in our own age the Pentecostal prophecy has been and is being fulfilled? Have we no young men nowadays who see visions, no old men who dream dreams, which it will be good for the world to see realized, even in part, of that divine order in which "God shall fulfil himself," not only "in many ways," but in the one way of perfectness—

> " When shall all men's good
> Be each man's rule, and universal peace
> Lie like a shaft of light across the land,
> And like a lane of beams athwart the sea,
> Through all the circle of the golden year? "

English churchmen, at any rate, cannot certainly at this time forget the example of one great English statesman whose body, just a year ago at Whitsuntide, they were burying in Westminster Abbey " with a nation's lamentation," whose splendid political achievements have left an indelible mark on English statesmanship and on English citizenship, whose voice, in the plenitude of his power and strength, had ever been raised, not only for what he thought the good of his own countrymen, but for the deliverance of the oppressed and downtrodden peoples in any part of Christendom, and whose example of Christian fortitude and patience at the last taught lessons to the English people concerning the reality of religion and the power of prayer in daily life, more potent for the inspiration and ennoblement of national life than all the splendid achievement of the strenuous years that lay behind.

And when we recall these things we cannot forget that it was also to Mr. Gladstone that we owe the Geneva Arbitration of 1872, an event by which two great nations, at a time of great bitterness of popular feeling, and when one side felt itself deeply injured, under circumstances which in all past history would have been thought to justify a declaration of war, deliberately controlled their passion of resentment and

determined to submit their differences to impartial arbitration, a decision which in its issue has not only largely contributed to the happy brotherly relationship of England and
America to-day, but has also thus enabled the modern world
to take probably the greatest step forward in history toward
the application of right reason and Christian wisdom to the
settlement of international disputes.

Nor can we forget many another occasion in which that
great Englishman seemed to be taking a prophet's stand, looking forth on the nations, reading the secret causes which
make them living or dying, and then, " looking beyond the
results of the moment," in the sure conviction of his long
and dearly bought experience, dreamed the old man's dreams,
among others—can we doubt it?—of the golden year of International Peace, " satisfied "—I quote his own words—
" that though to-day may not see it and to-morrow may not
see it, yet the fruits of patience and perseverance will be
reaped in the long future of the nation's existence, when the
reckoning cannot fail."

And, my friends, if, happily synchronizing with the holy
memories of Whitsuntide, the commemoration this week by
English churchmen of their great statesman's death-day a
year ago takes us back in thought to an old man's prophetic
dream, certainly the great event of this week in this place,
to be held by history—God grant it—as a perpetual memory
of blessing to all civilized peoples, speaks in unmistakable
tones of a young man's vision.

Can there be any Christian in this place to-day who, re-
calling the ancient Pentecostal prophecy and promise of
which I have spoken to you, would wish to think that these
last words of the young Tsar's rescript are anything but an
aspiration and a prayer, sincerely responsive to the leading,

piously pleading for the guidance, of God's holy Spirit of Wisdom, Peace, and Love?

"This Conference shall be, by the help of God, a happy presage for the century which is about to open. It would converge in one powerful focus the efforts of all the States which are sincerely seeking to make the great conception of Universal Peace triumph over the elements of trouble and discord. It would at the same time cement their agreement by a corporate consecration of the principles of equity and right on which rest the security of States and the welfare of peoples."

What is it that blocks the way—do we ask?—to this land of Utopia, to the present earthly realization of the young man's vision, the old man's dream?

I can only answer that the mountains of difficulty which some tell us stand in the way are moral difficulties for the most part, faults of character and will, failure of moral courage and purpose,—in a word, want of faith.

And yet, if we be Christians, we cannot, we must not, lose heart. The mountains of difficulty may be there. We cannot deny it. They do block the way to the promised land. But we walk by faith, not by sight. It was a saying of the great Napoleon, looking out from France on the neighboring country of Spain, "There are no more Pyrenees!" The power of the human will, the vaulting ambition of one man, was—so he thought—sufficient to remove this greatest of natural boundaries.

My friends, do we forget the promise of Him who said that by faith we too should remove mountains?

Mountains of difficulty, mountains of misunderstanding, mountains of prejudice, will only vanish before the courage which despises difficulty, before the insight which sees into the heart of stone, before the love which compels confidence.

Ah, yes! the true Christian faith is like that fabled sword of which one reads in the " Song of Roland," by which that renowned Paladin cleft a way for his army through those same Pyrenees mountains to the open land beyond. Such a breach of Roland, doubt it not, will one day be made through the mountain walls of national jealousy and national pride and national prejudice, and open out a way to the land of International Peace.

May God, of his great mercy, send into the hearts of each member of this Peace Congress his great gift of vision! Let us pray for them—and what words could we better use than those in which for so many generations the Church of Christ has yearly sung her Advent antiphon of preparation for the Christmas message of Peace on earth, good will to men—

"O Sapientia! quæ ex ore Altissimi prodiisti, attingens a fine atque ad finem; fortiter suaviterque disponens omnia: veni ad docendum eos viam Prudentiæ!"

A THANKSGIVING FOR WILLIAM SHAKESPEARE

THE BIRTHDAY SERMON PREACHED IN THE COLLEGIATE CHURCH OF THE HOLY TRINITY, STRATFORD-ON-AVON, APRIL 23, 1899

" What thanksgiving can we render again unto God for him, for all the joy? "—1 Thess. iii, 9.

THE special festival of this day—at once a saint's day of the English Church, and a hero-day of the English nation, for it is the Day of St. George, the Patron Saint of England and of Chivalry, and it is the birth-day and death-day of Shakespeare—happens to synchronize this year with the Third Sunday after Easter.

We have already, at our earliest service this morning, celebrated the greatest Eucharist of our Church, that sacrament of thanksgiving for the risen Lord which not only should throw its consecration over all our other acts of worship in this place to-day, but also should consecrate for us all realms of human thought and action. It is quite natural, therefore, that at this later service the "note of thanksgiving" which we would most wish to emphazise should be for him whose power and presence must always, I should imagine, be felt more vividly in this place than elsewhere in England.

In this memorial service, then, "let us render again unto God for him thanksgiving for all the joy," thanksgiving for all the mighty achievement of his poetic genius, of his prophetic vision as a supreme interpreter of human life—"how noble in reason! how infinite in faculty! in apprehension how like a God!"—thanksgiving for all the joy which has come down to us through the centuries as his gift to the English race, to the human race, forever.

And, that I may not be misunderstood, let me repeat that in rendering such debt in this place we need not think we shall be in any sense trenching upon His inviolable honor who must always remain the ever-present centre of our worship here. For it is only through the study of the many and varying qualities of his servants that we learn by degrees to welcome the fulness and the richness of his ideal manhood. Much less in doing this honor to Shakespeare to-day do we arrogate to ourselves any authority of final judgment as to his personal character or life.

In thanking God, then, for the gift of the heroes and the saints, the prophets and the kings of England, for their lives and thoughts, we are recognizing our national benefaction and so far acknowledging the power and love of God in those by whose ministry it was made known to us.

I have already indicated my desire to speak to you to-day of Shakespeare as a national prophet. You will rightly ask me in what sense I use this term. Let me answer you in the words of two modern poets.

In his magnificent prose essay on " The Defence of Poetry," the poet Shelley thus compares the functions of the poet and the prophet:

" Poets, according to the circumstance of the age and nation in which they appeared, were called, in the earlier epochs of the world, legislators or prophets. A poet essentially comprises and unites both these characters. For he not only beholds intensely the present as it is, and discovers those laws according to which present things ought to be ordered, but he beholds the future in the present, and his thoughts are the germs of the flower and fruit of latest time. Not that I assert poets to be prophets in the gross sense of that word, or that they can foretell the form as surely as they foreknow the spirit of events. Such is the pretence of superstition which would make poetry an attribute of prophecy rather than prophecy an attribute of poetry."

And this is how a great American poet, Russell Lowell, has expressed a similar thought in imperishable verse:

" To know the heart of all things was his duty,
    All things did speak to him to make him wise,
And with a sorrowful and conquering beauty
    The soul of all looked grandly from his eyes.
He gazed on all within him and without him,
    He watched the flowing of Time's steady tide,
And shapes of glory floated all about him
    And whispered to him, and he prophesied.
Than all men he more fearless was, and freer,
    And all his brethren cried with one accord—
' Behold the holy man! behold the seer!
    Him who hath spoken with the unseen Lord.' "

But you will ask me very probably, and some of you perhaps with some surprise—Can you really speak of Shakespeare, even in this sense, as a prophet? Can you speak of him in any sense even as a religious man?

My friends, I should not care to speak of him in this place at all if I did not think that he was both.

If the underlying and almighty essence of this world be good, then it is likely—is it not?—that the writer who most deeply approached to that essence will be himself good.

There is a religion of week-days as well as of Sundays, a religion of "cakes and ale" as well as of pews and altar-cloths. This England lay before Shakespeare as it lies before us all, with its green fields, and its long hedgerows, and its many trees, and its great towns, and its endless hamlets, and its motley society, and its long history, and its bold exploits, and its gathering power; and he saw that they were good.

To him, perhaps, more than to any one else, has it been given to see that they were a great unity, a great religious object; that if you could only descend to the inner life, to the deep things, to the secret principles of its noble vigor, to the essence of character, to what we know of Hamlet and seem to fancy of Ophelia, we might, so far as we are capable of so doing, understand the Nature which God has made. Let us, then, think of Shakespeare, not as a teacher of dry dogmas, or a sayer of hard sayings, but as—

> " A priest to us all
> Of the wonder and bloom of the world "—

—a teacher of the hearts of men and women; one from whom may be learned something of that inmost principle that ever modulates—

> " With murmurs of the air,
> And motions of the forest and the sea,
> And voice of living beings, and woven hymns
> Of night and day and the deep heart of man."

Shakespeare was not a prophet or preacher, of course, in the same sense as Mrs. Barbauld, or Dr. Doddridge, or Dr. Watts, or even John Keble But perhaps he was something better and higher. He rises above mere morals, and preaches to us, prophesies to us of life.

The Gospel of Jesus Christ, remember, is not morality only, not a book of morals, but the story of a life; a life in which all men can see the perfection of human character, the divinity of forgiveness, of perpetual mercy, of constant patience, of endless peace, of everlasting gentleness; and is there any prophet of our modern dispensation who knew these things better, or could prophesy of them more vividly through life, than did Shakespeare?

In an evil day too, remember, Shakespeare prophesied; he taught the most gracious and gentle precepts—too good, I fancy, almost to have been listened to, if men had quite known what they were receiving. There are some things in Shakespeare I almost fancy he might have been burnt for had he been a theologian—just as, certainly, there are things about politics, about civil liberty, which, had he been a politician or a statesman, would have brought him to the block. But God made him a player and neither of these other things. And so he could teach a message to his age which it much needed,—lessons of peace, gentleness, mercy, patience, long-suffering. He was no priest, it is true, he waved no censer, yet who can tell, when we consider the thousands of souls who have learned the lessons of Shakespeare, how much he has done to humanize, nay, to Christianize mankind. His doctrine may not be preached to men in set dogma and maxim. It may rather, perhaps, distil as dew. Yet many a man who has read " The Merchant of Venice," or pondered over that sad drama of a sinful soul in " Macbeth," or watched that terrible attempt of the wicked king to pray, in " Hamlet," or in " Measure for Measure " has grasped the key to that marvellously sad but most moral story in the lines :

> " He who the sword of Heaven would bear
> Must be holy as severe,"

—has heard sermons more precious probably than any homilies of the pulpit,—lessons, I venture to think, as sweet or sweeter than any that have fallen on the world since the days of the Apostles.   For think of it for a moment in this way.

We are all familiar with the thought that it is Christ's life which gives to the Master's words their force, and we confess that love of Jesus himself is the only motive strong enough to make men keep his Commandments.   St. John sums up the significance of all that in the phrase—" The Word was made flesh."

It is not irreverence, I think, to point out that Shakespeare's teaching has the same advantage over that of the ordinary preacher that the teaching of the Evangelists has over the teaching of Solomon.   He gives us a man to know instead of a proverb.   It is through words made flesh that he teaches us.

The time at our disposal is all too short, alas! to make this special interpretation of Shakespeare's method as a teacher, as a national prophet, plain to you.

But let me take two concrete examples of his method, which will at any rate furnish, I think, each one of us with two practical lessons for our own every-day working lives.   And the first lesson is an appropriate one for St. George's Day.   For it is a lesson of chivalry.

I am sure that many of you must be familiar with that noble passage in Mr. Ruskin's " Sesame and Lilies " in which that great writer calls attention to the fact that, in the strict sense of the word, Shakespeare has no heroes—only heroines. "There is not one entirely heroic figure," Mr. Ruskin says, "in all his plays, except the slight sketch of Henry the Fifth. . . . Whereas there is hardly a play that has not a perfect woman in it, steadfast in grave hope and errorless purpose; Cordelia, Desdemona, Isabella, Hermione, Imogen, Queen Catherine, Perdita, Sylvia, Viola, Rosalind, Helena, and last, and perhaps loveliest, Virgilia, are all faultless; conceived in the highest heroic type of humanity."

Now the lesson of this fact is not, I think, what Mr. Ruskin apparently conceives it to be. It is not, that is to say, that women are perfect in character—"infallibly faithful, and wise counsellors—incorruptibly just and pure examples—strong always to sanctify, even when they cannot save"—in a way which is not possible to men. But the lesson is surely this, that Shakespeare evidently thought them so. That is the point to be grasped. Shakespeare kept true through his whole life to the youthful, the chivalric, ideal of a good woman, expressed in words which, in "Measure for Measure," he puts into the mouth of the jesting Lucio, describing Isabella,—in her virginal strength and self-possessed dignity, perhaps the noblest of all the heroines of the plays:

> "I hold you as a thing enskyed and sainted;
> By your renouncement, an immortal spirit;
> And to be talked with in sincerity,
> As with a saint."

And, my friends, what is worth remembering about this reverence of Shakespeare for women, which surrounds them for him to the end of his days,—it is in "Winter's Tale," one of his latest plays, that he draws for us the gracious simplicity, the wifely perfection, of Hermione, and in "The Tempest,"

the latest of his plays, the peerless purity, the maiden sweet-
ness, of the most admired Miranda,—with an almost divine
light and glamour, is that it is just what the ordinary man of
the world too often despises as the mistake of his inexperi-
enced youth.

And yet who was more " the man of the world " than
Shakespeare? His knowledge of human nature was immense
and infallible, and in no sense did he avoid the world and its
temptations. He lived, too, in the midst of London town
life, of theatrical life, such as we know it to have been in
Elizabeth's day, coarse, corrupt, feculent; and yet he preserved in his heart the feeling—natural, I venture to assert,
to uncorrupted youth—of the divinity and sacredness of
womanhood, so that in his latest as in his earliest plays his
strong spirit, so keen to detect human weakness and sin, pays
woman the involuntary homage of laying aside, in face of
her excellence, its weapon of criticism. It is Iago, who is
nothing if not critical, who dares to doubt of Desdemona's
truth. He, it is true, as Mrs. Jameson says in her " Characteristics of Women," would have " bedevilled an angel."
But alas! there are men in our own day, who, with none of
Iago's wickedness, in either intention or act, are still tainted
by the evil spirit of the world, and in their inmost thought
dare to judge as he did of the virtue of woman. But such a
man was not Shakespeare. He, at fifty years of age, still
feels, in presence of his heroines, like a lover before his first
love.

Seriously, then, do I beg you to ponder this fact, that the
reverence for woman, which too many men affect to lose in
their teens, was retained by the myriad-minded Shakespeare
to the end of his days.

One further word and lesson. You remember the char-

acter of Prospero in " The Tempest." Did it ever strike you
to identify that great enchanter with Shakespeare himself in
the closing years of life? The thought is surely a fruitful
one. For " The Tempest," the latest of all his plays, is an
ideal allegory of human life, with under-meanings everywhere, in every line of it, for those who have eyes to see
and ears to hear; but with all its lessons unforced, unso-
phisticated, illusive, unperceived indeed by those whose eyes
are closed, whose ears are dull of hearing; the scene of it
nowhere, anywhere, for it is in the Fortunate Island of the
soul of man, that vexed land of Imagination hung between
the upper and the nether world; the characters of it, types,
abstractions—Womanhood, Youth, the People—all of them,
more or less, victims of illusion, all of them losing their way
in this enchanted Realm of Life, except only Prospero, the
great Mage, absolute lord of the Island, who could summon
to his service, at a moment's notice, every shape of merriment
or of passion, every figure in the great tragi-comedy of life,
and who, being none other surely than Shakespeare himself,
" not one, but all mankind's epitome," could run easily
through the whole scale of human passion and thought, from
" Nature's wood-notes wild," or the homely commonplaces of
existence, the chimney-corner wisdom of " Master Goodman
Dull," to the transcendental subtilties of—

> " No, Time, thou shalt not boast that I do change,
> Thy pyramids built up with newer light
> To me are nothing novel, nothing strange,
> They are but dressings of a former sight."

It is not only because Prospero was a great enchanter,
about to break his magic staff, to " drown his book deeper
than ever plummet sounded," to dismiss his " airy spirits,"
and to return to the practical service of the State, that we

identify the Philosopher Duke with Shakespeare the Poet
Prophet. It is rather because the temper of Prospero is the
temper of Shakespeare in those last days, when he came back
to the dear old English home here in Stratford, to its sweet-
est, simplest, homeliest things, finding the daily life of this
little place, the men and women here, the Nature all around,
the green fields, the sweet hedgerow flowers, the quiet woods,
the softly flowing Avon, good enough for him; despising
nothing as common or unclean; curious of all things and of
all men, but never scornful; humorous, sympathetic, toler-
ant; his wide-viewing mind at last looking back from the
altitudes of thought to which he had attained, on all the
pageantry of the lower world which he had abandoned,
through a strange, pathetic, ideal light.

> " Our revels now are ended: these our actors,
> As I foretold you, were all spirits, and
> Are melted into air, into thin air:
> And, like the baseless fabric of this vision,
> The cloud-capp'd towers, the gorgeous palaces,
> The solemn temples, the great globe itself,
> Yea, all which it inherit, shall dissolve;
> And, like this insubstantial pageant faded,
> Leave not a rack behind. We are such stuff
> As dreams are made of, and our little life
> Is rounded with a sleep. Sir, I am vex'd;
> Bear with my weakness; my old brain is troubled
> Be not disturb'd with my infirmity:
> If you be pleased, retire into my cell,
> And there repose; a turn or two I'll walk,
> To still my beating mind."

And so he ends—Prospero or Shakespeare. In the epilogue
to the play you have the keynote of this self-mastered character, this self-possessed grandeur of a completely disciplined
will which is common to both, to Shakespeare as to Prospero—Forgiveness and Freedom.

> " And my ending is despair,
> Unless I be relieved by prayer;
> Which pierces so, that it assaults
> Mercy itself, and frees all faults."

And so, too, I will end—how better?—with those lessons of Freedom and Forgiveness; the true Freedom which only comes from service, the true Pardon which only comes to those who forgive, because they have been forgiven.

Have you learned those lessons? The root of all true religion, believe me, lies there. What do you know of the true "service which is perfect freedom"? What is your definition of life? How do you conceive of it to yourself? Is it, do you think, as Shakespeare has elsewhere said—" a tale told by an idiot, signifying nothing"? or is it a mission of service to your fellows for Christ's sake?

God grant you may answer—Life is service! Life is duty! Life is mission! All for Love and the world well lost. For Jesus said—" Whosoever would save his life shall lose it; but whosoever shall lose his life for my sake shall save it."

And the lesson of Pardon—have you made that, too, yours? "The tongues of dying men"—our poet says—"enforce attention like deep harmony." And from the Cross of Jesus and his last dying prayer—" Father, forgive them; for they know not what they do"—we have all learned—God grant it!—to recognize the ethical beauty of the spirit of forgiveness; but do we equally acknowledge its moral power? its redeeming power? "Father! . . . forgive us our trespasses, as we forgive them that trespass against us."

So daily we pray. Brothers! Sisters! do we truly realize this power of forgiveness, this social power of remitting or retaining sins, this priestly power of humanity?

Ah! believe me, just so far as we exercise it lovingly and wisely in our lives and with our lips we help men away from sin; just so far as we do not exercise it, or exercise it wrongly, we drive men into sin. And, my friends, from which of your Christian teachers will you learn of that un-

strained " quality of mercy "—of that earthly power of free
forgiveness " which then shows likest God's when mercy sea-
sons justice "—more unerringly than you will from Shakespeare? He was no priest, I repeat; he waved no censer. But
just as in regard to that other lesson of Freedom, Shakespeare does seem to give to each one of us courage, and
energy, and strength to dedicate ourselves and our work to
that service, to that mission—whatever it may be—which life
has revealed to us as best, and highest, and most real,—so,
also, with regard to this other lesson of the redemptive power
of a priestly humanity, this social force of true forgiveness,
I do not hesitate to say that in Shakespeare's censer there
burns truly, and fragrantly, and steadily—

> " Such incense as of right belongs
>   To the true shrine,
> Where stands the Healer of all wrongs,
>   In light Divine."

PARNELL

CHARLES STEWART PARNELL, the greatest organizer whom the Irish people have ever known, with the doubtful exception of O'Connell, was born at Avondale, County Wicklow, Ireland, in 1846. His father was a country gentleman of good estate, belonging to an old and well-known Protestant family. Through his mother C. S. Parnell was a grandson of Commodore Stewart of the United States Navy. He was sent to the English University of Cambridge, and for some years after he obtained his baccalaureate degree it seemed likely that he would lead a quiet life on the paternal acres. In 1875, however, he entered Parliament as a supporter of the Home Rule movement, which was at that time directed by Mr. Isaac Butt. Mr. Parnell soon became convinced that Mr. Butt's method of furthering the agitation was academic and futile, and that Englishmen would never listen to Irish claims until they should be compelled to do so by the stoppage of the whole machinery of legislation through parliamentary obstruction. To offering such obstruction he devoted all his efforts, and with such effect as presently to wring from Englishmen as well as Irishmen an admission that he had discovered an almost irresistible instrument of constitutional propaganda. In 1879 he was made President of the Irish Land League, and under the Coercion Act of 1881–82 he was temporarily imprisoned. Thereafter he so thoroughly gained the confidence of his countrymen that at the general election of December, 1885, he succeeded in returning to the House of Commons a compact band of 86 Home Rulers, and thus acquired the balance of power in that body, where the Liberals and the Conservatives were nearly equal in respect of numbers. The outcome of the situation was an alliance between Mr. Parnell and Mr. Gladstone and the latter's introduction of the first Home Rule Bill, which, however, was defeated by the secession of the Unionist-Liberals. Some years later Mr. Parnell was deposed from the leadership of the Irish Nationalist Party by a majority of his followers, owing to his implication in the O'Shea divorce case as co respondent. He was shattered in body as well as spirit by the blow, and died in October, 1891, the year preceding that in which Mr. Gladstone was restored to power with a majority of 40 in the House of Commons. Had Parnell lived and remained the head of an undivided Nationalist party, the majority would probably have been a hundred instead of forty, and the second Home Rule bill, notwithstanding the opposition which it encountered in the House of Lords, would probably have become a law.

(10571)

AGAINST NONRESIDENT LANDLORDS

FROM THE SPEECH DELIVERED IN ST. LOUIS, MARCH 4, 1880

MR. PRESIDENT AND LADIES AND GENTLEMEN:—I thank you for this magnificent meeting—a splendid token of your sympathy and appreciation for the cause of suffering Ireland. It is a remarkable fact that while America, throughout the length and breadth of her country, does her very utmost to show her sympathy and send her practical help to our people; while there is scarcely any hand save America's between the starvation of large masses of the western peasantry, England alone of almost all the civilized nations does scarcely anything, although close beside Ireland, to help the terrible suffering and famine which now oppress that country. I speak a fact when I say that if it had not been for the help which has gone from America during the last two months among these, our people would have perished ere now of starvation. . . .

We are asked: "Why do you not recommend emigration to America?" and we are told that the lands of Ireland are too crowded. The lands of Ireland are not too crowded; they are less thickly populated than those of any civilized country in the world; they are far less thickly populated—the rich lands of Ireland—than any of your Western States. It is only on the barren hillsides of Connemara and along the west Atlantic coast that we have too thick a population, and it is only on the unfertile lands that our people are allowed to live. They are not allowed to occupy and till the rich lands; these rich lands are retained as preserves for landlords, and as vast grazing tracts for cattle.   And although emigration might be a temporary alleviation of the trouble in Ireland, it would be a cowardly step on our part; it would be running away from our difficulties in Ireland, and it would be an acknowledgment of the complete conquest of Ireland by England, an acknowledgment which, please God! Ireland shall never make.

No! we will stand by our country, and whether we are exterminated by famine to-day, or decimated by English bayonets to-morrow, the people of Ireland are determined to uphold the God-given right of Ireland—to take her place among the nations of the world.   Our tenantry are engaged in a struggle of life and death with the Irish landlords.   It is no use to attempt to conceal the issues which have been made there.   The landlords say that there is not room for both tenants and landlords, and that the people must go, and the people have said that the landlords must go.   But it may—it may, and it undoubtedly will happen in this struggle that some of our gallant tenantry will be driven from their homes and evicted.   In that case we will use some of the money with which you are intrusting us in this country for the purpose of finding happier homes in this far western land for those of our expatriated people, and it will place us in a position of great power, and give our people renewed confidence in their struggle, if they are assured that any of them who are evicted in their attempts to stand by their rights will get one hundred and fifty good acres of land in Minnesota, Illinois, or some of your fine Western States.

Now the cable announces to us to-day that the government is about to attempt to renew the famous Irish Coercion acts which expired this year. Let me explain to you what these Coercion acts are. Under them the Lord Lieutenant of Ireland is entitled at any time to proclaim in any Irish county, forbidding any inhabitant of that county to go outside of his door after dark, and subjecting him to a long term of imprisonment with hard labor if he is found outside his door after dark. No man is permitted to carry a gun, or to handle arms in his house; and the farmers of Ireland are not even permitted to shoot at the birds when they eat the seed corn on their freshly sowed land. Under these acts it is also possible for the Lord-Lieutenant of Ireland to have any man arrested and consigned to prison without charge, and without bringing him to trial; to keep him in prison as long as he pleases; and circumstances have been known where the government has arrested prisoners under these Coercion acts, and has kept them in solitary confinement for two years and not allowed them to see a single relative or to communicate with a friend during all that period, and has finally forgotten the existence of the helpless prisoners. And this is the infamous code which England is now seeking to re-enact. I tell you, when I read this despatch, strongly impressed as I am with the magnitude and vast importance of the work in which we are engaged in this country, that I felt strongly tempted to hurry back to Westminster in order to show this English Government whether it shall dare, in this year 1880, to renew this odious code with as much facility as it has done in former years. We shall then be able to put to a test the newly-forged gagging rules that they have invented for the purpose of depriving the Irish members of freedom of speech. And I wish to express my belief, my firm conviction, that if the Irish members do their duty that it will be impossible that this infamous statute can be re-enacted; and if it again finds its place upon the statute book, 1 say that the day upon which the royal assent is given to that Coercion Act will sound the knell of the political future of the Irish people. . . .

And now, I thank you in conclusion for the magnificent service that you are doing for the cause of Ireland. Keep up this work; help to destroy the Irish land system which hangs like a millstone around the necks of our people, and when we have killed the Irish land system we shall have done much to kill English misgovernment in Ireland.

We cannot give up the right of Ireland to be a nation, and although we may devote all our energies to remove the deadly upas tree of Irish landlordism, yet still you will trust us and believe that above and before all we recognize and are determined to work for the right of Ireland to regain her lost nationhood. We believe that Ireland is eminently fitted to take her place among the nations of the world. A people who can boast of such a history as ours; who can boast of martyrs like Robert Emmet, whose memory we celebrate to-day; who have had such leaders as Lord Edward Fitzgerald and Wolfe Tone; whose literature has been enriched by a Davis—I say that such a people has shown that although we may be kept down for a time, we cannot long continue deprived of our rights. And I, for one, feel just as convinced that Ireland will be a nation some day or other, as I feel convinced that in a year or two the last vestiges of landlordism will have disappeared from the face of our country.

B

ON THE COERCION BILL

[In the former part of this speech, delivered in the House of Commons, April 18, 1887, Mr. Parnell denounced as a forgery the letter purporting to have been written by him, as giving countenance to the Phœnix Park murders, and published in facsimile in " The Times " of this date.]

SIR,—The right honorable gentleman [Mr. A. J. Balfour] refrained from answering the speech which I delivered on the first reading of this Bill, and the Government refused to allow the adjournment of the debate, in order that some other member of the Government should have an opportunity of answering it the next day; and now, upon the second reading of this Bill, he goes back to the speech, and he attempts an answer to it, at a time of the night when he knows perfectly well that no reply can be made to him; and, with characteristic unfairness—an unfairness which I suppose we may expect to be continued in the future—he has refused to me the ten or twelve minutes that I should have craved to refer to a villainous and barefaced forgery which appeared in the " Times " of this morning, obviously for the purpose of influencing the Division, and for no other purpose.

I got up when the right honorable gentleman the member for Midlothian [Mr. Gladstone] sat down. I had not intended to have made a speech at all upon the second stage of this Bill. I should not have said more than a very few words in reference to this forgery; but I think I was entitled to have had from the right honorable gentleman an opportunity of exposing this deliberate attempt to blacken my character at some time when there would have been some chance of what I stated reaching the outside world.

I say there is no such chance now. I cannot suppose the right honorable gentleman, in refusing me the ten minutes which I crave, had not in his eye the design of practically preventing my denial of this unblushing calumny having that effect upon public opinion which it would otherwise have had if it had been spoken at a reasonable hour of the night.

It appears that, in addition to the passage of this Coercion Act, the dice are to be loaded—that your great organs of public opinion in this country are to be permitted to pay miserable creatures for the purpose of producing these calumnies. Who will be safe in such circumstances and under such conditions? I do not envy the right honorable gentleman the Chief Secretary for Ireland, this first commencement of suppression of defence—this first commencement of calumny and of forgery which has been made by his supporters.

We have heard of the misdeeds of Mr. Ford, the editor of the "Irish World," but Mr. Ford never did anything half so bad as this.

[Mr. A. J. Balfour.—I do not wish to interrupt the honorable member; but as he makes these accusations, I should like to explain that I intervened between the honorable gentleman and the House simply because I understood that it had been arranged that I should follow the right honorable member for Midlothian, and that the honorable member would follow me. No hint reached me that he was going to confine himself to an explanation of, or deal at all with, the accusation in the "Times" to which he has referred. No hint of that kind reached me, and I conceive that the honorable member might have risen, had he wished, at any time earlier in the evening.]

I was asked officially, at an early hour in the evening, whether I would speak after the right honorable member for Midlothian, and I replied that I would, and that I only intended to say a few words in reference to this calumny. I think I ought to have been given the opportunity which I desired.

Now, sir, when I first heard of this precious concoction—I heard of it before I saw it, because I do not take in or even read the " Times " usually—when I heard that a letter of this description, bearing my signature, had been published in the " Times," I supposed that some autograph of mine had fallen into the hands of some person for whom it had not been intended, and that it had been made use of in this way.

I supposed that some blank sheet containing my signature, such as many members who are asked for their signature frequently send—I supposed that such a blank sheet had fallen into hands for which it had not been intended, and that it had been misused in this fashion, or that something of that kind had happened.

But when I saw what purported to be my signature, I saw plainly that it was an audacious and unblushing fabrication. Why, sir, many members of this House have seen my signature, and if they will compare it with what purports to be my signature in the " Times " of this morning, they will see that there are only two letters in the whole name which bear any resemblance to letters in my own signature as I write it.

I cannot understand how the conductors of a responsible, and what used to be a respectable, journal, could have been so hoodwinked, so hoaxed, so bamboozled, and that is the most charitable interpretation which I can place on it, as to publish such a production as that as my signature.

My writing—its whole character—is entirely different. I unfortunately write a very cramped hand; my letters huddle into each other, and I write with very great difficulty and slowness. It is, in fact, a labor and a toil to me to write

anything at all. But the signature in question is written by
a ready penman, who has evidently covered as many leagues
of letter-paper in his life as I have yards.

Of course, this is not the time, as I have said, to enter into
full details and minutiæ as to comparisons of handwriting;
but if the House could see my signature, and the forged, the
fabricated signature, they would see that, except as regards
two letters, the whole signature bears no resemblance to
mine.

The same remark applies to the letter. The letter does
not purport to be in my handwriting. We are not informed
who has written it. It is not alleged even that it was written
by anybody who was ever associated with me. The name of
this anonymous letter-writer is not mentioned. I do not
know who he can be. The writing is strange to me. I think
I should insult myself if I said—I think, however, that I perhaps ought to say it, in order that my denial may be full and
complete—that I certainly never heard of the letter.

I never directed such a letter to be written. I never saw
such a letter before I saw it in the " Times " this morning.
The subject-matter of the letter is preposterous on the surface.
The phraseology of it is absurd—as absurd as any phraseology that could be attributed to me could possibly be. In
every part of it, it bears absolute and irrefutable evidence of
want of genuineness and want of authenticity.

Politics are come to a pretty pass in this country when a
leader of a party of eighty-six members has to stand up, at
ten minutes past one, in the House of Commons, in order to
defend himself from an anonymous fabrication, such as that
which is contained in the " Times " of this morning. I have
always held, with regard to the late Mr. Forster, that his treatment of his political prisoners was a humane treatment, and

a fair treatment; and I think for that reason alone, if for no other, he should have been shielded from such an attempt as was made on his life by the Invincible Association.

I never had the slightest notion in the world that the life of the late Mr. Forster was in danger, or that any conspiracy was on foot against him, or any other official in Ireland or elsewhere. I had no more notion than an unborn child that there was such a conspiracy as that of the Invincibles in existence, and no one was more surprised, more thunderstruck, and more astonished than I was when that bolt from the blue fell upon us in the Phœnix Park murders.

I know not in what direction to look for this calamity. It is no exaggeration to say that if I had been in the park that day I would gladly have stood between Lord Frederick Cavendish and the daggers of the assassins, and, for the matter of that, between their daggers and Mr. Burke too.

Now, sir, I leave this subject. I have suffered more than any other man from that terrible deed in the Phœnix Park, and the Irish nation has suffered more than any other nation through it.

I go for a moment to the noble Marquis the member for Rossendale [the Marquis of Hartington]. The noble Marquis made a rather curious complaint of me. He said that, having denied point-blank a charge that had been made by him against me and the National League during the general election last year, he was rather surprised that I did not again refer to the matter in the House of Commons.

Well, I was rather surprised that the noble Marquis made a charge which he advanced without a particle of truth. He advanced that charge again to-night without a particle of proof, and I deny that charge, as I denied it before, in point-blank terms.

I said it was absolutely untrue to say that the Irish National League or the Parliamentary Party had ever had any communication whatever, direct or indirect, with a Fenian organization in America or this country. I further said that I did not know who the leaders of the Fenian organization in this country or America were.

I say that still. But the noble Marquis says he knows who they are, at least he tells us that Mr. Alexander Sullivan—I believe that was the name mentioned—was president of the Clan-na-Gael, or Fenian organization. When I asked him how he obtained his knowledge, he said that he obtained it from information he received as a member of her Majesty's Government.

That may be. But I am not in possession of the information with regard to the Clan-na-Gael which is possessed by the members of the present, or of the late Government. The Clan-na-Gael is a secret organization; it is an oath-bound organization; it gives no information with regard to its members to persons who are not members. I presume that the Government, if they obtained their information with regard to Alexander Sullivan, obtained it through their secret agents in America, through means which are not open to me in any capacity as a private person or a public politician.

It is no answer to me to say that because the noble Marquis, a member of the late Government, with all the information obtainable by the wealth and resource of that Government at his disposal, believes Alexander Sullivan was a member and the leader of the Clan-na-Gael, or any secret organization in America.

I have never had any dealings with him, or anyone else, either in Ireland or America, in respect to the doings or proceedings of any secret society whatsoever.

All my doings on, and sayings and doings in Irish public life have been open and above board, and they have stood the test of the searching investigation of the three years' administration of the Crimes Act by Lord Spencer, who has left it on record that neither any of my colleagues nor myself were in any way connected with the commission of, or approving of the commission of, any crime. Here are Lord Spencer's words spoken at Newcastle on the 21st of April 1886:

"Foremost among the many objections are these: It is said that you are going to hand over the government of Ireland to men who have encouraged—nay, some I have heard say even have directed—outrage and crime in Ireland. That is a very grave accusation. Now, I have been in a position in my official capacity to see and know nearly all the evidence that has been given in Ireland in regard to the murder and conspiracies to murder that took place in 1881 and 1882, and I can say, without doubt or hesitation, that I have neither heard nor seen any evidence of complicity with those crimes against any of the Irish representatives.

"It is right that I should clearly and distinctly express my condemnation of many of the methods by which they carried on their agitation. They often used language and arguments that were as unjustifiable as they were unfounded. They sometimes, perhaps from financial grounds, were silent when words would have been golden, when words might have had a great influence on the state of the country. They might even have employed men for their own legitimate purposes who had been employed in illegal acts by others; this I must say, but, on the other hand, I believe those men to have an affection for, and a real interest in, the welfare of their country. Their ability has been shown and acknowledged in the House of Commons by all parties. I believe that, with full responsibility upon them, they will show that the only true way of obtaining the happiness and contentment of Ireland, is for the Government to maintain law and order, and defend the rights and privileges of every class and of every man in the country."

I cordially re-echo those words. I believe that that expresses the only real way of maintaining law and order in any country—that you must obtain from the majority of the people of the country sympathy toward the law, without which the maintenance of the law is impossible; that you must show the majority of the community that the law is not only made, but that it is also administered for their benefit, and fairly and justly to all classes.

In this way, and in this way only, can you ever obtain respect and sympathy for law and order in Ireland, or anywhere else. The present Bill may put down crime, or it may increase crime. If it puts it down, it will not put it down by instilling in the minds of the people a sympathy for law and order. Crime will die out only as the effect of sullen submission. You will be no farther, after you have been administering your Crimes Act, in the direction of the real maintenance of law and order than you were at the beginning; nay, not nearly so far.

You are crushing by this iron Coercion Bill those beneficial symptoms in Ireland which a Government of wise statesmen and wise administrators would cherish and foster. You are preventing that budding of friendship between the two countries which this generation would never have witnessed in Ireland had it not been for the great exertions of the right honorable member for Midlothian.

Who could have predicted, who would have ventured to predict, that the heat, the passion, the political antipathies engendered by the working of the Protection Act of 1881 and the Crimes Act of 1882 would have all disappeared in three or four short months, and that you would have had the English and the Irish people regarding each other as they did during that happy, that blessed period, and all this to be put an end to by the mad, the fatuous conduct of the present Government.

You are going to plunge everything back into the seething cauldron of disaffection. You cannot see what the results of all this may be. We can only point to the experience of what has happened in past times. We anticipate nothing beneficial from this Bill, either to your country or to ours; and we should not be honest men if we did not warn you, with all the little force at our command, of the terrible dangers that may be before you.

I trust before this Bill goes into Committee, or at all events, before it leaves Committee, the great English people will make their voices heard, and impress upon their representatives that they must not go on any further with this coercive legislation.

If this House and its majority have not sense enough to see this, the great heart of this country will see it, for I believe it is a great and generous heart, that can sympathize even when a question is concerned in reference to which there have been so many political antipathies. I am convinced, by what I have seen of the great meetings which have been held over the length and breadth of England and Scotland, that the heart of your nation has been reached—that it has been touched, and though our opponents may be in a majority to-day, that the real force of public opinion is not at their back.

A Bill which is supported by men, many of whom are looking over their shoulders and behind them, like the soldiers of an army which a panic is beginning to reach, to see which is their readiest mode of retreat, is not likely to get through the difficult times before it emerges from Committee. The result will be modifications of the provisions of the most drastic of the Coercion Acts ever introduced against Ireland since 1833.

Do not talk to me of comparing the suspension of the Habeas Corpus Act with the present Bill. We have suffered from both. We have suffered from some of the provisions of the present Bill, as well as from the Habeas Corpus Suspension Act, and we are able to compare the one with the other; and I tell you that the provisions of the Habeas Corpus Suspension Act empowered you to arrest and detain in prison those whom you suspected; but it guaranteed them humane treatment, which did much to soften the asperities that otherwise would have been bred between the two nations by that Act. Your prisoners under the Habeas Corpus Act were not starved and tortured as they will be under this. Your political prisoners were not put upon a plank bed, and fed on sixteen ounces of bread and water per day, and compelled to pick oakum, and perform hard labor, as they will be under this Bill.

The Bill will be the means by which you will be enabled to subject your political prisoners to treatment in your jails which you reserve in England for the worst of criminals, and it is idle to talk about comparison between the suspension of the Habeas Corpus Act, under which your prisoners were humanely and properly treated—although imprisonment is hard to bear under the best circumstances; but in the position in which this Bill will place them, your political prisoners will be deliberately starved with hunger and clammed with cold in your jails. I trust in God, sir, that this nation and this House may be saved from the degradation and the peril that the mistake of passing this Bill puts them in.

DAVITT

MICHAEL DAVITT, a noted Irish political leader, was born of peasant parentage at Straide, County Mayo, Ireland, March 25, 1846. His parents, being evicted in 1851, removed to Lancashire, where the son worked in a cotton factory until he was eleven, and then, after a few years' schooling, became a printer. Joining the Irish movement in 1865, he was tried in London in 1870 for " treason-felony " and sentenced to fifteen years' penal servitude, but after seven and a half years' confinement in Dartmoor prison he was released on a ticket of leave. With Parnell and others he founded the Irish Land League in 1879 and was arrested the same year for seditious speaking, but was soon released. In 1881 he was again arrested on a similar charge and was sent to Portland prison for fifteen months, and in 1883 was once more arrested and imprisoned for three months. While detained in the Portland prison he was elected to Parliament, but was disqualified by vote of the House of Commons, and when once again elected in 1892 was unseated. The same year, however, he entered unopposed for Cork, but resigned in 1893. In 1895 he was returned to the House of Commons from East Kerry and South Mayo, retaining his seat until 1899. He published " Leaves from a Prison Diary " (1884); " Defence of the Land League " (1891); " Life and Progress in Australia " (1898).

IN DEFENCE OF THE LAND LEAGUE

FROM SPEECH DELIVERED BEFORE THE SPECIAL COMMISSION,
OCTOBER, 1889

I AM only too sensible of the fact that I have trespassed upon the patience and forbearance of the court to an extent which, possibly, would not be permitted to a lawyer. I am thankful, therefore, for such latitude, as well as for the unfailing fairness and courtesy of your lordships toward me, personally, from the very commencement of this inquiry.

I know too well I have spoken hot words and resorted to hard phrases in arguments, which may have been out of place in the calm region of a court like this. But that was because

(10586)

I felt that the character of the charges I have tried to meet and to answer was such as merited the strongest possible language of condemnation. I came here to address this court contrary to the advice of Mr. Parnell, who was the central figure and chief object of the " Times's " malignant allegations.

I have therefore spoken only for myself. I felt that it was my duty to come here, no matter who should advise me to the contrary. I may be wrong in my opinion, but I thought and believed that if one with my record of suffering, physical and otherwise, at the hands of Irish landlordism and Castle rule; of the conflict of a lifetime with the law as it has been administered in Ireland, and of the punishment which that conflict has entailed: I felt and believed, if I came before this tribunal and pleaded, in my own way, the cause of the Celtic peasantry of Ireland, that perhaps the story which I have told and the case which I have submitted might possibly, in part or in whole, arrest the attention of the people of Great Britain when they come to study your lordships' labors and report.

And I thought and hoped that in the defence which I have made there might possibly be found some help in the task of finally solving this Anglo-Irish struggle. Should my hope be realized, should I have contributed but in the least possible degree to point to a just and feasible solution of a problem which would bring peace and some chance of prosperity to Ireland, I shall be happy in the recollection of the task which I am now bringing to a close.

I can only say that I represent the working classes of my country here as I did in the Land League movement, and I know they feel, as I do, that, no matter how bitter past memories have rankled in our hearts, no matter how much

we have suffered in the past in person or in our country's
cause, no matter how fiercely some of us have fought against
and denounced the injustice of alien misgovernment; I know
that, before a feeling of kindness and of good will on the
part of the people of England, Scotland, and Wales, and in
a belief in their awakening sense of justice toward our country, all distrust and opposition and bitter recollections will
die out of the Irish heart, and the Anglo-Irish strife will
terminate forever when landlordism and Castle rule are dethroned by Great Britain's verdict for reason and for right.

My lords, I now bring my observations to a close. Whatever legal points are to occupy your lordships' study and care
in this long and arduous investigation, it will appear to the
public, who will study the report or the decision of this
tribunal, that two institutions stood indicted before it.

One has had a life of centuries, the other an existence of
but a few brief years. They are charged, respectively, by
the accused and the accusers, with the responsibility for the
agrarian crimes of the period covered by this inquiry.

One is Irish Landlordism, the other is the Irish Land
League. The " Times " alleges that the younger institution
is the culprit. The Land League, through me, its founder,
repels the accusation, and counter-charges landlordism with
being the instigation and the cause, not alone of the agrarian
violence and crimes from 1879 to 1887, but of all which are
on record, from the times spoken of by Spenser and
Davis in the days of Elizabeth, down to the date of this
Commission.

To prove this real and hoary-headed culprit guilty, I have
not employed or purchased the venal talent of a forger, or
offered the tempting price of liberty for incriminatory
evidence to unhappy convicts in penal cells. Neither have

I brought convicted assassins or professional perjurers, like the Delaneys and Le Carons, before your lordships. I have not sought assistance such as this with which to sustain my case. Nor have I been aided by the Colemans, Buckleys, and Igos as confederates, or had to scour the purlieus of American cities for men who would sell evidence that might repair the case which Richard Pigott's confession destroyed, and which his self-inflicted death has sealed with tragic emphasis.

I did not go to such sources or resort to such means for testimony against Irish landlordism. I relied not upon the swearing of spies or informers, but upon disinterested facts, left as legacies to Truth by men who are held in reverence by England for services rendered to their country, to justice, to humanity.

I have reproduced the words which these men have placed on record against crime-begetting Irish landlordism. Among those quoted as authorities, but not of them, one with them in their verdicts, though not to be classed otherwise with honored names, I have placed the " Times " newspaper, which is the Land League's accuser: I have made it speak its own condemnation and compelled it historically to exculpate the League. The face of what the first editorial ever written in the " Times " likened to the pagan deity, Janus,—the face which circumstances have sometimes forced to look toward Truth by power akin to that which compels matter to look toward the sun,—I have made to confront and shame, by contrast, the other face of fraud and falsehood, which, like an evil genius, has led England to regard with hate and distrust every effort of the Irish people for right and justice.

I have made the " Times " of 1847 and of 1880 give the lie direct to the " Times " of this Commission, and have caused it to become my strongest historic accuser of the evil system which it now condemns by its very advocacy.

To this testimony I have added the sworn evidence of the persons whom it charges with the deeds of its client; the evidence of the living actors in the Land League movement, and of others who represent every class into which Ireland's population is divided—bishops, priests, members of Parliament, municipal representatives, journalists, merchants, traders, farmers, laborers, mechanics, who one and all say with the "Times's" Red Book of 1880 that eviction and threats of eviction are the chief source of all agrarian crime in Ireland.

But there is another and a higher interest involved in the drama of this Commission now rapidly drawing to a close; an interest far surpassing in importance, and the possible consequences of your lordships' judgment, anything else comprised in this investigation. It stands between the "Times" and landlordism, on the one hand; the persons here charged and the Land League, on the other. In bygone ages, historians, with some prophetic instinct, called it "The Isle of Destiny."

And Destiny seems to have reserved it for a career of trial, of suffering, and of sorrow. That same Destiny has linked this country close to England. Politically it has remained there for seven hundred years or more. During that period few people ever placed upon this earth have experienced more injustice or more criminal neglect at the hands of their rulers than we have.

This even English history will not and dare not deny. This land so tried and treated has nevertheless struggled, generation after generation, now with one means, now with another, to widen the sphere of its contracted religious, social, and political liberties—liberties so contracted by the deliberate policy of its English governing power; and ever and always were these struggles made against the prejudice and might, and often the cruelties, of this same power, backed by the support or the indifference of the British nation.

But, despite all this, the cause so fought and upheld has ever and always succeeded, sooner or later, in vindicating its underlying principles of truth and justice, and in winning from the power which failed to crush them an after-justification of their righteous demands.

A people so persevering in its fight for the most priceless and most cherished of human and civil rights, so opposed, but so invariably vindicated, might surely, in these days of progress and of enlightenment excite in the breasts of Englishmen other feelings than those of jealously, hate, revenge, and fear. To many, thank God, it has appealed successfully, at last, to what is good and what is best in English nature. It has spoken to the spirit of Liberty, and has turned the love of justice in the popular mind toward Ireland, and has asked the British people, in the interests of peace, to put force and mistrust away with every other abandoned weapon of Ireland's past misrule, and to place in their stead the soothing and healing remedies of confidence and friendship, based upon reason and equality.

The verdict of this court, the story that will be told in the report of this Commission, may or may not carry the appeal which Ireland's struggles and misfortunes have addressed to the conscience and fairness of the English nation much farther than it has already travelled in the British mind.

But one thing, at least, the history of this Commission will have to tell to future generations. It will narrate how this progress of conciliation between ruled and rulers was sought to be arrested; how a people asking for justice were answered by ferocious animosity; how men who had suffered imprisonment, degradation, and calumny in their country's service were foully attacked by the weapons of moral assassination, and how every dastard means known in the records of political warfare was purchased and employed to cripple or destroy the elected representative of the Irish nation.

This story will picture this once-powerful organ of English public opinion earning again the title of " literary assassin " which Richard Cobden gave it near thirty years ago. It will stand again in this light when its writers are seen plotting with Houston, planning with Pigott, and bargaining with Delaney how best to reawaken in the English mind the old hate and jealousy and fear of a people who were to be depicted in its columns in the most odious and repulsive character that forgers' or libellers' mercenary talent could delineate in " Parnellism and Crime."

This story will exhibit these men sitting in the editorial rooms of Printing House Square, with professions of loyalty on their lips and poison in their pens; with " honesty " loudly proclaimed in articles which salaried Falsehood had written; with simulated regard for truth, making " Shame ashamed " of their concocted fabrications.

And these men, with the salaries of the rich in their pockets and the smiles of London society as their reward, carrying on a deliberately planned system of infamous allegation against political opponents who were but striving to redeem the sad fortunes of their country, in efforts to bring to an end a strife of centuries' duration between neighboring nations and peoples.

Between the " Times " on the one hand, and the accused
on the other, your lordships are, however, first to judge. It
is, if I may say so without presumption, as serious and momentous a duty as judges of England were ever called upon
to perform. The traditions of your lordships' exalted position, elevated as that position is above the play of political
passion of the influence of fear or favor, will call, and will
not, I am sure, call in vain, for the exercise of all those great
qualities of trained ability, of calmness, of discernment, of
judgment, and of courage which are the proud boast of the
judicial bench of this land.

Whether or not the test of a cold, indiscriminating law will
alone decide an issue in which political passion has played so
great a part, and where party feeling has been a moving
principle in acts and words; whether the heated language of
platform oratory, or the sometimes crude attempts at political reform, are to be weighed in the balance of legal
scales,—scales never fashioned, at least in England, to measure the bounds of political action; or whether the test is to
lie with a discriminating judicial amalgam of law in its
highest attributes and of calm reason applied to the men and
motives and means of the Land League, as the accused, and
to the " Times," its charges and allegations, as the accuser,
I am, as a layman, unable to forecast.

But, be the test what it may, if it be only based upon
truth and guided by the simple monitor of common sense;
I say on my own behalf and on that of the Land League and
of the peasantry of Ireland, hopefully, confidently, fearlessly,
" Let justice be done though the heavens fall."

THE CRIMES OF IRISH LANDLORDISM

[A monster demonstration in favor of the Land League movement, which sought to reform the Irish land laws, was held at Straide, County Mayo, February 1, 1880. Mr. Davitt was among the speakers, and a peculiar interest was attached to the meeting from the fact that the platform from which he spoke was erected over the very ruins of the old homestead from which he, with his father and mother, had been evicted many years before. Mr. Davitt delivered the following speech:]

WHILE every nerve must be strained to stave off, if possible, the horrible fate which befel our famine-slaughtered kindred in 1847 and 1848, the attention of our people must not for a moment be withdrawn from the primary cause of these periodical calamities, nor their exertions be relaxed in this great social struggle for the overthrow of the odious system responsible for them. Portions of the English press had recently declared that the charity of Englishmen would be more spontaneous and generous if this agitation did not stand in the way. Well, Ireland's answer to this should be that she asks no English alms, and that she scorns charity which is offered her in lieu of the justice which is her right and her demand. Let landlordism be removed from our country, and labor be allowed the wealth which it creates instead of being given to legalized idlers, and no more famine will darken our land or hold Ireland up to the gaze of the civilized world as a nation of paupers. England deprives us annually of some seven millions of money for Imperial taxation, and she allows an infamous land system to rob our country of fifteen or twenty millions more each year to support some nine or twelve thousand lazy landlords, and then, when famine extends its destroying wings over the land, and the dread spectre of death stands sentinel at our thresholds, an appeal to English charity—a begging-box outside the London Mansion House—is paraded before the world, and expected to atone for every wrong inflicted upon Ireland by a heartless and hated government, and to blot out the records of the most monstrous land code that ever cursed a country or robbed humanity of its birthright. The press of England may bring whatever charges its prejudices can prompt against this land movement, the Duchess of Marlborough may hurl her gracious wrath at the heads of " heartless agitators," but neither the venomed scurrility of government organs nor the jealous tirades of politico-prompted charity can rob the much-abused land movement of the credit attached to the following acts. The cry of distress and national danger was first raised by the agitators, and all subsequent action, government, vice-regal, landlord, and Mansion House, to alleviate that distress, was precipitated by the action of the " heartless agitators." The destroying hand of rackrenting and eviction was stricken down for the moment by the influence of the agitation, and the farmers of Ireland were spared some two or three millions with which to meet the distress now looming on their families and country, while the rooftrees of thousands of homesteads were protected from the crowbar brigade; and the civilized world has been appealed to against the existence of a land monopoly which is responsible for a pauperized country, a starved and discontented population, and every social evil now afflicting a patient and industrious people, until a consensus of home and foreign opinion has been evoked in favor of a lasting and efficacious remedy. With these services rendered to Ireland, with a resolve to do the utmost possible to save our people from the danger immediately threatening them, the " heartless agitators " will not relax a single effort or swerve one iota from their original purposes,—to haul down the ensign of land monopoly and plant the banner of the " land for the people " upon the dismantled battlements of Irish landlordism. Against what have we declared this unceasing

strife, and whence the justification for the attitude we are
calling upon the people to assume? The resolution so elo-
quently proposed by my friend Mr. Brennan declares that the
present land code had its origin in conquest and national spo-
liation, and has ever since been the curse of our people and
the scourge of Ireland. Does not the scene of domestic devastation now spread before this vast meeting bear testimony
of the crimes with which landlordism stands charged before
God and man to-day? Can a more eloquent denunciation of
an accursed land code be found than what is witnessed here
in this depopulated district? In the memory of many now
listening to my words that peaceful little stream which
meanders by the outskirts of this multitude sang back the
merry voices of happy children and wended its way through
a once populous and prosperous village. Now, however, the
merry sounds are gone, the busy hum of hamlet life is hushed
in sad desolation, for the hands of the home destroyers have
been here and performed their hellish work, leaving Straide
but a name to mark the place where happy homesteads once
stood, and whence an inoffensive people were driven to the
four corners of the earth by the ruthless decrees of Irish
landlordism. How often in a strange land has my boyhood's
ear drunk in the tale of outrage and wrong and infamy per-
petrated here in the name of English laws and in the interest of territorial greed. In listening to the accounts
of famine and sorrow, of deaths from landlordism, of coffin-
less graves, of scenes—

> On highway's side, where oft were seen
> The wild dog and the vulture keen
> Tug for the limbs and gnaw the face
> Of some starved child of our Irish race,

what wonder that such laws should become hateful, and, when
felt by personal experience of their tyranny and injustice,

that a life of irreconcilable enmity to them should follow, and
that standing here on the spot where I first drew breath, in
sight of a levelled home, with memories of privation and tor-
tures crowding upon my mind, I should swear to devote the
remainder of that life to the destruction of what has blasted
my early years, pursued me with its vengeance through manhood, and leaves my family in exile to-day far from that Ireland which is itself wronged, robbed, and humiliated through
the agency of the same accursed system? It is no little con-
solation to know, however, that we are here to-day doing battle against a doomed monopoly, and that the power which has
so long domineered over Ireland and its people is brought to
its knees at last and on the point of being crushed forever. It
is humiliating to the last degree that a few thousand land-
sharks should have so long and so successfully trod upon the
necks of millions of Irishmen and defrauded them of the
fruits of their land, while at the same time robbing, insult-
ing, and dragooning our country with an inhumanity unsurpassed by the titled plunderers of the middle ages. An average landlord may be likened to a social vulture hovering over
the heads of the people and swooping down upon the earnings and the food which that industry produces whenever
his appetite or his avarice prompts him. The tenantry in
the past have stood by like a flock of frightened sheep, timid
and terrified, unable to prevent this human bird of prey from
devouring their own and their children's substance. While
rackrents were paid the farmer and his family must live in
semi-starvation, in wretched hovels, amid squalor and priva-
tions, barbed by the thought that the money earned by labor
and sweat from day to day was being spent by his own and
his children's deadly enemy in another land in voluptuous
ease and sensual gratification. If the rackrent was not paid

and this blackmail levied upon labor in the shape of rent
was not forthcoming, to be squandered by one who never
earned a penny of it, out upon the roadside the earners would
be cast, to take their choice of death by exposure, workhouse
degradation, or banishment from home and Ireland forever.
Is it possible that our fathers could have tolerated such a
giant wrong, submitted to so monstrous an infamy, and bequeathed to us an acceptance of it as an inevitable decree
of God, to be borne in meek submission, or to plod on in
sluggish servitude from sire to son, from age to age, proud
of our trampled nature? Such, however, is not our resolve.
We accept no such blasphemous excuse for the abrogation
of our manhood, nor will we allow a horde of vampires to
fatten upon our soil, to degrade us by their assumption of
superiority, and keep our country before the world as the
property and the preserve of the deadliest enemies to her
social and political welfare. We demand the right to live
like civilized men in our land; we demand the right to enjoy
life here, and we are resolved to labor unitedly and unceas-
ingly for the privilege to do so. We ask these demands
upon the God-given right to mankind to hold in proportion
to their wants and deserts the land which was created for
their sustenance. The principles upon which this land movement rests are founded upon obvious and natural justice,
and if in advocating them we outstep the barriers of political
conventionalities we are justified by the monstrous wrongs
which are upheld by a system that justice and reason alike
condemn, and which civilization has stamped out in every
other country. In demanding the land for the people we
are but claiming the right which is ours in virtue of our creation and the decrees of our Creator. Land was created for
man's sustenance, and declared to be the property of the

human family, to be worked by labor and made productive in food for the children of men. To hold that, because robbery and fraud have succeeded in gaining possession of the soil of Ireland, landlordism was in the Divine intention and has a right to the land of the country, is a libel on God's immutable ordinances and a doctrine opposed alike to reason and common sense. Landlordism has worked the deadliest wrong to our country and our race. Its gifts to Ireland are famines, discontent, bloodshed, national impoverishment, and national degradation. It robs our country of £20,000,000 annually and disposes of our people as so much vermin. It bars our social progress and deprives us of those advantages which are enjoyed by those who have freed themselves from landlordism. Remove the land monopoly, and famine will be exorcised from Ireland. Strike down this giant fraud upon a people, and peace and plenty will take the place of disturbance and starvation. Give labor its claim upon the wealth it creates, remove the restrictions which this feudal code places upon the proper cultivation of the soil of Ireland, and the charity of other lands will no more be appealed to on our behalf, or our national pride be humiliated by our being exhibited in the eyes of the world as a nation of paupers. Organize, then, for so glorious a consummation. Vow that you will never cease striking until land monopoly is crushed forever in Ireland. Forward with the glorious watchword of " The land for the people." The cause of Ireland to-day is that of humanity and labor throughout the world, and the sympathy of all civilized people is with us in the struggle. Stand together, then, in this contest for the soil of your fatherland, and victory will soon crown your efforts with success. Remember, with courage and with pride, that seven hundred years of wrong failed to crush the soul of Ireland.

ROSEBERY

ARCHIBALD PHILIP PRIMROSE, fifth Earl of Rosebery, a distinguished English statesman, was born in London, May 7, 1847, and was educated at Eton and Christ Church College, Oxford University. He succeeded to the title in 1868 by the death of his grandfather, before he reached his majority, and his first appearance in Parliament was in the House of Lords. His first speech was made in 1871, when he was selected by Mr. Gladstone to second the address in reply to the Queen's speech from the throne. During the next few years he mingled occasionally in the debates, always speaking with animation, but with no especial eloquence. A Liberal in politics, and a warm admirer of Gladstone, he sat in the latter's cabinet in 1881-83 as under-secretary of home affairs. During the brief Liberal rule of 1885 he was Lord Privy Seal and First Commissioner of Public Works, and in 1886 he was made Secretary of Foreign Affairs. While holding this position he conducted the foreign policy on the general lines followed in the preceding Conservative government and endeavored to keep it removed as far as possible from the influence of party strife. He was one of the most ardent supporters in the House of Lords of Gladstone's first Home Rule Bill. In 1888 he became a member of the London County Council and in the last Gladstone administration he was again at his post as Minister of Foreign Affairs. On the retirement of Gladstone in March, 1894, Lord Rosebery succeeded him as Prime Minister, holding office until the return of the Conservative party to power in 1895. Lord Rosebery is a man of wide sympathies, and manifested much interest in ameliorating the condition of the laboring classes. He served as Lord Rector of Aberdeen University 1878-81, and of Edinburgh University 1882-83. He was made honorary student of Christ Church, Oxford, in 1894. He published " Life of Pitt " (1891); " Speeches, 1874-96 " (1896); " Appreciations and Addresses " (1899).

THE TRUE LEVERAGE OF EMPIRE

DELIVERED AT THE SOCIAL SCIENCE CONGRESS, GLASGOW, SEPTEMBER 30, 1874

IF, in addressing this great meeting, I were to speak out of the fulness of my heart, I should tell of nothing but my own misgivings. But it is too much the practice on these occasions to take up time selfishly in apologies. You asked me kindly and generously to come here to-night. I thought it a clear duty to obey your summons and reciprocate your sympathy. But none the less sensible am I of my own deficiencies and of my need of your further large indulgence; none the less do I feel as if I were only placed in this prominent position to serve as a foil to the ripe wisdom of so many in this Congress.

It is impossible for any one at my age to pretend to instruct—few can have adequate knowledge; none sufficient experience. I can offer, then, no fresh contribution to your stock of information. I can only, as it were, set in motion my small share of electric current of sympathy and interest, which is surely not the least valuable of the features of this Congress. But I would before all express my pride and my joy at making this first visit to Glasgow under the auspices of your association. There are probably few places to which an Englishman can point with more pride than to Glasgow; none perhaps which a Scotchman can regard with so much.

I suppose that there are in this city 500,000 inhabitants; that the rental amounts to £2,500,000; that the shipbuilding of the Clyde is supreme in the world. How long has it taken to produce this immense result? What is the origin of this great population? Whence dates this easy predominance in shipping, this vast collection of material wealth?

Two centuries ago Glasgow was officially described as " a neat burghe town, consisting of foure streets." At that time she possessed twelve vessels carrying 957 tons. In the year 1718, little more than a century and a half ago, the first Scottish ship that ever crossed the Atlantic—a vessel of sixty tons—was launched in the Clyde, which has since witnessed the building of the Cunard line of steamers. And as for her rental of £2,500,000, it has been computed that the rental of the whole of Scotland did not a century ago exceed £1,000,000 sterling.

We could not, indeed, have chosen a more suggestive scene for our Congress, or one where social science should be more dear. For here we have a great material result rapidly produced by the exertions of a vast laboring population; and no one surely, in considering the labors of this Congress and its functions, can avoid seeing that the most vital and perpetual question before it is the well-being of our working classes; a vital question, because on the apt solution of it depends the commercial supremacy, the political solidarity, nay, the very existence of our empire. To my mind a body like ours has no more direct or important duties than the attempt to raise the condition of the nation by means which Parliament is unable or disdains to apply.

Here we have an illimitable field of operations. Parliament can give a workman a vote; it cannot give him a comfortable home. Nor can it sift and exhibit the many contrivances which may be placed before him for bettering himself or increasing his capacities and enlarging his enjoyments.

All this lies within our province, and it is work incalculably more important than the great mass of our parliamentary legislation. In this century we are surrounded by a great aggregation of humanity, seething, laboring, begrimed humanity; children of toil who have made Glasgow what she is and can alone raise and maintain her; not mere machines of production, but vehicles of intelligence, mixed in nationality and various in opinion.

You cannot appeal to them by common feelings or uniform interests. They are there, a dark and mighty power, like the Cyclopean inmates of Ætna. I must honestly avow my conviction—though to those who see how many there are who profess to represent and understand the working classes it may seem rash, while to others it may seem a truism—that this vast laboring population of ours has not made itself, its wants, its creeds, and its interests sufficiently intelligible to many of us. How indeed, if it be otherwise, is it that the problems connected with their condition have advanced so little toward solution? How is it, otherwise, that each political party claims with equal certainty and on every point to possess the sympathy and confidence of the workingman? How else is it that, when the working class makes its voice heard on any question, it comes upon us like thunder in a clear sky? I avow myself no exception to the rule, but for that very reason, perhaps, I can conceive no subjects more interesting than those which relate to the welfare of our laboring population.

Perhaps, then, you will allow me to disregard the ordinary precedent upon these occasions. The opening address of this Congress has commonly surveyed the present position of those questions with which your Society is accustomed to deal, or which it watches with interest. But speaking, as I do, in the presence of many who, in the various sections, will discuss such subjects with ripe authority of knowledge and experience, I should feel it presumptuous in me to poise a light sentence or hazard a shallow conjecture where my hearers can for themselves sound the very depth and perhaps approximate solution.

I will, then, if you please, attempt to-night to take stock in some degree of the various means by which it is sought to raise the condition of the working classes; a group of subjects some of which appear under different divisions in your programme, but which are ultimately—I had almost said solemnly—connected together; and I would do so rather as a sign of humble interest in them than with the slightest pretension of having anything original to advance.

The moment is as suitable as the place for the discussion of these vital and national questions. In times such as these, of high wage, of general peace, of immunity from furious political discord, the well-being of the laboring classes often appears secured and does not always attract the attention of statesmen. It is, however, precisely then that it is possible to take measures which, without exciting jealousy on one hand and suspicion on the other, may secure that well-being in less prosperous times. It is then that even the Greeks may innocently bring gifts.

But should there come a European war such as we weathered successfully at the beginning of the century, but which left us surrounded for the most part with battered wrecks and with stranded hulls, we might possibly find our teeming population, confined within so small an ark, a perilous and disheartening agency.

Moreover, while our numbers increase in a greater proportion daily, it would seem that for a few years our principal outlet for emigration may be partially blocked up. It appears more than probable that for some time, owing to late commercial disasters, and it may be because corn-growing in the West has been somewhat overdone, the United States will not find employment for that million and a quarter of emigrants, more or less, that we are accustomed annually to send to her. This is the most important problem which can occupy statesmen; and at the same time the most difficult for a statesman to face. For Parliament can seldom see its way to interference. Nor is it, indeed, desirable that it should do so.

Legislatures and governments have at various times, by

direct laws, attempted to benefit the working classes; but the most obvious instances of this—the National Workshops of 1848, and the decrees of the Parisian Commune in 1871—have been conspicuous failures.

It is well, then, that in this present time, so peaceful and blessed for us, we can here discuss, however slowly and imperfectly, the pregnant topics which our programmes suggest. And there is so much to be done; our civilization is so little removed from barbarism! At this moment there is a daily column in the newspapers devoted to recording brutal outrages, where human beings have behaved like wild beasts. Every policeman in London is assaulted on an average about once in two years. Within the memory of living men, the workmen at the salt-pans of Joppa, only a mile or two from Edinburgh, were serfs—*adscripti glebœ*—and sold along with the land on which they dwelt. Neither they nor their children could remove from the spot or alter their calling. The late Lord Provost of Edinburgh, who bears the honored name of Chambers, records his having talked to such men.

What a hell, too, was that described to Lord Ashley's Commission of 1842. In the mines were women and children employed as beasts; dragging trucks on all fours, pursuing in fetid tunnels the degraded tasks which no animal could be found to undertake. We know that equal horrors existed in the brickfields two or three years ago, where there were 30,000 children employed, looking like moving masses of the clay they bore, whose ages averaged from three and one-half years to seventeen; and when an average case was thus described:

"I had a child weighed very recently, and though he was somewhat over eight years old he weighed but 52½ pounds, and was employed carrying 43 pounds of clay on his head an

average distance of 15 miles daily, and worked 73 hours a
week.   This is only an average case of what many poor children are doing in England at the present time; and we need
not wonder at their stunted and haggard appearance when
we take into account the tender age at which they are sent to
their Egyptian tasks."

Then again:

"All goodness and purity seems to become stamped out of
these people; and were I to relate [says a witness who has
worked himself in the brickfields] what could be related, the
whole country would become sickened and horrified."

It would not indeed be difficult, and it would be painfully
instructive, to draw out a dismal catalogue of facts to prove
how little the splendor of our civilization differs from the
worst horrors of barbarism.

And yet, after all, we can only come to the hackneyed conclusion that the sole remedy for this state of things is education, a humanizing education.   It is not a particularly brilliant or original thing to say, but severe truth is seldom
brilliant and original.   There is a noble passage in De Tocque-
ville, known probably to all and too long to quote here, which
points out that knowledge is the arm of democracy; that
every intellectual discovery, every development of science,
is a new source of strength to the people; that thought and
eloquence and imagination, the divine gifts which know no
limit of class, even when bestowed on the enemies of the
popular cause, yet serve it by exalting the natural grandeur
of man; and that literature is the vast armory, open to all
indeed, but where the poor, who have hardly any other, may
always find their weapons.   These, I say, are features of
education which all recognize, though some may profess to
dread them.

But there is a general expediency besides. Take the case of machinery. The winter nights of 1830 were bright with blazing rick-yards. No farmer in the southern counties felt his stacks safe. There was a time of terror in England, and of retribution.

"In Kent," says Miss Martineau, "there were gibbets erected in Penenden Heath, and bodies swung there in the December winds, bodies of boys about eighteen or nineteen years old, but looking much younger; brothers who had said to each other on arriving at the gallows, 'That looks an awful thing!'"

Again, take the Luddite riots of 1812 and 1816, where cunning and furious mobs nearly stamped out lace manufacture at Nottingham. The broken frames and the burning ricks were ignorant protests against machinery. Well, intelligence has marched a little, and what is the case now? What do the associated masters—no unduly partial authority —affirm? The accuracy of this statement is manifest from the fact that the operatives are now the earnest advocates for improvements in machinery; whereas twenty years ago it was no uncommon thing for them to strike at the factory where they were introduced. Here, it seems to me, we can put our finger on definite and tangible progress, due solely to increased intelligence.

Take another case which shows the need of it. Wages were probably never so high in England as in 1873. Nine years before, an increasing spirit duty paid £9,692,515 to the Excise. In the last financial year the Excise receipts from spirits amounted to £14,639,562.

I am not one of those who are appalled, certainly not surprised, by this expenditure. But see how it strengthens the argument. A man who has but natural instincts to guide him comes into a fortune, and at once procures himself an increased quantity of what has been in smaller doses an enjoyment and a solace. Has he been educated to find his amusement elsewhere? If one of us should succeed to a large fortune to-morrow, we certainly should not spend our inheritance in drink; but the difference, I venture to say, is solely one of culture.

Well, my contention is that in an educated country, among a nation educated not in Shakespeare and the musical glasses, but so instructed as to be able to find amusement outside the skittle-alley and the public-house, a great increase in wages would not have been followed by so enormous an increase in the consumption of spirits; and an enormous consumption of spirits means an enormous amount of crime and pauperism. . . .

I now come to a large division of the subject where we may thankfully remember that much has been effected during the last session of Parliament.

We have considered some of the means, at any rate, of ameliorating, morally and physically, the great mass of the nation; and as we have discussed how, by education, we can ensure the progressive march of intellect among rising and future generations, so it will not be out of place if I dwell here for a moment on another question which relates to the physical preservation and improvement of our race.

We all know to a certain extent the history of factory legislation, how the sacred tradition of the great work was handed down by the first Sir Robert Peel, whose claims to national gratitude have been so beautifully obscured by the greater claims of his illustrious son: to Oastler and Vadler, and Hobhouse and Ashley, and Mundella. In the last session of Parliament the main principles of Mr. Mundella's

Factory Bill, embodied in a government measure, passed through both Houses, so that the hours of labor for women and children are now limited to fifty-six and a half in a week.

But although much has been effected, it may be regarded as serious that so keen and independent a thinker as Mr. Fawcett should have offered determined resistance to the bill. But his argument was founded on the assumption that those whom the bill is taking care of are well able to take care of themselves, which is at least a doubtful proposition; and that legislative interference, to be logical, should be complete, and should extend even to women employed in domestic service.

But no one would deny that if great injury to women were to be apprehended as an effect of domestic service,—that if, for example, every master was a Legree and every mistress a Brownrigg,—the legislature would have to interfere for the protection of maids. Nothing of the sort is, however, pretended.

Now we have evidence, and very complete evidence, that injury is done to women, and not merely to women but to their descendants, by their undue employment in factories. Parliament must in consequence determine what limitation must be placed on factory labor, not merely for the protection of weak women now, but in its own imperial interests for the preservation of health in the children of these women— the future citizens of the country.

Nor is it certain that Mr. Fawcett's other assumption, that the classes affected are well able to take care of themselves, is in any degree correct. It is certain that women, from love of approbation, as well as from those feelings of unselfishness which do honor to them as wives, are only too easily led to work beyond their powers. . . .

The conditions of life in this country are rapidly reversing themselves. Wealth is doubling itself and increasing the population; greater care in management and subtlety in mechanical appliances are diminishing, and must further diminish, the proportion of persons employed, especially in agriculture. Here is the problem: daily a greater population, daily in all probability less work, which means less subsistence.

We are shut up by a sea with our surging myriads,—a source of strength if guided and controlled; if not, an immeasurable volcanic power. Many of them must go forth to people the world. Our race has colonized and colonizes, has influenced and influences; and in future ages seems likely further to colonize and influence a great part of the habitable globe.

So great has been our field of influence that we can only view it with awe. It has been, and is, a great destiny for this country to sway so mightily the destinies of the universe. But the great privilege involves a sacred trust. We must look to it that the fertile race we send forth to the waste places of the earth is a race physically, morally, and intellectually equal to its high duties.

At present we will not compel our children to be educated, however rudely; at present, in one of our cities nearly a quarter of the infants born die before they are one year old. In one of your sections you propose to discuss, " What are the best means of drawing together the interests of the United Kingdom, India, and the Colonies?" I submit that the primary means are to send forth colonists who may be worthy the country they leave and the destiny they seek.

The different agencies I have noticed to-night all tend to this: Whether we keep them in England or they pass from us, we must look to the nurture of this race of kings. We annually distribute through the world a population nearly as large as that of Birmingham. In the last two years more emigrants have left our shores than there are inhabitants in Glasgow and Dundee put together. After all, whatever our commerce or political influence may be, this is the most gigantic enterprise in which this or any other nation can be engaged; and the responsibility for its success, not merely for the present, but for countless future generations, lies with us.

Will this great stream pass from us a turbid flood, composed of emigrants like some we now send forth, who shake the dust from their feet and swear undying enmity to us; or shall it be a broad and beneficent river of life, fertilizing as the Nile, beloved as the Ganges, sacred as the Jordan, separated from us indeed by the ocean, but, like that fabled fountain, Arethusa, which, passing under the sea from Greece into Sicily, retained its original source in Arcadia?

We do not know what our fate may be. We have no right, perhaps, to hope that we may be an exception to the rule by which nations have their period of growth, and of grandeur, and of decay. It may be that all we most esteem may fade away like the glories of Babylon. But if we have done our duty well, even though our history should pass away, and our country become—

> ——" an island salt and bare,
> The haunt of seals, and orcs, and seamews' clang,"

—she may be remembered, not ungratefully, as the mother of great commonwealths and peaceful empires that shall perpetuate the best qualities of the race.

I have only mentioned one of the topics with which a Social Science Congress is called upon to deal; yet how vast

this single subject appears! Indeed, it is difficult to see any
limit to the possible usefulness of a meeting like the present.

We live in remarkable times—times of social development
so ominous that we may be approaching a period of social
revolution. What a change from that old world whence this
fertile brood of nations sprang! On the one side, a dark
surging mass of barbarians; on the other, the inevitable,
stern immobility of the Roman Empire.

Now the whole universe seems undergoing the volcanic influence of social theory. Everywhere there is breaking out
some strange manifestation. The grotesque congregation of
the Shakers, the agricultural socialism of Harris, the polygamous socialism of Mormon, the lewd quackery of Free
Love, the mad, blank misery of Nihilism, the tragic frenzy
of the Parisian Commune, are portents no observer can neglect.

Some try to solve the problem by abolishing property;
some by a new religion. Most of these experiments thrive in
America, which alone has room for such diversities of opinion
and practice. It is too much the practice to treat these various organizations as a mixture of knavery and folly. Two,
indeed, of these phases of humanity will receive more attention from the historian of the future than they attract from
their contemporaries,—I mean the Commune of Paris, and
the Church of the Latter-Day Saints. That eccentric church
is a socialism founded on a polygamous religion and ruled
by a supreme pontiff. But it would be a mistake, I think,
to suppose that polygamy is an essential part of Mormonism.
The traveller in Utah will be struck most, not by the plu-
rality of wives, but by the prevailing industry and apparent
external brotherhood. These are the outward features of an
extraordinary community.

That it should largely increase; that it should have converted a desert into a garden; that it should, in the last few years, have attracted to it thousands of the working classes (not by polygamy, for that is expensive, and almost all the emigrants are poor), will seem, to a future age, a strange sign of our times.

Again, whatever may be thought of the Commune of Paris, which issued quaintly ingenuous decrees, and which ended in blood and iron, it will always remain one of the sinister facts of our age. Like the Ninevite king, it perished in a blazing pyre of what was fairest in its habitation; and the world lost so much in those flames that it cannot now pass judgment with complete impartiality.

But as a gigantic outbreak of class hostility, as a desperate attempt to found a new society in the very temple of the old, it has hardly, perhaps, received sufficient attention. Far be it from me to attempt to palliate the horrors of that disastrous conflict. They are, however, only terrible accessories. But the ominous fact of that sudden social revolution is a portent that cannot be blotted from the history of humanity. While human beings remain human beings, and while efforts like these are made for complete social reorganization, a Social Science Congress has even more scope than a Parliament. . . .

Never was a league of the friends of humanity more needed than now. Never was there, on all sides, so much of energy and skill given to the preparation of those efforts by which civilization is retarded and mankind made miserable. The armies of the four great military Powers, when on a war footing, engross three and a quarter millions of men in the prime and flower of life. Three and a quarter millions of men in four countries with their swords ready to the grind-

stone form a portentous, silent fact which we cannot ignore
in the halls where we discuss the efficacy of arbitration in
settling disputes between nations.

In Spain we see a war of dynasty; in America a conflict
of color. The night is dark and troubled; we can but labor
steadfastly, hoping for the dawn, united by the sympathy of
the living and animated by the example of the dead.

THURSTON

JOHN MELLEN THURSTON, an American politician, was born at Montpelier, Vermont, August 21, 1847, but removed with his parents to Wisconsin in 1854. His education was obtained in the public schools and at Wayland University at Beaver Dam, Wisconsin, while he supported himself by farm work and other manual labor. After studying law he was admitted to the bar in 1869, and in the same year he took up his residence in Omaha, Nebraska. In 1872 he was elected to the Omaha city council, and in 1874 became city attorney. He was a member of the Nebraska legislature in 1875, and was president of the Republican League of the United States, 1888-91. In 1877 he was appointed assistant attorney of the Union Pacific Railway Company, and in 1888 became general solicitor of the entire Union Pacific system, a position which he retained until his election to the United States Senate in 1895.

CUBA MUST BE FREE

DELIVERED IN THE UNITED STATES SENATE, MARCH 24, 1898

MR. PRESIDENT,—I am here by command of silent lips to speak once and for all upon the Cuban situation. I trust that no one has expected anything sensational from me. God forbid that the bitterness of a personal loss should induce me to color in the slightest degree the statement that I feel it my duty to make. I shall endeavor to be honest, conservative, and just. I have no purpose to stir the public passion to any action not necessary and imperative to meet the duties and necessities of American responsibility, Christian humanity, and national honor. I would shirk this task if I could, but I dare not. I cannot satisfy my conscience except by speaking, and speaking now.

Some three weeks since, three Senators and two Representatives in Congress accepted the invitation of a great metropolitan newspaper to make a trip to Cuba and person-

(10615)

ally investigate and report upon the situation there. Our invitation was from a newspaper whose political teachings I have never failed to antagonize and denounce, and whose journalism I have considered decidedly sensational. But let me say, for the credit of the proprietor of the paper in question, that I believe the invitation exended to us was inspired by his patriotic desire to have the actual condition of affairs in Cuba brought to the attention of the American people in such a way that the facts would no longer remain in controversy or dispute.

We were not asked to become the representatives of the paper; no conditions or restrictions were imposed upon us; we were left free to conduct the investigation in our own way, make our own plans, pursue our own methods, take our own time, and decide for ourselves upon the best manner of laying the results of our labors before the American people. For myself I went to Cuba firmly believing that the condition of affairs there had been greatly exaggerated by the press, and my own efforts were directed in the first instance to the attempted exposure of these supposed exaggerations.

Mr. President, there has undoubtedly been much sensationalism in the journalism of the time, but as to the condition of affairs in Cuba there has been no exaggeration, because exaggeration has been impossible. I have read the careful statement of the junior senator from Vermont [Mr. Proctor], and I find that he has anticipated me in almost every detail. From my own personal knowledge of the situation, I adopt every word of his concise, conservative, specific presentation as my own; nay, more, I am convinced that he has, in a measure, understated the facts. I absolutely agree with him in the following conclusions:

After three years of warfare and the use of 225,000

Spanish troops, Spain has lost control of every foot of Cuba not surrounded by an actual intrenchment and protected by a fortified picket line.

She holds possession with her armies of the fortified seaboard towns, not because the insurgents could not capture many of them, but because they are under the virtual protection of Spanish warships, with which the revolutionists cannot cope.

The revolutionists are in absolute and almost peaceful possession of nearly one half of the island, including the eastern provinces of Santiago de Cuba and Puerto Principe. In those provinces they have an established form of government, levy and collect taxes, maintain armies, and generally levy a tax or tribute upon the principal plantations in the other provinces, and, as is commonly believed, upon the entire railway system of the island.

In the four so-called Spanish provinces there is neither cultivation nor railway operation except under strong Spanish military protection or by consent of the revolutionists in consideration of tribute paid.

Under the inhuman policy of Weyler not less than 400,000 self-supporting, simple, peaceable, defenceless country people were driven from their homes in the agricultural portions of the Spanish provinces to the cities and imprisoned upon the barren waste outside the residence portions of these cities and within the lines of intrenchment established a little way beyond. Their humble homes were burned, their fields laid waste, their implements of husbandry destroyed, their live stock and food supplies for the most part confiscated. Most of these people were old men, women, and children. They were thus placed in hopeless imprisonment, without shelter or food. There was no work for them in the cities to which they were driven. They were left there with nothing to depend upon except the scanty charity of the inhabitants of the cities and with slow starvation their inevitable fate.

It is conceded upon the best ascertainable authority, and those who have had access to the public records do not hesitate to state, that upward of 210,000 of these people have already perished, all from starvation or from diseases incident to starvation.

The government of Spain has never contributed one dollar to house, shelter, feed, or provide medical attention for these its own citizens. Such a spectacle exceeds the scenes of the Inferno as painted by Dante.

There has been no amelioration of the situation except through the charity of the people of the United States. There has been no diminution in the death rate among these reconcentrados except as the death supply is constantly diminished. There can be no relief and no hope except through the continued charity of the American people until peace shall be fully restored in the island and until a humane government shall return these people to their homes and provide for them anew the means with which to begin again the cultivation of the soil.

Spain cannot put an end to the existing condition. She cannot conquer the insurgents. She cannot re-establish her sovereignty over any considerable portion of the interior of the island. The revolutionists, while able to maintain themselves, cannot drive the Spanish army from the fortified seacoast towns.

The situation, then, is not war as we understand it, but a chaos of devastation and depopulation of undefined duration, whose end no man can see.

I will cite but a few facts that came under my personal

observation, all tending to fully substantiate the absolute truth of the foregoing propositions. I could detail incidents by the hour and by the day, but the senator from Vermont has absolutely covered the case. I have no desire to deal in horrors. If I had my way, I would shield the American public even from the photographic reproductions of the awful scenes that I viewed in all their original ghastliness.

Spain has sent to Cuba more than 225,000 soldiers to subdue the island, whose entire male population capable of bearing arms did not exceed at the beginning that number. These soldiers were mostly boys, conscripts from the Spanish hills. They are well armed, but otherwise seem to be absolutely unprovided for. They have been without tents and practically without any of the necessary supplies and equipment for service in the field. They have been put in barracks, in warehouses, and old buildings in the cities where all sanitary surroundings have been of the worst possible character. They have seen but little discipline, and I could not ascertain that such a thing as a drill had taken place in the island.

There are less than 60,000 now available for duty. The balance are dead or sick in hospitals, or have been sent back to Spain as incapacitated for further service. It is currently stated that there are now 37,000 sick in hospital. I do not believe that the entire Spanish army in Cuba could stand an engagement in the open field against 20,000 well-disciplined American soldiers.

As an instance of the discipline among them I cite the fact that I bought the machete of a Spanish soldier on duty at the wharf in Matanzas, on his offer, for $3 in Spanish silver. He also seemed desirious of selling me his only remaining arm, a revolver.

The Spanish soldiers have not been paid for some months, and in my judgment they, of all the people on the earth, will most gladly welcome any result which would permit them to return to their homes in Spain.

The pictures in the American newspapers of the starving reconcentrados are true. They can all be duplicated by the thousands. I never saw, and please God I may never again see, so deplorable a sight as the reconcentrados in the suburbs of Matanzas. I can never forget to my dying day the hopeless anguish in their despairing eyes. Huddled about their little bark huts, they raised no voice of appeal to us for alms as we went among them.

There was almost no begging by the reconcentrados themselves. The streets of the cities are full of beggars of all ages and all conditions, but they are almost wholly of the residents of the cities and largely of the professional-beggar class. The reconcentrados—men, women, and children—stand silent, famishing with hunger. Their only appeal comes from their sad eyes, through which one looks as through an open window into their agonizing souls.

The present autonomist governor of Matanzas (who speaks excellent English) was inaugurated in November last. His records disclose that at the city of Matanzas there were 1,200 deaths in November, 1,200 in December, 700 in January, and 500 in February—3,600 in four months, and those four months under the administration of a governor whom I believe to be a truly humane man. He stated to me that on the day of his inauguration, which I think was the 12th of last November, to his personal knowledge fifteen persons died in the public square in front of the executive mansion. Think of it, oh, my countrymen! Fifteen human beings dying from starvation in the public square, in the shade of the palm-trees, and amid the beautiful flowers, in sight of the open windows of the executive mansion!

The governor of Matanzas told us that for the most part the people of the city of Matanzas had done all they could for the reconcentrados; and after studying the situation over I believe his statement is true. He said the condition of affairs in the island had destroyed the trade, the commerce, and the business of the city; that most of the people who had the means assisted the reconcentrados with food just as long as they could, but he said to us that there were thousands of the people living in fine houses on marble floors who were in deep need themselves and who did not know from one day to the other where their food supply was coming from.

The ability of the people of Matanzas to aid is practically exhausted. The governor told us that he had expended all of his salary and all that he could possibly afford of his private means in relief work. He is willing that the reconcentrados shall repass the picket line and go back to seek work in the interior of the island. He expresses his willingness to give them passes for that purpose, but they are no longer physically able to take advantage of that offer. They have no homes to return to; their fields have grown up to weeds; they have no oxen, no implements of husbandry with which to begin anew the cultivation of the soil. Their only hope is to remain where they are, to live as long as they can on an insufficient charity, and then die. What is true at Matanzas is true at all the other cities where these reconcentrados have been gathered.

The government of Spain has not and will not appropriate one dollar to save these people. They are now being attended and nursed and administered to by the charity of the United States. Think of the spectacle! We are feeding these citizens of Spain; we are nursing their sick; we are saving such as can be saved, and yet there are those who still say it is right for us to send food, but we must keep hands off. I say that the time has come when muskets ought to go with the food.

We asked the governor if he knew of any relief for these people except through the charity of the United States. He did not.

We then asked him, " Can you see any end to this condition of affairs? " He could not.

We asked him, " When do you think the time will come that these people can be placed in a position of self-support? "

He replied to us, with deep feeling, " Only the good God or the great government of the United States can answer that question."

I hope and believe that the good God by the great government of the United States will answer that question.

I shall refer to these horrible things no further. They are there. God pity me; I have seen them; they will remain in my mind forever—and this is almost the twentieth century. Christ died nineteen hundred years ago, and Spain is a Christian nation. She has set up more crosses in more lands, beneath more skies, and under them has butchered more people than all the other nations of the earth combined.

Europe may tolerate her existence as long as the people of the Old World wish. God grant that before another Christmas morning the last vestige of Spanish tyranny and oppression will have vanished from the Western Hemisphere.

Mr. President, the distinguished senator from Vermont has seen all these things; he knows all these things; he has described all these things; but after describing them he says he has nothing to propose, no remedy to suggest. I have. I am only an humble unit in the great government of the United States, but I should feel myself a traitor did I remain silent now.

I counselled silence and moderation from this floor when the passion of the nation seemed at white heat over the destruction of the " Maine; " but it seems to me the time for action has now come. Not action in the " Maine " case! I hope and trust that this government will take action on the Cuban situation entirely outside of the " Maine " case. When the " Maine " report is received, if it be found that our ship and sailors were blown up by some outside explosive, we will have ample reparation without quibble or delay; and if the explosion can be traced to Spanish official sources there will be such swift and terrible punishment adjudged as will remain a warning to the world forever.

What shall the United States do, Mr. President?

I am a Republican, and I turn to the last platform of my party and I read:

" From the hour of achieving their own independence the people of the United States have regarded with sympathy the struggles of other American people to free themselves from European domination. We watch with deep and abiding interest the heroic battle of the Cuban patriots against cruelty and oppression, and our best hopes go out for the full success of their determined contest for liberty.

" The government of Spain having lost control of Cuba and being unable to protect the property or lives of resident American citizens, or to comply with its treaty obligations, we believe that the government of the United States should actively use its influence and good offices to restore peace and give independence to the island."

Mr. President, when that declaration was read before the St. Louis convention, over which I had the distinguished honor to preside, it was greeted with a mighty shout which seemed to lift the very roof of that great convention hall, and it was adopted as a part of the platform of the Republican party by unanimous vote. On the 29th day of June, 1896, William McKinley, standing upon his vine-clad porch at Canton, Ohio, in accepting the nomination then officially tendered him, said:

" The platform adopted by the Republican national convention has received my careful consideration and has my unqualified approval. It is a matter of gratification to me, as I am sure it must be to you and Republicans everywhere and to all our people, that the expressions of its declaration of principles are so direct, clear, and emphatic. They are too plain and positive to leave any chance for doubt or question as to their purport and meaning."

That platform of the Republican party, that indorsement by its nominee for President, was ratified by more than seven million American voters. That platform has marked my path of duty from the hour of its adoption up to the present time.

It is an honored boast of the Republican party that it always keeps its promises and that its platform declarations are always carried out by its administrations. I have no reason to doubt, I have every reason to believe, that the present Chief Magistrate of the United States still stands upon the platform of the Republican party. I have no reason to doubt, I have every reason to believe, that he will make its fulfilment a part of the glorious history of the world.

Mr. President, that platform was adopted almost two years ago. Has there been any such change in the Cuban situation as to relieve the Republican party from its obligations? None whatever. There has been no change except such as to strengthen the force of our platform assertion that Spain has lost control of the island. Twice within the last two years I have voted for a resolution according the rights of belligerents to the Cuban revolutionists.

I believed at those times, I still believe, that such a recognition on our part would have enabled the Cuban patriots to have achieved independence for themselves; that it would have given them such a standing in the money markets of the world, such rights on the sea, such flag on the land, that ere this the independence of Cuba would have been secured, and that without cost or loss of blood or treasure to the people of the United States. But that time has passed; it is too late to talk about resolutions according belligerent rights; and mere resolutions recognizing the independence of the Cuban republic would avail but little. Our platform demands that the United States shall actively use its influence for the independence of the island.

I am not here to criticize the present administration. I yield to no man living in my respect, my admiration for, and my confidence in the judgment, the wisdom, the patriotism, the Americanism of William McKinley. When he entered upon his administration he faced a difficult situation. It was his duty to proceed with care and caution. At the first available opportunity he addressed a note to Spain, in which he gave that government notice, as set forth in his message to the Congress of the United States, that the United States—

—" could be required to wait only a reasonable time for the mother country to establish its authority and restore peace and order within the borders of the island; that we could not contemplate an indefinite period for the accomplishment of this result."

The President further advised us:

" This government has never in any way abrogated its sovereign prerogative of reserving to itself the determination of its policy and course according to its own high sense of right and in consonance with the dearest interests and convictions of our own people should the prolongation of the strife so demand."

This was the proper, the statesmanlike beginning of the performance of the promise of the Republican platform. It was in accordance with the diplomatic usages and customs of civilized nations. In the meantime the whole situation apparently changed. In Spain the liberal ministry of Sagasta succeeded that of Canovas; the cruel and inhuman Weyler was recalled, and succeeded by the humane Blanco, who, under the Sagasta ministry, has unquestionably made every effort to bring about peace in the island of Cuba under the promise of autonomy—a decided advance beyond any proposition ever before made for the participation of the Cubans in their own domestic affairs.

It was the plain duty of the President of the United States to give to the liberal ministry of Spain a reasonable time in which to test its proposed autonomy. That time has been given. Autonomy is conceded the wide world over to be a conspicuous failure. The situation in Cuba has only changed for the worse. Sagasta is powerless; Blanco is powerless to put an end to the conflict, to rehabilitate the island, or to relieve the suffering, starvation, and distress.

The time for action has, then, come. No greater reason for it can exist to-morrow than exists to-day. Every hour's delay only adds another chapter to the awful story of misery and death. Only one Power can intervene—the United States of America. Ours is the one great nation of the New World, the mother of American republics. She holds a position of trust and responsibility toward the peoples and the affairs of the whole Western Hemisphere.

It was her glorious example which inspired the patriots of Cuba to raise the flag of liberty in her eternal hills. We cannot refuse to accept this responsibility which the God of the universe has placed upon us as the one great power in the New World. We must act! What shall our action be? Some say the acknowledgment of the belligerency of the revolutionists. As I have already shown, the hour and the opportunity for that have passed away.

Others say, Let us by resolution or official proclamation recognize the independence of the Cubans. It is too late even for such recognition to be of great avail. Others say, Annexation to the United States. God forbid! I would oppose annexation with my latest breath. The people of Cuba are not our people; they cannot assimilate with us; and beyond all that I am utterly and unalterably opposed to any departure from the declared policy of the fathers which would start this Republic for the first time upon a career of conquest and dominion utterly at variance with the avowed purposes and manifest destiny of popular government.

Let the world understand that the United States does not propose to annex Cuba, that it is not seeking a foot of Cuban soil or a dollar of Spanish treasure. Others say, Let us intervene for the pacification the island, giving to its people the greatest measure of autonomy consistent with the continued sovereignty of Spain. Such a result is no longer possible. It is enough to say that it would be resisted by all classes ot the Cuban population, and its attempt would simply transfer the putting down of the revolution and the subjugation of the Cuban patriots to the armies of the United States.

There is also said to be a syndicate organization in this country, representing the holders of Spanish bonds, who are urging that the intervention of the United States shall be for the purchase of the island or for the guaranteeing of the Spanish debt incurred in the attempted subjugation of the Cuban revolutionists. Mr. President, it is idle to think for a single moment of such a plan. The American people will never consent to the payment of one dollar, to the guaranteeing of one bond, as the price paid to Spain for her relinquishment of the island she has so wantonly outraged and devastated.

Mr. President, there is only one action possible, if any is taken; that is, intervention for the independence of the island; intervention that means the landing of an American army on Cuban soil, the deploying of an American fleet off Havana; intervention which says to Spain, Leave the island, withdraw your soldiers, leave the Cubans, these brothers of ours in the New World, to form and carry on government for themselves. Such intervention on our part would not of itself be war. It would undoubtedly lead to war. But if war came it would come by act of Spain in resistance of the liberty and the independence of the Cuban people.

Some say these Cubans are incapable of self-government; that they cannot be trusted to set up a republic. Will they ever become better qualified under Spanish rule than they are to-day? Sometime or other the dominion of kings must cease on the Western continent.

The senator from Vermont has done full justice to the native population of Cuba. He has studied them, and he knows that of all the people on the island they are the best qualified and fitted for government. Certainly any government by the Cuban people would be better than the tyranny of Spain.

Mr. President, there was a time when "jingoism" was abroad in the land; when sensationalism prevailed, and when there was a distinct effort to inflame the passions and prejudices of the American people and precipitate a war with Spain. That time has passed away. "Jingoism" is long since dead. The American people have waited and waited and waited in patience; yea, in patience and confidence—confidence in the belief that decisive action would be taken in due season and in a proper way. To-day all over this land the appeal comes up to us; it reaches us from every section and from every class. That appeal is now for action.

In an interview of yesterday, the senior senator from Maine [Mr. Hale] is reported as saying: "Events have crowded on too rapidly, and the President has been carried off his feet."

I know of no warrant for such an assertion, but I do know this, that unless Congress acts promptly, meeting this grave crisis as it should be met, we will be swept away, and we ought to be swept away, by the tidal wave of American indignation.

The President has not been carried off his feet.

The administration has been doing its whole duty. With rare foresight and statesmanship it has hastened to make every possible preparation for any emergency. If it be true that the report in the "Maine" case has been delayed, it has been delayed in order that we might be prepared at all points for defensive and offensive action. There are some who say, but they are mostly those who have procrastinated from the beginning up to the present time, "Let Congress hold its peace, adjourn, go home, and leave the President to act."

I for one believe that the Congress of the United States is an equal and co-ordinate branch of the federal government, representing the combined judgment and wisdom of the many. It can more safely be depended on than the individual judgment and wisdom of any one man. I am a Senator of the United States, and I will never consent to abdicate my right to participate in the determination as to what is the solemn duty of this great Republic in this momentous and fateful hour. We are not in session to hamper or cripple the President; we are here to advise and assist him. Congress can alone declare war; Congress can alone levy taxes; and to this Congress the united people of this broad land, from sea to sea, from lake to gulf, look to voice their wishes and execute their will.

Mr. President, against the intervention of the United States in this holy cause there is but one voice of dissent; that voice is the voice of the money-changers. They fear war! Not because of any Christian or ennobling sentiment against war and in favor of peace, but because they fear that a declaration of war, or the intervention which might result in war, would have a depressing effect upon the stock market.

Mr. President, I do not read my duty from the ticker; I do not accept my lessons in patriotism from Wall Street. I deprecate war. I hope and pray for the speedy coming of the time when the sword of the soldier will no longer leap from its scabbard to settle disputes between civilized nations. But, it is evident, looking at the cold facts, that a war with Spain would not permanently depreciate the value of a single American stock or bond.

War with Spain would increase the business and the earnings of every American railroad, it would increase the output of every American factory, it would stimulate every branch of industry and domestic commerce, it would greatly increase the demand for American labor, and in the end every certificate that represented a share in an American business enterprise would be worth more money than it is to-day. But in the meantime the spectre of war would stride through the stock exchanges, and many of the gamblers around the board would find their ill-gotten gains passing to the other side of the table.

Let them go; what one man loses at the gambling-table his fellow gambler wins. It is no concern of yours, it is no concern of mine, whether the " bulls " or the " bears " have the best of these stock-deals. They do not represent American sentiment; they do not represent American patriotism. Let them take their chances as they can. Their weal or woe is of but little importance to the liberty-loving people of the United States. They will not do the fighting; their blood will not flow; they will keep on dealing in options on human life. Let the men whose loyalty is to the dollar stand aside while the men whose loyalty is to the flag come to the front.

There are some who lift their voices in the land and in the open light of day insist that the Republican party will not act, for they say it sold out to the capitalists and the money-changers at the last national election.

It is not so. God forbid! The 7,000,000 freemen who voted for the Republican party and for William McKinley did not mortgage the honor of this nation for a campaign fund, and if the time ever comes when the Republican party hesitates in its course of duty because of any undue anxiety for the welfare of the accumulated wealth of the nation, then let the Republican party be swept from the face of the earth and be succeeded by some other party, by whatever name it may be called, which will represent the patriotism, the honesty, the loyalty, and the devotion that the Republican party exhibited under Abraham Lincoln in 1861.

Mr. President, there are those who say that the affairs of

Cuba are not the affairs of the United Sates, who insist that we can stand idly by and see that island devastated and depopulated, its business interests destroyed, its commercial intercourse with us cut off, its people starved, degraded, and enslaved. It may be the naked legal right of the United States to stand thus idly by.

I have the legal right to pass along the street and see a helpless dog stamped into the earth under the heels of a ruffian. I can pass by and say that is not my dog. I can sit in my comfortable parlor with my loved ones gathered about me, and through my plate-glass window see a fiend outraging a helpless woman near by, and I can legally say this is no affair of mine—it is not happening on my premises; and I can turn away and take my little ones in my arms, and, with the memory of their sainted mother in my heart, look up to the motto on the wall and read, " God bless our home."

But if I do I am a coward and a cur unfit to live, and, God knows, unfit to die. And yet I cannot protect the dog or save the woman without the exercise of force.

We cannot intervene and save Cuba without the exercise of force, and force means war; war means blood. The lowly Nazarene on the shores of Galilee preached the divine doctrine of love, " Peace on earth, good will toward men." Not peace on earth at the expense of liberty and humanity. Not good will toward men who despoil, enslave, degrade, and starve to death their fellow men. I believe in the doctrine of Christ. I believe in the doctrine of peace; but, Mr. President, men must have liberty before there can come abiding peace.

Intervention means force. Force means war. War means blood. But it will be God's force. When has a battle for humanity and liberty ever been won except by force?

What barricade of wrong, injustice, and oppression has ever been carried except by force?

Force compelled the signature of unwilling royalty to the great Magna Charter; force put life into the Declaration of Independence and made effective the Emancipation Proclamation; force beat with naked hands upon the iron gateway of the Bastile and made reprisal in one awful hour for centuries of kingly crime; force waved the flag of revolution over Bunker Hill and marked the snows of Valley Forge with blood-stained feet; force held the broken line at Shiloh, climbed the flame-swept hill at Chattanooga, and stormed the clouds on Lookout Heights; force marched with Sherman to the sea, rode with Sheridan in the valley of the Shenandoah, and gave Grant victory at Appomattox; force saved the Union, kept the stars in the flag, made " niggers " men. The time for God's force has come again. Let the impassioned lips of American patriots once more take up the song:

" In the beauty of the lilies Christ was born across the sea,
With a glory in his bosom that transfigured you and me,
As he died to make men holy, let us die to make men free,
For God is marching on."

Others may hesitate, others may procrastinate, others may plead for further diplomatic negotiation, which means delay, but for me, I am ready to act now, and for my action I am ready to answer to my conscience, my country, and my God.

Mr. President, in the cable that moored me to life and hope the strongest strands are broken. I have but little left to offer at the altar of Freedom's sacrifice, but all I have I am glad to give. I am ready to serve my country as best I can in the Senate or in the field. My dearest wish, my most earnest prayer to God is this, that when death comes to end all, I may meet it calmly and fearlessly as did my beloved, in the cause of humanity, under the American flag.

FOSTER

GEORGE EULAS FOSTER, a Canadian statesman and orator of the Liberal-Conservative party, was born in Carleton County, New Brunswick, September 3, 1847. After receiving a common-school education and working for a time in a grocery store, he entered the University of New Brunswick, whence he graduated at the head of his class, and in 1871 was appointed professor of history. He resigned in 1879 and devoted himself to lecturing on temperance and prohibition. In 1882 he was elected to the House of Commons and immediately made his mark as a parliamentary speaker. In 1885 he was appointed Minister of Marine and Fisheries and took charge of the Canadian interests in the Joint Commission that sat at Washington in 1888. That same year he succeeded Sir Charles Tupper as Minister of Finance, a position which he held through four administrations until July, 1896. He was returned to the Eighth Dominion Parliament as a member for York. Mr. Foster advocated the building of the Canadian Pacific Railway and favored the idea of an imperial federation of the British dominions, in which each country, while free to manage its own domestic affairs, should be leagued with all the others in a community of trade and defence. At the unveiling of the Macdonald monument in Montreal in June, 1895, he delivered an impressive oration.

DEFENCE AND PROTECTION

[Extract from a speech delivered in the Canadian House of Commons, January 16, 1896, during the debate on the Address in reply to the Speech from the Throne delivered by his Excellency in opening the session of Parliament.]

MY honorable friend also drew attention to the section in the Address which refers to the arming and the strengthening of the militia and defences of Canada. He spoke words none too hearty, he spoke none too approvingly of the militia of this country, and he voiced what is the general sentiment of this House and the country, that its militia deserves well at its hands, and it is the duty of the country to put the best and the newest arms in the hands of the militia, and see that they are well taken care of and equipped in this respect.

(10634)

But he had to qualify that by saying that he could perceive in it the flavor of a " jingo " policy.

Well, sir, I leave it to the honorable gentleman and all reasonable men to say if, taking up that paragraph in reply to the Speech, they can see anything in it which savors of defiance or in the least approaches to a jingo policy. It is a modest and straightforward expression, meaning exactly what he says and nothing more, and my honorable friend, I think, will agree that it does not in the least show a tendency in the direction suggested.

No person in Canada who loves his country and desires its peace and prosperity can, in the present juncture of circumstances, whatever may be said at other times, think of breathing a spirit of defiance and jingoism. This would be furthest removed possible from the sensible and well-developed sentiment of Canada, which, while it honors love of country, feels the evidence of strength in its arms, and cherishes in its heart the full purpose to defend that country and stand by it whenever it is threatened, yet, relying on its own calmness, force, and strength, does not ask for declamation and does not flaunt itself in defiance.

But he would read the signs of the times not aright in these somewhat troublesome days, when the great mother Empire stands splendidly isolated in Europe, with interests stretching over the wide world, with a commerce the greatest any nation of the world has ever possessed and vulnerable on every quarter of the sea, who did not feel as Britain feels to-day, and is showing it, that the country's weal, the country's progress, the country's stability, all of the country's pride and glory must base itself upon the strong arms and willing, loyal hearts of the citizenship of that Empire from one end of it to the other.

It is the right and duty of Britain herself and of every dependency that belongs to her to be ready, aye, ready as well as steady in its sentiments of loyalty and devotion for the Empire as a whole. It is in that spirit, and not in any spirit that asks for war or trouble, that that modest reference was placed in the Queen's Speech. And in pursuance of that it is the determination of this government to put the militia and the defences of this country, so far as can possibly be done by Canada, into a state which is adequate to the feelings, the interests, and the security of this country in itself, and as a portion of the Empire.

Now, sir, my honorable friend [Mr. Laurier] has referred to the development of foreign markets. I would not speak of that for a single moment except that he introduced a specious fallacy which is often thrown at the Liberal-Conservative party.

It is this: You tell me that the farmer of Great Britain is seeking for protection, that to-day the weight of competition is being felt by the English farmer who, when raising his wheat one hundred miles from London, is at a disadvantage in competition with the man who raises his wheat three thousand miles away under other and freer conditions; and that therefore the British farmer is looking for protection to aid him in the unequal competition. But, says my honorable friend, if the British farmer gets the protection that he needs, it is a death-blow to you as a protectionist in Canada.

That I think, sir, is not a view that takes in the whole of the situation. We shall have time to discuss that by and by, but there is just one great question to-day which is pressing itself to the front, which is becoming every day more and more considered by the best statesmen of Great Britain and the colonies, and that is as to whether, these forces and outside circumstances conjoining together, the time is not approaching when it shall not become a question simply as to whether Great Britain shall give protection to her farmers, but when the greater problem will appear for solution as to whether the needs of the Empire cannot be best met within the Empire itself; as to whether the Empire's markets cannot be supplied by the Empire's producers, and practical independence of foreign countries in food-supplies be secured, so that in time of trial and war the Empire's producers may be rid of that great danger of the present time, in this, that the Empire itself shall be sufficient to feed and to produce for the needs of the Empire.

FOODS FOR THE HOMELAND

CLOSING ARGUMENT AND PERORATION OF SPEECH DELIVERED IN
THE CANADIAN HOUSE OF COMMONS, JANUARY 31, 1896

IS there any reason why we should change our line of reasonable protection in order to adopt any of those facile political faiths which have been confessed from time to time by honorable gentlemen opposite? Is there any reason for change to be found in the general circumstances of the world to-day? If in 1878 the people of this country thought that a reasonable protection was necessary to give them the vantage-ground in competing with the world and building up and establishing industrial life in this country, is it any less necessary to-day? Is the competition less keen to-day than it was in 1878? Are the tariff lines of the various countries of the world lower to-day than in 1878?

Is the tendency of the commercial countries of the world changed in the direction of freer trade and lower duties?

No, sir, they have changed and are changing in the direction of greater stringency and more prohibitive tariffs and circumstances. If they have changed from 1878 to this time, they are stronger to-day in the direction of making Canada keep, for the sake of her trade and business interests, to the line of reasonable protection, instead of taking the line of free trade or partial free trade.

Why, to-day, after the Democratic administration had lowered the duties to a small extent, but so far away from free trade that they enjoy a tariff with an average of 42 per cent on dutiable articles for home consumption in that country, when they had given Canada some little better footing in their market by lowering to some extent duties on agricultural products, what to-day has happened? A Republican majority in the House of Representatives has sent to the Senate a bill which proposes to raise the rate of taxation on all those articles, and to raise them so as to be prohibitive as regards the introduction of the products of Canada into the United States. Is that a reason why we should change our line of policy? If in 1878 there was a reason for the adoption of this policy, in 1895 there is greater reason that this policy should be continued and we should hold to it in Canada.

But there is a line which I think it is possible, and I believe it is right, that the statesmanship of this country as well as of Great Britain and other colonies of the Empire should consider and ponder carefully and well, and that is whether it is not possible for statesmanship in the colonies and Great Britain to bring about between the colonies as among themselves, and between the colonies and Great Britain, concurrent action which will be conducive to the commercial interests of both, and which will result in greater power and strength. I read an article but a little time ago in the " Nineteenth Century Review," in which the general question which is agitating many thoughtful minds at the present day was raised and discussed, as to whether the Empire would be able to feed itself in the event of war against Great Britain which would cut off her supplies from hostile nations.

Feed itself! Why, sir, if statesmanship is not able practically to solve that question, statesmanship must find it impossible to solve any of the great questions which from time to time present themselves for consideration. The Empire able to feed itself! Yes. This article showed that 100,000,-000 bushels of wheat were necessary to England other than what the colonies afforded her at the present time, in order to feed the people of the Empire there.

One hundred million bushels of wheat! Why, 50,000 Canadian farmers with 100 acres each in wheat, and raising twenty bushels to the acre, would produce the 100,000,000 of bushels of wheat needed by Great Britain. And what is 50,000 farmers cultivating 5,000,000 of acres, compared with the English farmers wanting employment and the numbers of millions of acres of good wheat land in Manitoba and the Northwest Territories, which has not yet been scratched by the plow?

Meats to the value of $140,000,000 would need to be supplied by the colonies to make up for Great Britain's deficiency supplied now from foreign countries. Well, cattle and horses and pigs in illimitable quantity could be raised in this country. As to butter and cheese: 50,000 farmers owning each
D 50 cows, amounting to 2,500,000 in numbers, would supply

butter and cheese going far to meet the demands of Great
Britain for such supplies.   And, with the vast lands of the
Northwest, that is not an estimate which cannot be reached
if adequate means were taken to bring it about.

So, sir, I might go on to amplify this.   The sugar which
is necessary for the consumption of Great Britain could be
supplied by the West Indies, and by the East Indies, with
the cultivation of the cane lands which are now going out
of use, and which by its diminution is impoverishing the
planters and the laborers of the West Indies.   That industry
might again have its period of flourishing and its reward of
remunerative production were concurrent action taken in
Britain and the islands.

So all the way through.   It is a problem which requires
only time and good statesmanship to solve.   And, as I said
before, it is for Canada, for Australia, for the other colonies
of Great Britain, and for Great Britain herself, to ponder
seriously and carefully; to consider whether or not an arrangement cannot become to which will make the Empire and
its dependencies sufficient within themselves to feed the Empire, and by doing that add to the volume of business and to
a mutually remunerative production.   And, sir, the statesmanship which could formulate some such policy of mutually
beneficial trade would achieve an end infinitely higher and
more wide-reaching.   It would evolve from the dark fore-
ground of the not-distant future a national life of singular
strength and beauty, in which Canadian Britain, and
Australasian Britain, the Britain of Asia and Africa and of
the Isles of the Sea, would group themselves in grand imperial unity; the old enriching the new, and the new imparting fresh strength to the old,—through whose world-wide
realm the blood of a common commerce should mingle with

the blood of a common patriotism, whose power would compel peace, and whose millions of happy people would march in the van of the fullest freedom and the highest civilization.

PRUDENT COMPROMISE

[Peroration of speech on the Manitoba Remedial Separate School Bill, delivered in the Canadian House of Commons, March 13, 1896.]

AFTER six years, sir, we stand here under circumstances such as I have detailed. What is it, then, for this Parliament to do? On the one hand, there is a well-founded repugnance to interfere, and do what, even though clearly within our right to do, the province can do more easily and far better than ourselves. There is along with that a number of subordinate reasons arising, either from considerations of principle or of personal concern, or of party interests that tend to induce some to vote against this bill and against remedial legislation.

On the other hand, what is there? There is the genius and spirit of the constitutional compacts of this country. There is the splendid lesson of toleration and of compromise which has been read to you in that constitution, and which has been evidenced in its harmonious workings for nearly thirty years. There is the cry of the minority, small in the area of those who directly suffer, but large, let me tell you, in the area of those who sympathize with it in this country from one end to the other. There are the minorities in other provinces demanding of you where they shall stand and how they shall be treated if in future years their time of trial comes, and they will have to appeal to this same high court of Parliament and invoke this same jurisdiction.

There is the Parliament, sir, invested, knowingly, definitely, positively invested by the fathers of confederation in the constitution with the jurisdiction to maintain these rights and to restore them if they are taken away. This Parliament is appealed to. It is watched by Canada, it is watched by the world. On grounds of courage, on grounds of justice, on grounds of good faith, make you answer to those who appeal, make you answer to Canada, which is watching you, and to the world, which will judge of your actions. History, sir, is making itself in these eventful days. Shall the chapter be a record of nobleness and adequacy, or a record of weakness and inefficiency? Shall we stamp ourselves as petty and provincial, or shall we be recorded to future ages as magnanimous and imperial? Let us plant our feet in the firm paths of constitutional compact and agreement of good faith, and of honest, fair dealing. Let us take and pass on that gleaming touch of prudent compromise under whose kindly light the fathers of confederation marched safely through in times far more troublous and far less advanced than ours into an era of harmony and continued peace.

Let us do justice to a weak and patient minority, and thus settle forever the question of the sufficiency of the guarantees of confederation. Let us follow with cheerful emulation the shining example of our great mother country, whose foundations were laid on the solid granite of good faith, and whose world-wide and wondrous superstructure has been joined together with the cement of a strong and generous toleration.

Let us prove ourselves now, in the thirtieth year of our existence as in the stress of our natal days, a people fit for Empire, and worthy to rank among the best and greatest of nations.

BALFOUR

ARTHUR JAMES BALFOUR, a noted English statesman and author, was born in Scotland, July 25, 1848, and was educated at Eton and Trinity College, Cambridge. He entered Parliament in 1874 as member for Hertford, which he represented till 1885, since which time he has sat for East Manchester. He was private secretary to his uncle, Lord Salisbury, 1878-80, and for a short period acted with a few Conservatives led by Lord Randolph Churchill, and known as the "Fourth Party." He was Privy Councillor in 1885, Secretary for Scotland, 1886-87, and Chief Secretary for Ireland, 1887-91, his Irish policy being not altogether to the liking of some of the Conservatives. He was First Lord of the Treasury, 1891-92, and again in 1895. He became Conservative leader of the House in 1891 and in the following year delivered many speeches against the Home Rule Bill. Balfour was Lord Rector of St. Andrew's University in 1880, and of Glasgow University in 1890. His writings comprise "A Defence of Philosophic Doubt" (1879); "Essays and Addresses" (1893); "The Foundations of Belief," a book which has attracted general attention (1895).

THE PLEASURES OF READING

DELIVERED AT ST. ANDREW'S UNIVERSITY, DECEMBER 10, 1887

TRULY it is a subject for astonishment that, instead of expanding to the utmost the employment of this pleasure-giving faculty, so many persons should set themselves to work to limit its exercise by all kinds of arbitrary regulations.

Some persons, for example, tell us that the acquisition of knowledge is all very well, but that it must be useful knowledge,—meaning usually thereby that it must enable a man to get on in a profession, pass an examination, shine in conversation, or obtain a reputation for learning. But even if they mean something higher than this—even if they mean that knowledge, to be worth anything, must subserve ulti-

(10643)

mately, if not immediately, the material or spiritual interests of mankind,—the doctrine is one which should be energetically repudiated.

I admit, of course, at once, that discoveries the most apparently remote from human concerns have often proved themselves of the utmost commercial or manufacturing value. But they require no such justification for their existence, nor were they striven for with any such object.

Navigation is not the final cause of astronomy, nor telegraphy of electro-dynamics, nor dye-works of chemistry. And if it be true that the desire of knowledge for the sake of knowledge was the animating motives of the great men who first wrested her secrets from nature, why should it not also be enough for us, to whom it is not given to discover, but only to learn as best we may what has been discovered by others?

Another maxim, more plausible but equally pernicious, is that superficial knowledge is worse than no knowledge at all. That " a little knowledge is a dangerous thing " is a saying which has now got currency as a proverb stamped in the mint of Pope's versification,—of Pope who, with the most imperfect knowledge of Greek, translated Homer; with the most imperfect knowledge of the Elizabethan drama, edited Shakespeare; and with the most imperfect knowledge of philosophy, wrote the " Essay on Man."

But what is this " little knowledge " which is supposed to be so dangerous? What is it " little " in relation to? If in relation to what there is to know, then all human knowledge is little. If in relation to what actually is known by somebody, then we must condemn as " dangerous " the knowledge which Archimedes possessed of mechanics, or Copernicus of astronomy; for a shilling primer and a few weeks' study will enable any student to outstrip in mere information some of the greatest teachers of the past.

No doubt that little knowledge which thinks itself to be great many possibly be a dangerous, as it certainly is a most ridiculous, thing. We have all suffered under that eminently absurd individual who, on the strength of one or two volumes, imperfectly apprehended by himself and long discredited in the estimation of every one else, is prepared to supply you on the shortest notice with a dogmatic solution of every problem suggested by this " unintelligible world; " or the political variety of the same pernicious genus whose statecraft consists in the ready application to the most complex question of national interest of some high-sounding commonplace which has done weary duty on a thousand platforms, and which even in its palmiest days was never fit for anything better than a peroration.

But in our dislike of the individual do not let us mistake the diagnosis of his disease. He suffers not from ignorance, but from stupidity. Give him learning, and you make him, not wise, but only more pretentious in his folly.

I say, then, that so far from a little knowledge being undesirable a little knowledge is all that on most subjects any of us can hope to attain, and that as a source, not of worldly profit, but of personal pleasure, it may be of incalculable value to its possessor.

But it will naturally be asked, " How are we to select from among the infinite number of things which may be known those which it is best worth while for us to know? " We are constantly being told to concern ourselves with learning what is important, and not to waste our energies upon what is insignificant.

But what are the marks by which we shall recognize the

important, and how is it to be distinguished from the insignificant? A precise and complete answer to this question which shall be true for all men cannot be given. I am considering knowledge, recollect, as it ministers to enjoyment, and from this point of view each unit of information is obviously of importance in proportion as it increases the general sum of enjoyment which we obtain from knowledge. This, of course, makes it impossible to lay down precise rules which shall be an equally sure guide to all sorts and conditions of men; for in this, as in other matters, tastes must differ, and against real difference of taste there is no appeal.

There is, however, one caution which it may be worth your while to keep in view,—Do not be persuaded into applying any general proposition on this subject with a foolish impartiality to every kind of knowledge. There are those who tell you that it is the broad generalities and the far-reaching principles which govern the world, which are alone worthy of your attention.

A fact which is not an illustration of a law, in the opinion of these persons, appears to lose all its value. Incidents which do not fit into some great generalization, events which are merely picturesque, details which are merely curious— they dismiss as unworthy the interest of a reasoning being.

Now, even in science, this doctrine in its extreme form does not hold good. The most scientific of men have taken profound interest in the investigation of facts from the determination of which they do not anticipate any material addition to our knowledge of the laws which regulate the universe. In these matters I need hardly say that I speak wholly without authority. But I have always been under the impression that an investigation which has cost hundreds of thousands of pounds; which has stirred on three occasions the whole scientific community throughout the civilized world; on which has been expended the utmost skill in the construction of instruments and their application to purposes of research (I refer to the attempts made to determine the distance of the sun by observations of the transit of Venus), would, even if they had been brought to a successful issue, have furnished mankind with the knowledge of no new astronomical principle.

The laws which govern the motions of the solar system, the proportions which the various elements in that system bear to one another, have long been known. The distance of the sun itself is known within limits of error, relatively speaking, not very considerable. Were the measuring-rod we apply to the heavens, based on an estimate of the sun's distance from the earth, which was wrong by (say) three per cent, it would not, to the lay mind, seem to affect very materially our view either of the distribution of the heavenly bodies or of their motions. And yet this information, this piece of celestial gossip, would seem to be that which was chiefly expected from the successful prosecution of an investigation in which whole nations have interested themselves.

But though no one can, I think, pretend that science does not concern itself, and properly concern itself, with facts which are not in themselves, to all appearance, illustrations of law, it is undoubtedly true that for those who desire to extract the greatest pleasure from science, a knowledge, however elementary, of the leading principles of investigation and the larger laws of nature, is the acquisition most to be desired. To him who is not a specialist, a comprehension of the broad outlines of the universe as it presents itself to the scientific imagination, is the thing most worth striving to attain.

But when we turn from science to what is rather vaguely called history, the same principles of study do not, I think, altogether apply, and mainly for this reason,—that while the recognition of the reign of law is the chief amongst the pleasures imparted by science, our inevitable ignorance makes it the least among the pleasures imparted by history.

It is no doubt true that we are surrounded by advisers who tell us that all study of the past is barren except in so far as it enables us to determine the laws by which the evolution of human societies is governed. How far such an investigation has been up to the present time fruitful in results I will not inquire. That it will ever enable us to trace with accuracy the course which states and nations are destined to pursue in the future, or to account in detail for their history in the past, I do not indeed believe.

We are borne along like travellers on some unexplored stream. We may know enough of the general configuration of the globe to be sure that we are making our way towards the ocean. We may know enough by experience or theory of the laws regulating the flow of liquids, to conjecture how the river will behave under the varying influences to which it may be subject. More than this we cannot know. It will depend largely upon causes which, in relation to any laws which we are ever likely to discover, may properly be called accidental, whether we are destined sluggishly to drift among fever-stricken swamps, to hurry down perilous rapids, or to glide gently through fair scenes of peaceful cultivation.

But leaving on one side ambitious sociological speculations, and even those more modest but hitherto more successful investigations into the causes which have in particular cases been principally operative in producing great political changes, there are still two modes in which we can derive what I may call " spectacular " enjoyment from the study of history.

There is first the pleasure which arises from the contemplation of some great historic drama, or some broad and well-marked phase of social development. The story of the rise, greatness, and decay of a nation is like some vast epic which contains as subsidiary episodes the varied stories of the rise, greatness, and decay of creeds, of parties and of statesmen. The imagination is moved by the slow unrolling of this great picture of human mutability, as it is moved by the contrasted permanence of the abiding stars. The ceaseless conflict, the strange echoes of long-forgotten controversies, the confusion of purpose, the successes which lay deep the seeds of future evils, the failures that ultimately divert the otherwise inevitable danger, the heroism which struggles to the last for a cause foredoomed to defeat, the wickedness which sides with right, and the wisdom which huzzas at the triumph of folly— fate, meanwhile, through all this turmoil and perplexity, working silently toward the predestined end,—all these form together a subject the contemplation of which need surely never weary.

But there is yet another and very different species of enjoyment to be derived from the records of the past, which require a somewhat different method of study in order that it may be fully tasted. Instead of contemplating, as it were, from a distance, the larger aspects of the human drama, we may elect to move in familiar fellowship amid the scenes and actors of special periods.

We may add to the interest we derive from the contemplation of contemporary politics, a similar interest derived from a not less minute and probably more accurate knowledge of some comparatively brief passage in the political history of the past. We may extend the social circle in which we move—a circle perhaps narrowed and restricted through circumstances beyond our control—by making intimate acquaintances, perhaps even close friends, among a society long departed, but which, when we have once learnt the trick of it, it rests with us to revive.

It is this kind of historical reading which is usually branded as frivolous and useless, and persons who indulge in it often delude themselves into thinking that the real motive of their investigation into bygone scenes and ancient scandals is philosophic interest in an important historical episode, whereas in truth it is not the philosophy which glorifies the details, but the details which make tolerable the philosophy.

Consider, for example, the case of the French Revolution. The period from the taking of the Bastille to the fall of Robespierre is of about the same length as very commonly intervenes between two of our general elections. On these comparatively few months libraries have been written. The incidents of every week are matters of familiar knowledge. The character and the biography of every actor in the drama has been made the subject of minute study; and by common admission, there is no more fascinating page in the history of the world.

But the interest is not what is commonly called philosophic, it is personal. Because the Revolution is the dominant fact in modern history, therefore people suppose that the doings of this or that provincial lawyer, tossed into temporary eminence and eternal infamy by some freak of the revolutionary wave, or the atrocities committed by this or that mob, half-drunk with blood, rhetoric and alcohol, are of transcendent importance.

In truth their interest is great, but their importance is small. What we are concerned to know as students of the philosophy of history is, not the character of each turn and eddy in the great social cataract, but the manner in which the currents of the upper stream drew surely in toward the final plunge, and slowly collected themselves after the catastrophe, again to pursue, at a different level, their renewed and comparatively tranquil course.

Now, if so much of the interest of the French Revolution depends upon our minute knowledge of each passing incident, how much more necessary is such knowledge when we are dealing with the quiet nooks and corners of history—when we are seeking an introduction, let us say, into the literary society of Johnson or the fashionable society of Walpole! Society, dead or alive, can have no charm without intimacy, and no intimacy without interest in trifles which I fear Mr. Harrison would describe as " merely curious."

If we would feel at our ease in any company, if we wish to find humor in its jokes and point in its repartees, we must know something of the beliefs and the prejudices of its various members—their loves and their hates, their hopes and their fears, their maladies, their marriages, and their flirtations. If these things are beneath our notice, we shall not be the less qualified to serve our queen and country, but need make no attempt to extract pleasure out of one of the most delightful departments of literature.

That there is such a thing as trifling information, I do not of course question; but the frame of mind in which the reader is constantly weighing the exact importance to the universe at large of each circumstance which the author presents to his notice, is not one conducive to the true enjoyment of a picture whose effect depends upon a multitude of slight and seemingly insignificant touches, which impress the mind often without remaining in the memory.

The best method of guarding against the danger of reading what is useless is to read only what is interesting,—a truth which will seem a paradox to a whole class of readers, fitting objects of our commiseration, who may be often recognized by their habit of asking some adviser for a list of books, and then marking out a scheme of study in the course of which all these are to be conscientiously perused.

These unfortunate persons apparently read a book principally with the object of getting to the end of it. They reach the word "*Finis*" with the same sensation of triumph as an Indian feels who strings a fresh scalp to his girdle. They are not happy unless they mark by some definite performance each step in the weary path of self-improvement. To begin a volume and not to finish it would be to deprive themselves of this satisfaction; it would be to lose all the reward of their earlier self-denial by a lapse from virtue at the end. The skip, according to their literary code, is a form of cheating: it is a mode of obtaining credit for erudition on false pretences; a plan by which the advantages of learning are surreptitiously obtained by those who have not won them by honest toil. But all this is quite wrong. In matters literary, works have no saving efficacy. He has only half learned the art of reading who has not added to it the even more refined accomplishments of skipping and of skimming; and the first step has hardly been taken in the direction of making literature a pleasure, until interest in the subject, and not a desire to spare (so to speak) the author's feelings, or to accomplish an appointed task, is the prevailing motive of the reader.

CHURCHILL

RANDOLPH HENRY SPENCER CHURCHILL, a noted English politician, was the third son of the seventh Duke of Marlborough, and was born at Blenheim Palace, Woodstock, England, February 15, 1849. He was educated at Merton College, Oxford, and entered the House of Commons as member for Woodstock in 1874. After 1880 he was conspicuous for his attacks upon the Liberal party and was the leader of the so-called "Fourth Party." He was Secretary of State for India in 1885, and Chancellor of the Exchequer and leader of the House during Lord Salisbury's second administration in 1886. He resigned in December of that year and was then returned to the House as member for South Paddington, and again in 1892. He travelled in South Africa in 1891 on account of his failing health, and on his return to England was especially active in Parliament as a leader of the Opposition and in making platform speeches about the country. It was evident that he was more or less unbalanced as a result of disease, and his death occurred in London, January 24, 1895. He was one of the most prominent Tory politicians of his time, and an eloquent speaker, but his political course was erratic and misleading. He was the author of " Speeches " (1889); " Men, Mines, and Animals in South Africa " (1892).

ON THE EGYPTIAN CRISIS

A SPEECH DELIVERED IN PRINCE'S HALL, PICCADILLY, FEBRUARY, 16, 1884

[The fall of Sinkat and the massacre of its garrison excited indignation in all Conservative minds. When the announcement was made in the House of Lords on the twelfth inst., Lord Salisbury moved a vote of censure on the government, describing its policy pursued in Egypt as " vacillating and inconsistent," and also as " an act of blood-guiltiness." A similar vote was moved in the House of Commons by Sir Stafford Northcote. Indignation meetings were held everywhere, and the Liberal government seemed tottering to its fall.]

MY LORDS AND GENTLEMEN,—I rise for the purpose of moving the first resolution, and in order that we may consider that resolution with advantage I would beg all these gentlemen here who do not altogether concur with the views which we are going to expound, to listen to the discussion with equanimity, and, if possible, to reply to the arguments we may urge.

(10653)

It would conduce more to the dignity of a London meeting, it will conduce more to the maintenance of the high character of the citizens of this great metropolis, if any gentleman who have counter-opinions to urge to those of the majority of the meeting will come to the platform and address us. We have, gentlemen, to-day to set an example to the country: let us first set an example of order. The resolution which I have to propose is in these terms:

" That in the opinion of this meeting, her Majesty's government are solely responsible for the anarchy which prevails in Egypt, and the bloodshed which has occurred, and which is imminent in the Soudan, and that the vacillitating and pusillanimous policy of the Ministers deserve the severest censure of the country."

We are gathered together this afternoon for a serious purpose; no other, indeed, than to pronounce, after due deliberation, the strongest and most resolute condemnation of Mr. Gladstone's Egyptian policy, and our detestation and abhorrence of the bloodshed and misery of which he has been the immediate and direct cause. I say Mr. Gladstone's Egyptian policy, because I utterly decline to recognize as responsible agents either his ministerial colleagues or his parliamentary supporters.

Those parties have so wallowed in a stifling morass of the most degraded and servile worship of the Prime Minister that they have sunk below the level of slaves; they have become mere puppets, the objects of derision and contempt; they have lost all claim to the title of Englishmen, and I think they have lost all claim to the title of rational human beings.

To give you an instance of the abject imbecility which has struck down the Liberal party, I would mention what occurred in the House of Commons on Thursday night. Mr.

Forster, in that great speech which he made that evening— a speech in which he promised one vote to the government in the House of Commons, and alienated a hundred thousand votes from the government in the country—Mr. Forster, I say, expressed the opinion that the government ought to have rescued the garrison of Sinkat.

" How ? " cried out some importunate Liberals. " How ? " was the plaintive cry they raised.

" How ? " shouted Mr. Forster, turning upon them, so that they wished themselves a hundred leagues under the sea, " How ? why, by doing a fortnight earlier what they are doing now, sending British soldiers to the garrison's rescue."

There is a good instance of the hopeless and incurable mental alienation to which the once free and independent Liberal party have been reduced by Mr. Gladstone! It was indeed a melancholy spectacle.

I said that our purpose this afternoon was a serious one, and it is so. It is a serious thing for Englishmen to meet together in open day for the purpose of doing all they can to destroy a government. But we are not alone. Thousands of your countrymen have already met, and thousands more will meet, animated by the same feelings as yourselves, and, like yourselves, resolved to exhaust their energies in a supreme effort to avert further disgrace from our names, future defeat from our army, and ultimate ruin from our country, by dashing from his pride of place the evil and moonstruck minister who has brought England into grievous peril.

Perilous, I say, is our condition, for it is perilous for a country to shed human blood in vain; it is perilous for a country to assume responsibilities which it is too cowardly to discharge; it is perilous for a country to permit its foreign interests to be in such a condition that any morning we may awake to hear Europe demanding reparation and even vengeance.

Once again, for the fourth time in four years, do the ministry, whose programme was peace, and whose component parts were Quakers, call upon you to give them authority to wage a bloody war.

Of their former wars the results have been either infamous or futile—infamy in the south of Africa; futility in the north of Africa. Will you, I ask, with these memories still fresh in your minds, permit these false guides again to direct your course?

There can be but one answer. If war is again to be urged; if British blood and British treasure are again to be poured forth; if the regeneration of Egypt and the East is once more to be taken in hand, then other heads must do the work and other policies must be pursued.

A Parliament which has long ceased to represent England must be dissolved, and a ministry, for a parallel to which you must go back to the days of Shaftesbury or Lord North, must be placed on its trial by the people.

We have to provide for the safety of the hero Gordon; for the safety of the 4,000 British soldiers sent to Suakim; for the safety of the garrisons of the Soudan, 30,000 souls in all, whose one and only hope is now reposed in you. Above all, we have to provide for the safety of our position in the Delta of the Nile.

Shall labors such as these, interests so tremendous and so vital, be committed to the hands of Mr. Gladstone and his colleagues, men who have on their souls the blood of the massacre of Maiwand, the blood of the massacre of Laing's Nek, the blood of Sir George Colley, the blood of Lord Frederick Cavendish and Mr. Burke, and many other true and loyal subjects of the Crown in Ireland, the blood of Hicks Pasha and his 10,000 soldiers, the blood of the army of General Baker, the blood of Tewfik Bey and his 500 heroes?

For four years this ministry has literally waded in blood; their hands are literally dripping and reeking with blood. From massacre to massacre they march, and their course is ineffaceably stamped upon the history of the world by an overflowing stream of blood. How many more of England's heroes—how many more of England's best and bravest, are to be sacrificed to the Moloch of Midlothian?

This, too, is shocking and horrible—the heartless indifference and callousness of the Liberal party to narratives of slaughter and unutterable woe. Fifteen times did Mr. Gladstone on Tuesday night, in his reply to the grave and measured accusations of Sir Stafford Northcote,—fifteen times, I say, did he excite the laughter of his Liberal supporters with a frivolity which was too hideous to contemplate.

Talk of Bulgarian atrocities! Add them together, and even multiply them if you will, and you will not exceed the total of the atrocities and the infamies which have distinguished with an awful reputation the most blood-stained and withal the most cowardly government which England has ever seen.

Well, we are met together this afternoon, as loyal subjects of the Queen and as lovers of our country, for this purpose, and this purpose only,—to put a stop to further wicked and wanton bloodshed. We know that great empires must sometimes fight great battles, and that empires which fear to fight battles will soon cease to be empires; but we are resolved that the battles which we have to fight shall be fought for definite objects and for noble ends, and that poltroons and traitors, in the garb of ministers of the Crown, shall sacrifice no longer, for worthless and degraded aims, the life-blood of our country. The supporters of the present government exclaim that the Tory party, although prodigal of censure, is deficient in a policy of its own; and with many taunts they call upon us to disclose the direction in which our efforts would be turned in the event of a change in the councils of the Crown.

The demand cannot be considered unfair, and the reply is not so difficult as some people seem to think. We recognize to the very uttermost the immense responsibilities which this country has incurred toward Egypt, and toward the interests of Europe there, and to the discharge of these responsibilities we would be prepared to apply all the resources, if need be, of the Empire of the Queen; and till those responsibilities are satisfied we would neither stop nor stay.

The history of the Tory party in the past is, I fearlessly assent, an ample guarantee that the recognition of a responsibility and the full discharge of a responsibility are inseparable and consequential. I cannot claim to have the smallest share in the councils of the leaders of the Tory party, whoever they may be—and therefore, as far as they are concerned, I speak without authority.

But having studied with some care the history of our party in the past, possessing an unbounded faith in its future, and being not altogether ignorant of the state of public opinion, I will venture to say this much—that the policy of the Tory party, should it be placed in power, will be the policy of calling things by their right names. The occupation of Egypt by the British forces will be called a Protectorate of Egypt by the British Empire, having for its object the establishment, in process of time, of a government at Cairo which shall be consonant with the legitimate and laudable aspirations of the Egyptian people; which shall be able to protect itself alike from internal tumult and from foreign intrigue; which, while it shall develop the undoubted resources of Egypt, shall faithfully discharge the equitable liabilities of its people; and which, as far as human governments can do, shall give promise of prosperity and happiness in the land of the Nile.

We are now in Egypt by the sufferance of Europe, but we must endeavor to be in Egypt by the mandate of Europe. Our Protectorate, to be effective, and authoritative, and secure, should be acquiesced in by a European Congress in which Turkey shall be adequately represented and the rights and powers of the Sultan loyally secured. Our Protectorate, if it is to be crowned with success, must not shrink from dealing comprehensively and boldly with the financial indebtedness of Egypt, even though such dealing should involve some pecuniary liability on ourselves.

The work, if you undertake it, will be a work of time,— perhaps a long time. It will be a work of difficulty, and perhaps a work of danger; but it would also be a work of duty and a work of honor; and from work of that kind Britain has never yet recoiled. It is a work which, if courageously persisted in, will bind more closely to us than heretofore the sympathies of the Mohammedan races, and will establish on deeper foundations our dominions in the East. Our aims are honor, peace, and freedom, and we should not shrink from prosecuting those aims, if need be, by force of arms. Conscious of their magnanimity, we would go boldly forward, knowing well that the results of our policy would surely be to undo the heavy burdens and to let the oppressed go free.

BIRRELL

AUGUSTINE BIRRELL, a brilliant English essayist, was born near
Liverpool, January 19, 1850. He was the son of the Rev. Charles
Birrell, a Baptist minister; received his education at Amersham and Trinity
Hall, Cambridge, where he graduated in 1872, was called to the bar in 1875,
and fourteen years later was elected Liberal member of Parliament for
West Fife. In 1896 he was appointed Quain professor of law at University
College, London. Among his best-known publications are " Obiter Dicta "
(1884 and 1887); " Life of Charlotte Brontë " (1885); " Res Judicatæ "
(1892); " Men, Women, and Books " (1894); " Lectures on the Duties and
Liabilities of Trustees " (1896).

EDMUND BURKE

A LECTURE DELIVERED BEFORE THE EDINBURGH PHILOSOPHICAL
SOCIETY

MR. JOHN MORLEY, who among other things has
written two admirable books about Edmund Burke,
is to be found in the Preface to the second of them
apologizing for having introduced into the body of the work
extracts from his former volume — conduct which he seeks to
justify by quoting from the Greek (always a desirable thing
to do when in a difficulty), to prove that, though you may
say what you have to say well once, you cannot so say it
twice.

A difficulty somewhat of the same kind cannot fail to be
felt by every one who takes upon himself to write on Burke;
for, however innocent a man's own past life may be of any
public references to the subject, the very many good things
other men have said about it must seriously interfere with
true liberty of treatment.

Hardly any man, and certainly no politician, has been so

(10660)

bepraised as Burke, whose very name, suggesting, as it does, splendor of diction, has tempted those who would praise him to do so in a highly decorated style, and it would have been easy work to have brought together a sufficient number of animated passages from the works of well-known writers all dedicated to the greater glory of Edmund Burke, and then to have tagged on half-a-dozen specimens of his own resplendent rhetoric, and so to have come to an apparently natural and long desired conclusion without exciting any more than the usual post-lectorial grumble.

This course, however, not recommending itself, some other method had to be discovered. Happily, it is out of the question within present limits to give any proper summary of Burke's public life. This great man was not, like some modern politicians, a specialist, confining his activities within the prospectus of an association; nor was he, like some others, a thing of shreds and patches, busily employed to-day picking up the facts with which he will overwhelm his opponents on the morrow; but was one ever ready to engage with all comers on all subjects from out the stores of his accumulated knowledge.

Even were we to confine ourselves to those questions only which engaged Burke's most powerful attention, enlisted his most active sympathy, elicited his most bewitching rhetoric, we should still find ourselves called upon to grapple with problems as vast and varied as Economic Reform, the Status of our Colonies, our Empire in India, our Relations with Ireland both in respect to her trade and her prevalent religion; and then, blurring the picture, as some may think—certainly rendering it titanesque and gloomy—we have the spectacle of Burke in his old age, like another Laocoön, writhing and wrestling with the French Revolution; and it may serve to

give us some dim notion of how great a man Burke was,
of how affluent a mind, of how potent an imagination, of
how resistless an energy, that even when his sole unassisted
name is pitted against the outcome of centuries, and we say
Burke and the French Revolution, we are not overwhelmed
by any sense of obvious absurdity or incongruity.

What I propose to do is merely to consider a little Burke's
life prior to his obtaining a seat in Parliament, and then
to refer to any circumstances which may help us to account for the fact that this truly extraordinary man, whose intellectual resources beggar the imagination, and who devoted
himself to politics with all the forces of his nature, never so
much as attained to a seat in the Cabinet,—a feat one has
known to be accomplished by persons of no proved intellectual
agility. Having done this, I shall then, bearing in mind the
aphorism of Lord Beaconsfield, that it is always better to be
impudent than servile, essay an analysis of the essential elements of Burke's character.

The first great fact to remember is, that the Edmund Burke
we are all agreed in regarding as one of the proudest memories of the House of Commons was an Irishman. When we
are in our next fit of political depression about that island,
and are about piously to wish, as the poet Spenser tells us
men were wishing even in his time, that it were not adjacent,
let us do a little national stocktaking, and calculate profits as
well as losses.

Burke was not only an Irishman, but a typical one—of
the very kind many Englishmen, and even possibly some
Scotchmen, make a point of disliking. I do not say he was
an aboriginal Irishman, but his ancestors are said to have
settled in the county of Galway, under Strongbow, in King
Henry the Second's time, when Ireland was first conquered

and our troubles began. This, at all events, is a better Irish pedigree than Mr. Parnell's.

Skipping six centuries, we find Burke's father an attorney in Dublin—which somehow sounds a very Irish thing to be —who in 1725 married a Miss Nagle and had fifteen children. The marriage of Burke's parents was of the kind called mixed—a term which doubtless admits of wide application, but when employed technically signifies that the religious faith of the spouses was different; one, the father, being a Protestant, and the lady an adherent to what used to be pleasantly called the " old religion." The severer spirit now dominating Catholic councils has condemned these marriages on the score of their bad theology and their lax morality; but the practical politician, who is not usually much of a theologian—though Lord Melbourne and Mr. Gladstone are distinguished exceptions—and whose moral conscience is apt to be robust (and here I believe there are no exceptions), cannot but regret that so good an opportunity of lubricating religious differences with the sweet oil of the domestic affections should be lost to us in these days of bitterness and dissension.

Burke was brought up in the Protestant faith of his father, and was never in any real danger of deviating from it; but I cannot doubt that his regard for his Catholic fellow subjects, his fierce repudiation of the infamies of the penal code—whose horrors he did something to mitigate—his respect for antiquity, and his historic sense, were all quickened by the fact that a tenderly loved and loving mother belonged through life and in death to an ancient and an outraged faith.

The great majority of Burke's brothers and sisters, like those of Laurence Sterne, were " not made to live; " and out of the fifteen but three, beside himself, attained maturity.

These were his eldest brother, Garrett, on whose death Edmund succeeded to the patrimonial Irish estate, which he sold; his younger brother, Richard, a highly speculative gentleman, who always lost; and his sister, Juliana, who married a Mr. French, and was, as became her mother's daughter, a rigid Roman Catholic—who, so we read, was accustomed every Christmas Day to invite to the Hall the maimed, the aged, and distressed of her vicinity to a plentiful repast, during which she waited upon them as a servant. A sister like this never did any man any serious harm.

Edmund Burke was born in 1729, in Dublin, and was taught his rudiments in the country—first by a Mr. O'Halloran, and afterwards by a Mr. FitzGerald, village pedagogues both, who at all events succeeded in giving their charge a brogue which death alone could silence.

Burke passed from their hands to an academy at Ballitore, kept by a Quaker, from whence he proceeded to Trinity College, Dublin. He was thus not only Irish born, but Irish bred.

His intellectual habit of mind exhibited itself early. He belonged to the happy family of omnivorous readers, and, in the language of his latest schoolmaster, he went to college with a larger miscellaneous stock of reading than was usual with one of his years; which, being interpreted out of pedagogic into plain English, means that "our good Edmund" was an enormous devourer of poetry and novels, and so he remained to the end of his days.

That he always preferred Fielding to Richardson is satisfactory, since it pairs him off nicely with Dr. Johnson, whose preference was the other way, and so helps to keep an interesting question wide open. His passion for the poetry of Virgil is significant. His early devotion to Edward Young, the grandiose author of the " Night Thoughts," is not to be wondered at; though the inspiration of the youthful Burke, either as poet or critic, may be questioned when we find him rapturously scribbling in the margin of his copy:

" Jove claimed the verse old Homer sung,
But God himself inspired Dr. Young."

But a boy's enthusiasm for a favorite poet is a thing to rejoice over. The years that bring the philosophic mind will not bring—they must find—enthusiasm.

In 1750, Burke (being then twenty-one) came for the first time to London, to do what so many of his lively young countrymen are still doing—though they are beginning to make a grievance even of that—eat his dinners at the Middle Temple, and so qualify himself for the Bar. Certainly that student was in luck who found himself in the same mess with Burke; and yet so stupid are men—so prone to rest with their full weight on the immaterial and slide over the essential—that had that good fortune been ours we should probably have been more taken up with Burke's brogue than with his brains.

Burke came to London with a cultivated curiosity, and in no spirit of desperate determination to make his fortune. That the study of the law interested him cannot be doubted, for everything interested him, particularly the stage. Like the sensible Irishman he was, he lost his heart to Peg Woffington on the first opportunity. He was fond of roaming about the country, during, it is to be hoped, vacation-time only, and is to be found writing the most cheerful letters to his friends in Ireland (all of whom are persuaded that he is going some day to be somebody, though sorely puzzled to surmise what thing or when, so pleasantly does he take life), from all sorts of out-of-the-way country places, where he lodges with quaint old landladies who wonder maternally why he never gets drunk, and generally mistake him for an author until he pays his bill.

When in town he frequented debating societies in Fleet Street and Covent Garden, and made his first speeches; for which purpose he would, unlike some debaters, devote studious hours to getting up the subjects to be discussed. There is good reason to believe that it was in this manner his attention was first directed to India. He was at all times a great talker, and, Dr. Johnson's dictum notwithstanding, a good listener. He was endlessly interested in everything—in the state of the crops, in the last play, in the details of all trades, the rhythm of all poems, the plots of all novels, and indeed in the course of every manufacture. And so for six years he went up and down, to and fro, gathering information, imparting knowledge, and preparing himself, though he knew not for what.

The attorney in Dublin grew anxious, and searched for precedents of a son behaving like his, and rising to eminence. Had his son got the legal mind?—which, according to a keen observer, chiefly displays itself by illustrating the obvious, explaining the evident, and expatiating on the commonplace.

Edmund's powers of illustration, explanation, and expatiation could not indeed be questioned; but then the subjects selected for the exhibition of those powers were very far indeed from being obvious, evident, or commonplace; and the attorney's heart grew heavy within him. The paternal displeasure was signified in the usual manner—the supplies were cut off. Edmund Burke, however, was no ordinary prodigal, and his reply to his father's expostulations took the unexpected and unprecedented shape of a copy of a second and enlarged edition of his treatise on the " Sublime and

Beautiful," which he had published in 1756 at the price of three shillings. Burke's father promptly sent the author a bank-bill for £100,—conduct on his part which, considering he had sent his son to London and maintained him there for six years to study law, was, in my judgment, both sublime and beautiful.

In the same year Burke published another pamphlet—a one-and-sixpenny affair—written ironically, in the style of Lord Bolingbroke, and called "A Vindication of Natural Society; or, a View of the Miseries and Evils Arising to Mankind from Every Species of Civil Society." Irony is a dangerous weapon for a public man to have ever employed, and in after-life Burke had frequently to explain that he was not serious.

On these two pamphlets' airy pinions Burke floated into the harbor of literary fame. No less a man than the great David Hume referred to him, in a letter to the hardly less great Adam Smith, as an Irish gentleman who had written a "very pretty treatise on the Sublime." After these efforts, Burke, as became an established wit, went to Bath to recruit, and there, fitly enough, fell in love. The lady was Miss Jane Mary Nugent, the daughter of a celebrated Bath physician; and it is pleasant to be able to say of the marriage that was shortly solemnized between the young couple, that it was a happy one, and then to go on our way, leaving them—where man and wife ought to be left—alone.

Oddly enough, Burke's wife was also the offspring of a "mixed marriage"—only in her case it was the father who was the Catholic; consequently both Mr. and Mrs. Edmund Burke were of the same way of thinking, but each had a parent of the other way. Although getting married is no part of the curriculum of a law-student, Burke's father seems to have come to the conclusion that after all it was a greater distinction for an attorney in Dublin to have a son living amongst the wits in London, and discoursing familiarly on the "Sublime and Beautiful," than one prosecuting some poor countryman, with a brogue as rich as his own, for stealing a pair of breeches; for we find him generously allowing the young couple £200 a year, which no doubt went some way toward maintaining them. Burke, who was now in his twenty-eighth year, seems to have given up all notion of the law. In 1758 he wrote for Dodsley the first volume of the "Annual Register," a melancholy series which continues to this day. For doing this he got £100.

Burke was by this time a well-known figure in London literary society, and was busy making for himself a huge private reputation. The Christmas Day of 1758 witnessed a singular scene at the dinner-table of David Garrick. Dr. Johnson, then in the full vigor of his mind, and with the all-dreaded weapons of his dialectics kept burnished by daily use, was flatly contradicted by a fellow guest some twenty years his junior, and, what is more, submitted to it without a murmur. One of the diners, Arthur Murphy, was so struck by this occurrence, unique in his long experience of the Doctor, that on returning home he recorded the fact in his journal, but ventured no explanation of it.

It can only be accounted for—so at least I venture to think—by the combined effect of four wholly independent circumstances: First, the day was Christmas Day, a day of peace and good will, and our beloved Doctor was amongst the sincerest, though most argumentative of Christians, and a great observer of days. Second, the house was David Garrick's, and consequently we may be certain that the dinner had been a superlatively good one; and has not Boswell

placed on record Johnson's opinion of a man who professed
to be indifferent about his dinner? Third, the subject under
discussion was India, about which Johnson knew he knew
next to nothing. And fourth, the offender was Edmund
Burke, whom Johnson loved from the first day he set eyes
upon him to their last sad parting by the waters of death.

In 1761 that shrewd old gossip, Horace Walpole, met
Burke for the first time at dinner, and remarks of him in a
letter to George Montague:—

"I dined at Hamilton's yesterday; there were Garrick,
and young Mr. Burke, who wrote a book in the style of
Lord Bolingbroke, that was much admired. He is a sensible
man, but has not worn off his authorism yet, and thinks there
is nothing so charming as writers, and to be one. He will
know better one of these days."

But great as were Burke's literary powers, and passionate
as was his fondness for letters and for literary society, he
never seems to have felt that the main burden of his life lay
in that direction. He looked to the public service, and this
though he always believed that the pen of a great writer was
a more powerful and glorious weapon than any to be found
in the armory of politics. This faith of his comes out sometimes queerly enough. For example, when Dr. Robertson
in 1777 sent Burke his cheerful "History of America" in
quarto volumes, Burke, in the most perfect good faith, closes
a long letter of thanks thus:

"You will smile when I send you a trifling temporary production made for the occasion of the day, and to perish with
it, in return for your immortal work."

I have no desire, least of all in Edinburgh, to say anything
disrespectful of Principal Robertson; but still, when we re-

member that the temporary production he got in exchange for his "History of America" was Burke's immortal letter to the sheriffs of Bristol on the American war, we must, I think, be forced to admit that, as so often happens when a Scotchman and an Irishman do business together, the former got the better of the bargain.

Burke's first public employment was of an humble character, and might well have been passed over in a sentence had it not terminated in a most delightful quarrel, in which Burke conducted himself like an Irishman of genius.

Some time in 1759 he became acquainted with William Gerard Hamilton, commonly called "Single-Speech Hamilton," on account of the celebrity he gained from his first speech in Parliament, and the steady way in which his oratorical reputation went on waning ever after. In 1761 this gentleman went over to Ireland as Chief Secretary, and Burke accompanied him as the Secretary's secretary, or, in the unlicensed speech of Dublin, as Hamilton's jackal.

This arrangement was eminently satisfactory to Hamilton, who found, as generations of men have found after him, Burke's brains very useful, and he determined to borrow them for the period of their joint lives. Animated by this desire, in itself praiseworthy, he busied himself in procuring for Burke a pension of £300 a year on the Irish establishment, and then the simple "Single-Speech" thought the transaction closed. He had bought his poor man of genius, and paid for him on the nail with other people's money. Nothing remained but for Burke to draw his pension and devote the rest of his life to maintaining Hamilton's reputation. There is nothing at all unusual in this, and I have no doubt Burke would have stuck to his bargain had not Hamilton conceived the fatal idea that Burke's brains were exclusively his (Hamilton's). Then the situation became one of risk and apparent danger.

Burke's imagination began playing round the subject: he saw himself a slave, blotted out of existence—mere fuel for Hamilton's flame. In a week he was in a towering passion. Few men can afford to be angry. It is a run upon their intellectual resources they cannot meet. But Burke's treasury could well afford the luxury; and his letters to Hamilton make delightful reading to those who, like myself, dearly love a dispute when conducted according to the rules of the game by men of great intellectual wealth.

Hamilton demolished and reduced to stony silence, Burke sat down again and wrote long letters to all his friends, telling them the whole story from beginning to end. I must be allowed a quotation from one of these letters, for this really is not so frivolous a matter as I am afraid I have made it appear—a quotation of which this much may be said, that nothing more delightfully Burkean is to be found anywhere:

" My Dear Mason,—I am hardly able to tell you how much satisfaction I had in your letter. Your approbation of my conduct makes me believe much the better of you and myself; and I assure you that that approbation came to me very seasonably. Such proofs of a warm, sincere, and disinterested friendship were not wholly unnecessary to my support at a time when I experienced such bitter effects of the perfidy, and ingratitude of much longer and much closer connections. The way in which you take up my affairs binds me to you in a manner I cannot express; for, to tell you the truth, I never can (knowing as I do the principles upon which I always endeavor to act) submit to any sort of compromise of my character; and I shall never, therefore, look upon those who, after hearing the whole story, do not think me perfectly in the right, and do not consider Hamilton an infamous scoundrel, to be in the smallest degree my friends, or even

E   to be persons for whom I am bound to have the slightest es-

teem, as fair and just estimators of the characters and conduct of men.

"Situated as I am, and feeling as I do, I should be just as
well pleased that they totally condemned me, as that they
should say there were faults on both sides, or that it was a
disputable case, as I hear is (I cannot forbear saying) the
affected language of some persons. . . . You cannot avoid
remarking, my dear Mason, and I hope not without some indignation, the unparalleled singularity of my situation. Was
ever a man before me expected to enter into formal, direct,
and undisguised slavery? Did ever man before him confess an
attempt to decoy a man into such an alleged contract, not to
say anything of the impudence of regularly pleading it? If
such an attempt be wicked and unlawful (and I am sure no
one ever doubted it), I have only to confess his charge, and
to admit myself his dupe, to make him pass, on his own showing, for the most consummate villain that ever lived.

"The only difference between us is, not whether he is not
a rogue—for he not only admits but pleads the facts that
demonstrate him to be so; but only whether I was such a
fool as to sell myself absolutely for a consideration which, so
far from being adequate, if any such could be adequate, is
not even so much as certain. Not to value myself as a
gentleman, a free man, a man of education, and one pretend-
ing to literature; is there any situation in life so low, or
even so criminal, that can subject a man to the possibility
of such an engagement? Would you dare attempt to bind
your footman to such terms? Will the law suffer a felon
sent to the plantations to bind himself for his life, and to
renounce all possibility either of elevation or quiet? And
am I to defend myself for not doing what no man is suffered
to do, and what it would be criminal in any man to submit to?
You will excuse me for this heat."

I not only excuse Burke for his heat, but love him for
letting me warm my hands at it after a lapse of a hundred
and twenty years.

Burke was more fortunate in his second master, for in
1765, being then thirty-six years of age, he became private

secretary to the new Prime Minister, the Marquis of Rockingham; was by the interest of Lord Verney returned to
Parliament for Wendover, in Bucks; and on January 27,
1766, his voice was first heard in the House of Commons.

The Rockingham Ministry deserves well of the historian,
and on the whole has received its deserts. Lord Rockingham, the Duke of Richmond, Lord John Cavendish, Mr.
Dowdeswell, and the rest of them, were good men and true,
judged by an ordinary standard; and when contrasted with
most of their political competitors, they almost approach the
ranks of saints and angels. However, after a year and
twenty days, his Majesty King George III managed to get
rid of them, and to keep them at bay for fifteen years.

But their first term of office, though short, lasted long
enough to establish a friendship of no ordinary powers of endurance between the chief members of the party and the
Prime Minister's private secretary, who was at first, so ran
the report, supposed to be a wild Irishman, whose real name
was O'Burke, and whose brogue seemed to require the allegation that its owner was a popish emissary.

It is satisfactory to notice how from the very first Burke's
intellectual pre-eminence, character, and aims were clearly
admitted and most cheerfully recognized by his political and
social superiors; and in the long correspondence in which he
engaged with most of them, there is not a trace to be found,
on one side or the other, of anything approaching to either
patronage or servility. Burke advises them, exhorts them,
expostulates with them, condemns their aristocratic languor,
fans their feeble flames, drafts their motions, dictates their
protests, visits their houses, and generally supplies them with
facts, figures, poetry, and romance.

To all this they submit with much humility. The Duke of

Richmond once indeed ventured to hint to Burke, with ex-
ceeding delicacy, that he (the Duke) had a small private estate to attend to as well as public affairs; but the validity of
the excuse was not admitted. The part Burke played for the
next fifteen years with relation to the Rockingham party reminds me of the functions I have observed performed in lazy
families by a soberly clad and eminently respectable person
who pays them domiciliary visits, and, having admission
everywhere, goes about mysteriously from room to room,
winding up all the clocks. This is what Burke did for the
Rockingham party—he kept it going.

But fortunately for us, Burke was not content with private
adjuration, or even public speech. His literary instincts, his
dominating desire to persuade everybody that he, Edmund
Burke, was absolutely in the right, and every one of his opponents hopelessly wrong, made him turn to the pamphlet as
a propaganda, and in his hands—

> " The thing became a trumpet, whence he blew
> Soul-animating strains."

So accustomed are we to regard Burke's pamphlets as specimens of our noblest literature, and to see them printed in
comfortable volumes, that we are apt to forget that in their
origin they were but the children of the pavement, the publications of the hour.

If, however, you ever visit any old public library, and
grope about a little, you are likely enough to find a shelf
holding some twenty-five or thirty musty, ugly little books,
usually lettered " Burke," and on opening any of them you
will come across one of Burke's pamphlets as originally issued, bound up with the replies and counter-pamphlets it
occasioned. I have frequently tried, but always in vain, to
read these replies, which are pretentious enough—usually

the works of deans, members of Parliament, and other dignitaries of the class Carlyle used compendiously to describe as " shovel-hatted "—and each of whom was as much entitled to publish pamphlets as Burke himself.

There are some things it is very easy to do, and to write a pamphlet is one of them; but to write such a pamphlet as future generations will read with delight is perhaps the most difficult feat in literature. Milton, Swift, Burke, and Sydney Smith are, I think, our only great pamphleteers.

I have now rather more than kept my word so far as Burke's pre-parliamentary life is concerned, and will proceed to mention some of the circumstances that may serve to account for the fact, that when the Rockingham party came into power for the second time in 1782, Burke, who was their life and soul, was only rewarded with a minor office.

First, then, it must be recorded sorrowfully of Burke that he was always desperately in debt, and in this country no politician under the rank of a baronet can ever safely be in debt. Burke's finances are, and always have been, marvels and mysteries; but one thing must be said of them—that the malignity of his enemies, both Tory enemies and Radical enemies, has never succeeded in formulating any charge of dishonesty against him that has not been at once completely pulverized, and shown on the facts to be impossible.

Burke's purchase of the estate at Beaconsfield in 1768, only two years after he entered Parliament, consisting as it did of a good house and 1,600 acres of land, has puzzled a great many good men—much more than it ever did Edmund Burke. But how did he get the money? After an Irish fashion—by not getting it at all.

Two thirds of the purchase-money remained on mortgage, and the balance he borrowed; or, as he puts it, " With all I could collect of my own, and by the aid of my friends, I have established a root in the country." That is how Burke bought Beaconsfield, where he lived till his end came; whither he always hastened when his sensitive mind was tortured by the thought of how badly men governed the world; where he entertained all sorts and conditions of men— Quakers, Brahmins (for whose ancient rites he provided suitable accommodation in a greenhouse), nobles and abbés flying from revolutionary France, poets, painters, and peers; no one of whom ever long remained a stranger to his charm.

Burke flung himself into farming with all the enthusiasm of his nature. His letters to Arthur Young on the subject of carrots still tremble with emotion. You all know Burke's "Thoughts on the Present Discontents." You remember— it is hard to forget—his speech on Conciliation with America, particularly the magnificent passage beginning, "Magnanimity in politics is not seldom the truest wisdom, and a great empire and little minds go ill together."

You have echoed back the words in which, in his letter to the sheriffs of Bristol on the hateful American war, he protests that it was not instantly he could be brought to rejoice when he heard of the slaughter and captivity of long lists of those whose names had been familiar in his ears from his infancy, and you would all join with me in subscribing to a fund which would have for its object the printing and hanging up over every editor's desk in town and country a subsequent passage from the same letter:

" A conscientious man would be cautious how he dealt in blood. He would feel some apprehension at being called to a tremendous account for engaging in so deep a play without any knowledge of the game. It is no excuse for presumptuous ignorance that it is directed by insolent passion. The poorest being that crawls on earth, contending to save itself from injustice and oppression, is an object respectable in the eyes of God and man.

"But I cannot conceive any existence under heaven (which in the depths of its wisdom tolerates all sorts of things) that is more truly odious and disgusting than an impotent, helpless creature, without civil wisdom or military skill, bloated with pride and arrogance, calling for battles which he is not to fight, and contending for a violent dominion which he can never exercise. . . .

"If you and I find our talents not of the great and ruling kind, our conduct at least is conformable to our faculties. No man's life pays the forfeit of our rashness. No desolate widow weeps tears of blood over our ignorance. Scrupulous and sober in a well-grounded distrust of ourselves, we would keep in the port of peace and security; and perhaps in recommending to others something of the same diffidence, we should show ourselves more charitable to their welfare than injurious to their abilities."

You have laughed over Burke's account of how all Lord Talbot's schemes for the reform of the king's household were dashed to pieces because the turnspit of the king's kitchen was a Member of Parliament. You have often pondered over that miraculous passage in his speech on the Nabob of Arcot's debts, describing the devastation of the Carnatic by Hyder Ali—a passage which Mr. John Morley says fills the young orator with the same emotions of enthusiasm, emulation, and despair that (according to the same authority) invariably torment the artist who first gazes on "The Madonna" at Dresden, or the figures of "Night" and "Dawn" at Florence.

All these things you know, else are you mighty self-denying of your pleasures. But it is just possible you may have forgotten the following extract from one of Burke's farming letters to Arthur Young:

"One of the grand points in controversy (a controversy indeed chiefly carried on between practice and speculation) is that of deep plowing. In your last volumes you seem, on the whole, rather against that practice, and have given several reasons for your judgment which deserve to be very well considered. In order to know how we ought to plow, we ought to know what end it is we propose to ourselves in that operation. The first and instrumental end is to divide the soil; the last and ultimate end, so far as regards the plants, is to facilitate the pushing of the blade upward and the shooting of the roots in all the inferior directions.

"There is further proposed a more ready admission of external influences—the rain, the sun, the air, charged with all those heterogeneous contents, some, possibly all, of which are necessary for the nourishment of the plants. By plowing deep you answer these ends in a greater mass of the soil. This would seem in favor of deep plowing as nothing else than accomplishing, in a more perfect manner, those very ends for which you are induced to plow at all.

"But doubts here arise, only to be solved by experiment. First, it is quite certain that it is good for the ear and grain of farinaceous plants that their roots should spread and descend into the ground to the greatest possible distances and depths? Is there not some limit in this? We know that in timber, what makes one part flourish does not equally conduce to the benefit of all; and that which may be beneficial to the wood does not equally contribute to the quantity and goodness of the fruit; and, *vice versa*, that what increases the fruit largely is often far from serviceable to the tree.

"Secondly, is that looseness to great depths, supposing it is useful to one of the species of plants, equally useful to all?

"Thirdly, though the external influences—the rain, the sun, the air—act undoubtedly a part, and a large part, in vegetation, does it follow that they are equally salutary in any quantities, at any depths? Or that, though it may be useful to diffuse one of these agents as extensively as may be in the earth, that therefore it will be equally useful to render the earth in the same degree pervious to all.

"It is a dangerous way of reasoning in physics, as well as morals, to conclude, because a given proportion of anything is advantageous, that the double will be quite as good, or that it will be good at all. Neither in the one nor the other is it always true that two and two make four."

This is magnificent, but it is not farming, and you will easily believe that Burke's attempts to till the soil were more costly than productive. Farming, if it is to pay, is a pursuit of small economies; and Burke was far too Asiatic, tropical, and splendid to have anything to do with small economies. His expenditure, like his rhetoric, was in the "grand style." He belongs to Charles Lamb's great race, "the men who borrow." But indeed it was not so much that Burke borrowed as that men lent.

Right-feeling men did not wait to be asked. Dr. Brocklesby, that good physician, whose name breathes like a benediction through the pages of the biographies of the best men of his time, who soothed Dr. Johnson's last melancholy hours, and for whose supposed heterodoxy the dying man displayed so tender a solicitude, wrote to Burke, in the strain of a timid suitor proposing for the hand of a proud heiress, to know whether Burke would be so good as to accept £1,000 at once, instead of waiting for the writer's death. Burke felt no hesitation in obliging so old a friend.

Garrick, who, though fond of money, was as generous-hearted a fellow as ever brought down a house, lent Burke £1,000. Sir Joshua Reynolds, who has been reckoned stingy, by his will left Burke £2,000, and forgave him another £2,000 which he had lent him. The Marquis of Rockingham, by his will, directed all Burke's bonds held by him to be cancelled. They amounted to £30,000. Burke's patrimonial estate was sold by him for £4,000; and I have seen it stated that he had received altogether from family sources as much as £20,000. And yet he was always poor, and was glad at the last to accept pensions from the Crown in order that he might not leave his wife a beggar. This good lady survived her illustrious husband twelve years, and seemed, as his widow, to have some success in paying his bills, for at her death all remaining demands were found to be discharged.

For receiving this pension Burke was assailed by the Duke of Bedford, a most pleasing act of ducal fatuity, since it enabled the pensioner, not bankrupt of his wit, to write a pamphlet, now of course a cherished classic, and introduce into it a few paragraphs about the House of Russell and the cognate subject of grants from the Crown. But each of Burke's debts and difficulties, which I only mention because all through his life they were cast up against him.

Had Burke been a moralist of the calibre of Charles James Fox, he might have amassed a fortune large enough to keep up half a dozen Beaconsfields, by simply doing what all his predecessors in the office he held, including Fox's own father, the truly infamous first Lord Holland, had done—namely, by retaining for his own use the interest on all balances of the public money from time to time in his hands as Paymaster of the Forces. But Burke carried his passion for good government into actual practice, and, cutting down the emoluments of his office to a salary (a high one, no doubt), effected a saving to the country of some £25,000 a year, every farthing of which might have gone without remark into his own pocket.

Burke had no vices save of style and temper; nor was any of his expenditure a profligate squandering of money. It all went in giving employment or disseminating kindness. He sent the painter Barry to study art in Italy. He saved the poet Crabbe from starvation and despair, and thus secured to the country one who owns the unrivalled distinction of having been the favorite poet of the three greatest intellectual factors of the age (scientific men excepted),—Lord Byron, Sir Walter Scott, and Cardinal Newman.

Yet so distorted are men's views that the odious and anti-social excesses of Fox at the gambling-table are visited with a blame usually wreathed in smiles, whilst the financial irregularities of a noble and pure-minded man are thought fit matter for the fiercest censure or the most lordly contempt.

Next to Burke's debts, some of his companions and intimates did him harm and injured his consequence. His brother Richard, whose brogue we are given to understand was simply appalling, was a good-for-nothing, with a dilapidated reputation. Then there was another Mr. Burke, who was no relation, but none the less was always about, and to whom it was not safe to lend money. Burke's son, too, whose death he mourned so pathetically, seems to have been a failure, and is described by a candid friend as a nauseating person To have a decent following is important in politics.

A third reason must be given: Burke's judgment of men and things was often both wrong and violent. The story of Powell and Bembridge, two knaves in Burke's own office, whose cause he espoused, and whom he insisted on reinstating in the public service after they had been dismissed, and maintaining them there, in spite of all protests, till the one had the grace to cut his throat and the other was sentenced by the Queen's Bench to a term of imprisonment and a heavy fine, is too long to be told, though it makes interesting reading in the twenty-second volume of Howell's "State Trials," where at the end of the report is to be found the following note:—

"The proceedings against Messrs. Powell and Bembridge

occasioned much animated discussion in the House of Commons, in which Mr. Burke warmly supported the accused. The compassion which on these and all other occasions was manifested by Mr. Burke for the sufferings of those public delinquents, the zeal with which he advocated their cause, and the eagerness with which he endeavored to extenuate their criminality, have received severe reprehension, and in particular when contrasted with his subsequent conduct in the prosecution of Mr. Hastings."

The real reason for Burke's belief in Bembridge is, I think, to be found in the evidence Burke gave on his behalf at the trial before Lord Mansfield. Bembridge had rendered Burke invaluable assistance in carrying out his reforms at the Paymaster's Office, and Burke was constitutionally unable to believe that a rogue could be on his side; but, indeed, Burke was too apt to defend bad causes with a scream of passion, and a politician who screams is never likely to occupy a commanding place in the House of Commons.

A last reason for Burke's exclusion from high office is to be found in his aversion to any measure of Parliamentary reform. An ardent reformer like the Duke of Richmond—the then Duke of Richmond—who was in favor of annual Parliaments, universal suffrage, and payment of members, was not likely to wish to associate himself too closely with a politician who wept with emotion at the bare thought of depriving Old Sarum of parliamentary representation.

These reasons account for Burke's exclusion, and jealous as we naturally and properly are of genius being snubbed by mediocrity, my reading at all events does not justify me in blaming any one but the Fates for the circumstance that Burke was never a Secretary of State. And after all, does it matter much what he was? Burke no doubt occasionally felt his exclusion a little hard; but he is the victor who remains in possession of the field; and Burke is now, for us and for all coming after us, in such possession.

It now only remains for me, drawing upon my stock of assurance, to essay the analysis of the essential elements of Burke's mental character, and I therefore at once proceed to say that it was Burke's peculiarity and his glory to apply the imagination of a poet of the first order to the facts and the business of life. Arnold says of Sophocles—

" He saw life steadily, and saw it whole."

Substitute for the word " life " the words " organized society," and you get a peep into Burke's mind.

There was a catholicity about his gaze. He knew how the whole world lived. Everything contributed to this; his vast desultory reading; his education, neither wholly academical nor entirely professional; his long years of apprenticeship in the service of knowledge; his wanderings up and down the country; his vast conversational powers; his enormous correspondence with all sorts of people; his unfailing interest in all pursuits, trades, manufactures,—all helped to keep before him, like motes dancing in a sunbeam, the huge organism of modern society, which requires for its existence and for its development the maintenance of credit and of order.

Burke's imagination led him to look out over the whole land: the legislator devising new laws, the judge expounding and enforcing old ones, the merchant despatching his goods and extending his credit, the banker advancing the money of his customers upon the credit of the merchant, the frugal man slowly accumulating the store which is to support him in old age, the ancient institutions of Church and University with their seemly provisions for sound learning and true religion, the parson in his pulpit, the poet pondering his rhymes, the farmer eyeing his crops, the painter covering his canvases, the player educating the feelings.

Burke saw all this with the fancy of a poet, and dwelt on it with the eye of a lover. But love is the parent of fear, and none knew better than Burke how thin is the lava layer between the costly fabric of society and the volcanic heats and destroying flames of anarchy. He trembled for the fair frame of all established things, and to his horror saw men, instead of covering the thin surface with the concrete, digging in it for abstractions, and asking fundamental questions about the origin of society, and why one man should be born rich and another poor.

Burke was no prating optimist: it was his very knowledge how much could be said against society that quickened his fears for it. There is no shallower criticism than that which accuses Burke in his later years of apostasy from so-called Liberal opinions. Burke was all his life through a passionate maintainer of the established order of things, and a ferocious hater of abstractions and metaphysical politics.

The same ideas that explode like bombs through his diatribes against the French Revolution are to be found shining with a mild effulgence in the comparative calm of his earlier writings. I have often been struck with a resemblance, which I hope is not wholly fanciful, between the attitude of Burke's mind toward government and that of Cardinal Newman toward religion.

Both these great men belong, by virtue of their imaginations, to the poetic order, and they both are to be found dwelling with amazing eloquence, detail, and wealth of illustration on the varied elements of society. Both seem as they write to have one hand on the pulse of the world, and to be forever alive to the throb of its action; and Burke, as he regarded humanity swarming like bees into and out of their hives of industry, is ever asking himself, How are these men to be saved from anarchy? whilst Newman puts to himself the question, How are these men to be saved from atheism? Both saw the perils of free inquiry divorced from practical affairs.

"Civil freedom," says Burke, "is not, as many have endeavored to persuade you, a thing that lies hid in the depth of abstruse science. It is a blessing and a benefit, not an abstract speculation; and all the just reasoning that can be upon it is of so coarse a texture as perfectly to suit the ordinary capacities of those who are to enjoy and of those who are to defend it."

"Tell men," says Cardinal Newman, "to gain notions of a Creator from his works, and if they were to set about it (which nobody does), they would be jaded and wearied by the labyrinth they were tracing; their minds would be gorged and surfeited by the logical operation. To most men argument makes the point in hand more doubtful and considerably less impressive. After all, man is not a reasoning animal, he is a seeing, feeling, contemplating, acting animal."

Burke is fond of telling us that he is no lawyer, no antiquarian, but a plain, practical man; and the Cardinal, in like manner, is ever insisting that he is no theologian—he leaves everything of that sort to the Schools, whatever they may be, and simply deals with religion on its practical side as a benefit to mankind.

If either of these great men has been guilty of intellectual excesses, those of Burke may be attributed to his dread of anarchy, those of Newman to his dread of atheism. Neither of them was prepared to rest content with a scientific frontier, an imaginary line. So much did they dread their enemy, so alive were they to the terrible strength of some of his positions, that they could not agree to dispense with the protection afforded by the huge mountains of prejudice and the ancient rivers of custom. The sincerity of either man can only be doubted by the bigot and the fool.

But Burke, apart from his fears, had a constitutional love for old things, simply because they were old. Anything mankind had ever worshipped, or venerated, or obeyed, was dear to him. I have already referred to his providing his Brahmins with a greenhouse for the purpose of their rites, which he watched from outside with great interest. One cannot fancy Cardinal Newman peeping through a window to see men worshipping false though ancient gods. Warren Hastings's hind-handed dealings with the temples and time-honored if scandalous customs of the Hindoos filled Burke with horror. So, too, he respected Quakers, Presbyterians, Independents, Baptists, and all those whom he called Constitutional Dissenters.

He has a fine passage somewhere about Rust, for with all his passion for good government he dearly loved a little rust.   In this phase of character he reminds one not a little of another great writer—whose death literature has still reason to deplore—George Eliot; who, in her love for old hedgerows and barns and crumbling moss-grown walls, was a writer after Burke's own heart, whose novels he would have sat up all night to devour; for did he not deny with warmth Gibbon's statement that he had read all five volumes of "Evelina" in a day? "The thing is impossible," cried Burke; "they took me three days, doing nothing else." Now, "Evelina" is a good novel, but "Silas Marner" is a better.

Wordsworth has been called the High Priest of Nature.

Burke may be called the High Priest of Order—a lover of settled ways, of justice, peace, and security. His writings are a storehouse of wisdom, not the cheap shrewdness of the mere man of the world, but the noble, animating wisdom of one who has the poet's heart as well as the statesman's brain.

Nobody is fit to govern this country who has not drunk deep at the springs of Burke. "Have you read your Burke?" is at least as sensible a question to put to a parliamentary candidate, as to ask him whether he is a total abstainer or a desperate drunkard. Something there may be about Burke to regret, and more to dispute; but that he loved justice and hated iniquity is certain, as also it is that for the most part he dwelt in the paths of purity, humanity, and good sense. May we be found adhering to them!

LODGE

HENRY CABOT LODGE, an American politician and author, was born in Boston, Massachusetts, May 12, 1850. He was graduated at Harvard College in 1871, and at the Law School in 1874. In 1875 he received the degree of Ph.D. for his thesis on the " Land Law of the Anglo-Saxons." He was university lecturer on American history at Harvard from 1876 to 1879, and edited the " North American Review " in 1873-76, and the " International Review " in 1879-81. He served two terms in the Massachusetts legislature in 1880-81, and was a delegate to the Republican national conventions of 1880 and 1884. He was for two years chairman of the Republican state committee, and in 1886 was elected to Congress. He served through the fiftieth, fifty-first and fifty-second congresses and was re-elected to the fifty-third, but, having been elected to the United States Senate on January 17, 1893, to succeed Henry L. Dawes, he resigned his seat in the House and took his seat on the 4th of March in that year. During his congressional career Mr. Lodge was a member of several important committees, made several able speeches upon tariff, financial, and election laws, and presented the Force Bill in the Fifty-first Congress. His career in the Senate has also been signalized by notable speeches on many important measures. He was elected Overseer of Harvard University in 1884, and was awarded the honorary degree of LL.D. by Williams College in 1895. He published many notable works, among which may be mentioned the lives of " Alexander Hamilton " (1882); " Daniel Webster " (1883); " George Washington " (1889); " History of Boston " (1891); " Certain Accepted Heroes, and Other Essays " (1897).

ORATION ON DANIEL WEBSTER

DELIVERED AT THE UNVEILING OF HIS STATUE IN WASHINGTON, JANUARY 18, 1900

STATUES and monuments can justify their existence on only two grounds—the nature of the subject they commemorate or as works of art. They ought, of course, to possess both qualifications in the fullest measure. Theoretically, at least, a great art should ever illustrate and should always have a great subject.

But art cannot command at will a fit subject, and it is therefore fortunately true that if the art be great it is its own all-sufficient warrant for existence. That Michael Angelo's unsurpassed figure called "Meditation" should be in theory a portrait statue and bear the name of one of the most worthless of the evil Medicean race is, after all, of slight moment. The immortal art remains to delight and to uplift every one who looks upon it with considerate eyes; and it matters little that all the marvellous figures which the chapel of the Medici enshrines were commanded and carved in order to keep alive the memory of a family steeped in crime and a curse to every people among whom they came.

On the other hand, hard as it often is, we can endure bad art if there be no question that the great man or the shining deed deserves the commemoration of bronze or marble. But when the art is bad and the subject unworthy or ephemeral, then the monument, as was said of Sir John Vanbrugh's palaces, is simply a heavy load to the patient earth and an offence to the eyes of succeeding generations.

In these days the world sins often and grievously in this way, and is much given to the raising of monuments, too frequently upon trifling provocation. Yet the fault lies not in the mere multiplication of monuments. The genius of Greece and of the Renaissance multiplied statues, and very wisely, too, because art then was at once splendid and exuberant. But great sculptors and painters are as few now as they were plentiful in the age of Phidias or of Michael Angelo and Donatello, and we erect statues and monuments with a prodigal hand chiefly because we are very rich, and because mechanical appliances have made easy the molding of metal and the carving of stone.

It behooves us, therefore, not only to choose with care artists who can give us work worthy for posterity to look upon, but also to avoid recklessness in rearing monuments upon slight grounds. At present there seems no disposition to heed these salutary principles. The cities and towns of Europe and of England swarm with modern statues and monuments, as a rule ugly or commonplace, too often glaring and vulgar, and very frequently erected to the memory and the glory of the illustrious obscure and of the parish hero.

We Americans sin less numerously, I think, in these respects than the Old World, but we follow their practice none the less and with many melancholy results. We should break away from the example of Europe and realize that the erection of an enduring monument in a public place is a very serious matter. We should seek out the best artists and should permit no monuments to deeds or to men who do not deserve them and who will not themselves be monumental in history and before the eyes of posterity.

Here in Washington, especially, we should bear this principle in mind, for this is the city of the nation, and it should have no place for local glories or provincial heroes. Yet even here we have been so careless that while we have given space to one or more statues of estimable persons, the fact of whose existence will be known only by their effigies, we have found as yet no place for a statue of Hamilton, the greatest constructive statesman of our history, or of the great soldier whose genius made the campaign of Vicksburg rival that of Ulm.

To-day no such doubts or criticisms need haunt or perplex us. We can thank the artist who has conceived, and most unreservedly can we thank the generous and public-spirited citizen of New Hampshire who has given the statue which we unveil this morning. If anyone among our statesmen has a title to a statue in Washington it is Daniel Webster, for this is the national capital, and no man was ever more national in his conceptions and his achievements than he.

Born and bred in New Hampshire, which first elected him to the House, he long represented Massachusetts, the State of his adoption, in the Congress of the United States, and thus two historic Commonwealths cherish his memory. But much as he loved them both, his public service was given to the nation, and so given that no man doubts his title to a statue here in this city. Why is there neither doubt nor question as to Webster's right to this great and lasting honor half a century after his death?

If we cannot answer this question so plainly that he who runs may read, then we unveil our own ignorance when we unveil his statue and leave the act without excuse. I shall try, briefly, to put the answer to this essential question into words. We all feel in our hearts and minds the reply that should be made. It has fallen to me to give expression to that feeling.

What, then, are the real reasons for the great place which Webster fills in our history? I do not propose to answer this question by reviewing the history of his time or by retelling his biography. Both history and biography contain the answer, yet neither is the answer. They are indeed much more, for they carry with them, of necessity, everything concerning the man, his strength and his weakness, his virtues and his defects, all the criticism, all the differences of opinion which such a career was sure to arouse and which such an influence upon his country and upon its thought, upon his own time and upon the future, was equally sure to generate.

There is a place for all this, but not here to-day. We do not raise a monument to Webster upon debatable grounds, and thus make it the silent champion of one side of a dead controversy. We do not set up his statue because he changed his early opinions upon the tariff, because he remained in Tyler's cabinet after that President's quarrel with the Whigs, or because he made upon the 7th of March a speech about which men have differed always and probably always will differ. Still less do we place here his graven image in memory of his failings or his shortcomings. History, with her cool hands, will put all these things into her scales and mete out her measure with calm, unflinching eyes. But this is history's task, not ours, and we raise this statue on other grounds.

> " Not ours to gauge the more or less,
> The will's defect, the blood's excess,
> The earthy humors that oppress
>   The radiant mind.
> His greatness, not his littleness,
>   Concerns mankind."

To his greatness, then, we rear this monument. In what does that greatness, acknowledged by all, unquestioned and undenied by any one, consist? Is it in the fact that he held high office? He was a brilliant member of Congress; for nineteen years a great senator; twice Secretary of State. But " the peerage solicited him, not he the peerage."

Tenure of office is nothing, no matter how high the place. A name recorded in the list of holders of high office is little better than one writ in water if the office-holding be all. We do not raise this statue to the member of Congress, to the senator of the United States, or to the Secretary of State, but to Daniel Webster.

That which concerns us is what he did with these great places which were given to him; for to him, as to all others, they were mere opportunities. What did he do with these large opportunities? Still more, what did he do with the splendid faculties which nature gave him? In the answer lies the greatness which lifts him out of the ranks and warrants statues to his memory.

First, then, of those qualities which he inherited from the strong New England stock that gave him birth, and which Nature, the fairy who stands by every cradle, poured out upon him. How generous, how lavish she was to that " infant crying in the night; that infant crying for the light " in the rough frontier village of New Hampshire a hundred and eighteen years ago. She gave him the strong, untainted blood of a vigorous race—the English Puritans—who in the New World had been for five generations fighting the hard battle of existence against the wilderness and the savage.

His father was a high type of this class, a farmer and a frontiersman, a pioneer and Indian fighter, then a soldier of the Revolution. On guard the night of Arnold's treason, Washington in that dark hour declared that Captain Webster was a man who could be trusted; simple words, but an order of merit higher and more precious than any glowing ribbon or shining star. So fathered and so descended, the child was endowed with physical attributes at once rare and inestimable.

When developed into manhood he was of commanding stature and seemed always even larger and taller than he really was. Strong, massive, and handsome, he stood before his fellow men looking upon them with wonderful eyes, if we may judge from all that those who saw him tell us. " Dull anthracite furnaces under overhanging brows, waiting only to be blown," says Carlyle, and those deep-set, glowing eyes pursue us still in all that we read of Webster, just as they seemed to haunt everyone who looked upon them in life.

When in a burst of passion or of solemn eloquence he fixed his eyes upon his hearers, each man in a vast audience felt that the burning glance rested upon him alone and that there was no escape.

Above the eyes were the high, broad brow and the great leonine head; below them the massive jaw and the firm mouth " accurately closed." All was in keeping.

No one could see him and not be impressed. The English navvy with his " There goes a king," Sydney Smith, who compared Webster to " a walking cathedral," and the great Scotchman, harsh in judgment and grudging of praise, who set him down as a " Parliamentary Hercules," all alike felt the subduing force of that personal presence.

Look upon some of the daguerreotypes taken of him in his old age, when the end was near. I think the face is one of the most extraordinary, in its dark power and tragic sadness, of all the heads which any form of human portraiture has preserved. So imposing was he that when he rose to speak, even on the most unimportant occasions, he looked, as Parton says, like " Jupiter in a yellow waistcoat," and even if he uttered nothing but commonplaces, or if he merely sat still, such was his " might and majesty " that all who listened felt that every phrase was charged with deep and solemn meaning, and all who gazed at him were awed and impressed. Add to all this a voice of great compass, with deep organ tones, and we have an assemblage of physical gifts concentrated in this one man which would have sufficed to have made even common abilities seem splendid.

But the abilities were far from common. The intellect within answered to the outward vesture. Very early does it appear when we hear of " Webster's boy " lifted upon a stone wall to read or recite to the teamsters stopping to water their horses near the Webster farm. They were a rough, hardy set, but there was something in the child with the great dark eyes that held them and made them listen. And the father, gallant and quite pathetic soul, with a dumb and very manifest love of higher things, resolved that this boy should have all the advantages which had been denied to himself.

Like the Scottish peasants, who toiled and moiled and pinched and saved that their boy might go to the university to cultivate learning on a little oatmeal, so with many silent sacrifices Ebenezer Webster sent his son to school and college and gave him every opportunity the little State afforded. The boy was not slow to make the most of all that was thus opened to him. The dormant talents grew and burgeoned in the congenial soil. Love of books made him their reader and master. Rare powers of memory and of acquisition showed themselves; a strong imagination led him to the great makers of verse, and natural taste took him to the masters of style, both in English and Latin.

When he passed out of college his capacity for work brought him hardly earned pittances as a school teacher, and then carried him through the toilsome, early stages of the law.

As he advanced, the eager delight of acquisition was succeeded, as is ever the case, by the passionate desire for expression, and soon the signs come of the power of analysis, of the instinct of lucid statement at once so clear and so forcible as to amount to demonstration. We see before us as we study those early years the promise of the great master of words to whom a whole nation was one day to listen.

And with all these gifts, physical and mental, possibly, but not necessarily, the outcome of them all, we see that Webster had that indefinable quality which for lack of a better name we call " charm." He exercised a fascination upon men and women alike, upon old and young, upon all who came in contact with him. When as a boy he returned from the country fair, his mother said to him, " Daniel, what did you do with your quarter ? "

" Spent it."

" Ezekiel, what did you do with yours ? "

" Lent it to Daniel."

As with the elder brother then, so it was through life. Webster strode along the pathway of his great career in solemn state, and there were always people about him ready to lend to him and to give to him; not money, merely, but love and loyalty and service, ungrudging and unreasoning, without either question or hope of reward. A wonderful power this, as impalpable as the tints of the rainbow, and yet as certain as the sun which paints the colors on the clouds and makes all mankind look toward them for the bow of hope and promise.

So he went on and up from the college, the schoolhouse, and the country jury, until he stood at the head of the American bar before the supreme court of the nation. On and up he went, from the early, florid orations of youth until he became the first orator of his time, without superior or rival. He frightened and disappointed his father by refusing the safe harbor of a clerk of court, and strode onward and upward until he stood at the head of the Senate and directed from the State Department the foreign policy of his country. Up and on from the farmhouse and the schoolhouse, from the stone wall whence he read to the rude audience of teamsters, to the times when thousands hung upon his words, when he created public opinion and shaped the political thought of his nation.

What a triumphant progress it was, and of it all what now

remains to make men say fifty years after his death that he merits not only a statue but lasting remembrance? Is it to be found in his success as a great advocate and lawyer, the acknowledged head of his profession? There is nothing which demands or calls forth greater intellectual powers or larger mental resources than the highest success at the bar, and yet no reputation is more evanescent. The decisions of judges remain and become part of the law of the land, lasting monuments of the learning and the thought which brought them forth. But the arguments which enlightened courts, which swayed juries, upon which public attention was fixed in admiration, fade almost in the hour, while the brilliant lawyer who uttered them soon becomes a tradition and a memory.

We must look beyond his triumphs at the bar to find the Webster of history. Beyond his work as a lawmaker, also, for, although he had a lion's share in the legislation of his time, it is not as a constructive statesman that he lives for us to-day. In the first rank as a lawmaker and as a lawyer, something very great must remain behind if we can readily and justly set aside such claims as these and say the highest remembrance rests on other grounds.

Yet such is the case, and the first, but the lesser, of these other grounds is his power of speech. Eminent as a legislator, still more distinguished as a lawyer, Webster was supreme as an orator. I had occasion some years ago to make a very careful study of Webster's speeches and orations. I read with them, and in strict comparison, all that was best in Greek, Latin, French, and English oratory, and all that is best and finest—I do not say all that is fine and good—is is to be found in those four languages. Webster stood the comparison without need of deduction or apology. I do not think that I am influenced by national feeling, for my object was to exclude the historical as well as the personal valuation, and to reach a real estimate.

When all was done, it seemed to me that Webster was un-equalled. I am sure that he is unsurpassed as an orator. There was no need for him to put pebbles in his mouth to cure stammering, or to rehearse his speeches on the seashore in conflict with the noise of the wave. He had from the hand of nature all the graces of person and presence, of voice and delivery, which the most exacting critic could demand, and these natural gifts were trained, enhanced, and perfected by years of practice in the Senate, the court room, and before the people.

In what he said he always had distinction—rarest of qual-ities—and he had also the great manner, just as Milton has it in verse. To lucid statement, to that simplicity in dis-cussion which modern times demand for practical questions, to nervous force, he added, at his best, wealth of imagery, richness of diction, humor, and pathos, all combined with the power of soaring on easy wing to the loftiest flights of eloquence. Above all he had that highest quality, the "σπουδαιότην" or high and excellent seriousness which Aristo-tle sets down as one of the supreme virtues of poetry, and without which neither oratory nor poetry can attain to supremacy.

Charles Fox was the author of the famous aphorism that "no good speech ever read well." This is the declaration in epigrammatic form that the speech which is prepared like an essay and read or recited, which, in other words, is litera-ture before it is oratory, is not thoroughly good, and of the soundness of the doctrine there can be, I think, no doubt. But this proposition is not without its dangers.

Charles Fox lived up to his own principle. He was, in my opinion, the greatest of English orators at the moment of speech, but he is little read and seldom quoted now. What he said has faded from the minds of men despite its enchanting, its enormous effect at the moment.

On the other hand, the speech which is literature before it is spoken is ineffective or only partially effective at the moment, and if it is read afterwards, however much we may enjoy the essay, we never mistake it for the genuine eloquence of the spoken word. Macaulay is an example of this latter class, as Fox is of the former. Macaulay's speeches are essays, eloquent and rhetorical, but still essays, literature, and not speeches. He was listened to with interest and delight, but he was not a great parliamentary debater or speaker.

The highest oratory, therefore, must combine in exact balance the living force and freshness of the spoken word with the literary qualities which alone ensure endurance. The best examples of this perfection are to be found in the world of imagination, in the two speeches of Brutus and Mark Antony in the play of Julius Cæsar. They are speeches and nothing else—one cool, stately, reasonable; the other a passionate, revolutionary appeal, hot from the heart and pouring from the lips with unpremeditated art, and yet they both have the literary quality, absolutely supreme in this instance, because Shakespeare wrote them.

It is not the preparation or even the writing out beforehand, therefore, which makes a speech into an essay, for these things can both be done without detracting from the spontaneity, without dulling the sound of the voice which the wholly great speech must have, even on the printed page. The speech loses when the literary quality becomes predominant, and absolute success as high as it is rare comes only from the nice balance of the two essential ingredients.

You find this balance, this combination, in Demosthenes and Isocrates, although I venture to think that those two great masters lean, if at all, too much to the literary side. In Cicero, although in matter and manner the best judges would rank him below the Greek masters, the combination is quite perfect. One of his most famous speeches, it is said, was never delivered at all, and none the less it is a speech and nothing else, instinct with life and yet with the impalpable literary feeling all through it, the perfect production of a very beautiful and subtle art.

Among English orators Burke undoubtedly comes nearest to the union of the two qualities, and while the words of Fox and Pitt are unread and unquoted, except by students, Burke's gorgeous sentences are recited and repeated by successive generations. Yet there is no doubt that Burke erred on the literary side, and we find the proof of it in the fact that he often spoke to empty benches, and that Goldsmith could say of him :

> " Too deep for his hearers, still went on refining,
> And thought of convincing while they thought of dining."

Burke was a literary man as well as an orator and a statesman. Webster was not a literary man at all. He never wrote books or essays, although, in Dr. Johnson's phrase, he had literature and loved it. He was an orator, pure and simple; his speeches, good, bad, or indifferent, are speeches— never essays or anything but speeches—and yet upon all alike is the literary touch. In all is the fine literary quality, always felt, never seen, ever present, never obtrusive. He had the combination of Shakespeare's Brutus or Antony, of

Demosthenes or Cicero, and when he rose to his greatest heights he reached a place beyond the fear of rivalry.

Would you have a practical proof and exhibition of this fact, turn to any serious and large debate in Congress, and you will find Webster constantly quoted, as he is in every session, quoted twenty times as often as any other public man in our history. He said many profound, many luminous, many suggestive things; he was an authority on many policies and on the interpretation of the constitution. But there have been others of whom all this might be said; there were kings before Agamemnon, but they are rarely quoted, while Webster is quoted constantly.

He had strong competitors in his own day and in his own field, able, acute, and brilliant men. He rose superior to them, I think, in his lifetime, but now that they are all dead Webster is familiar to hundreds to whom his rivals are little more than names. So far as familiarity in the mouths of men goes, it is Eclipse first and the rest nowhere. It is the rare combination of speech and literature; it is the literary quality, the literary savor, which keeps what Webster said fresh, strong, and living. When we open the volumes of his speeches it is not like unrolling the wrappings of an Egyptian mummy, to find within a dried and shrivelled form, a faint perfume alone surviving to faintly recall the vanished days, as when—

"Some queen, long dead, was young."

Rather it is like the opening of Charlemagne's tomb, when his imperial successor started back before the enthroned figure of the great emperor looking out upon him, instinct with life under the red glare of the torches.

Let us apply another and surer test. How many speeches to a jury in a criminal trial possessing neither political nor public interest survive in fresh remembrance seventy years after their delivery? I confess I can think of no jury speeches of any kind which stand this ordeal except, in a limited way, some speeches of Erskine, and those all have the advantage of historical significance, dealing as they do with constitutional and political questions of great moment. But there is one of Webster's speeches to a jury which lives to-day, and no more crucial test could be applied than the accomplishment of such a feat. The White murder case was simply a criminal trial, without a vestige of historical, political, or general public interest. Yet Webster's speech for the prosecution has been read and recited until well-nigh hackneyed. It is in readers and manuals; and is still declaimed by schoolboys. Some of its phrases are familiar quotations and have passed into general speech. Let me recall a single passage:

" He has done the murder. No eye has seen him; no ear has heard him. The secret is his own, and it is safe.

" Ah, gentlemen, that was a dreadful mistake. Such a secret can be safe nowhere. The whole creation of God has neither nook nor corner where the guilty can bestow it and say it is safe. . . . A thousand eyes turn at once to explore every man, everything, every circumstance connected with the time and place; a thousand ears catch every whisper; a thousand excited minds intensely dwell on the scene, shedding all their light, and ready to kindle the slighest circumstance into a blaze of discovery. Meantime the guilty soul cannot keep its own secret. It is false to itself; or, rather, it feels an irresistible impulse of conscience to be true to itself. It labors under its guilty possession, and knows not what to do with it. The human heart was not made for the residence of such an inhabitant. It finds itself preyed on by a torment which it dares not acknowledge to God or man. A vulture is devouring it, and it can ask no sympathy or assistance either from heaven or earth. The secret which the murderer possesses soon comes to possess him, and, like the evil spirits of which we read, it overcomes him, and leads him whithersoever it will. He feels it beating at his heart, rising to his throat, and demanding disclosure. He thinks the whole world sees it in his face, reads it in his eyes, and almost hears its workings in the very silence of his thoughts. It has become his master. It betrays his discretion, it breaks down his courage, it conquers his prudence. When suspicions from without begin to embarrass him and the net of circumstance to entangle him, the fatal secret struggles with still greater violence to burst forth. It must be confessed; it will be confessed. There is no refuge from confession but suicide, and suicide is confession."

Those are words spoken to men, not written for them. It is a speech and nothing else, and yet we feel all through it the literary value and quality which make it imperishable.

Take another example. When Webster stood one summer morning on the ramparts of Quebec and heard the sound of drums and saw the English troops on parade, the thought of England's vast world-empire came strongly to his mind. The thought was very natural under the circumstances, not at all remarkable nor in the least original. Some years later, in a speech in the Senate, he put his thought into words, and this, as everyone knows, is the way he did it:

"A Power which has dotted over the surface of the whole globe with her possessions and military posts, whose morning drumbeat, following the sun and keeping company with the hours, circles the earth with one continuous and unbroken strain of the martial airs of England."

The sentence has followed the drumbeat round the world, and has been repeated in England and in the Antipodes by men who never heard of Webster and probably did not know that this splendid description of the British empire was due to an American. It is not the thought which has carried these words so far through time and space. It is the beauty of the imagery and the magic of the style.

Let me take one more very simple example of the quality which distinguishes Webster's speeches above those of others, which makes his words and serious thoughts live on when others, equally weighty and serious, perhaps, sleep or die. In his first Bunker Hill oration he apostrophized the monument, just as anyone else might have tried to do, and this is what he said:

" Let it rise, let it rise till it meet the sun in his coming; let the earliest light of morning gild it, and parting day linger and play on its summit."

Here the thought is nothing, the style everything. No one can repeat those words and be deaf to their music on insensible to the rhythm and beauty of the prose with the Saxon words relieved just sufficiently by the Latin derivatives.

The ease with which it is done may be due to training, but the ability to do it comes from natural gifts which, as Goethe says, " we value more as we get older because they cannot be stuck on." Possibly to some people it may seem very simple to utter such a sentence as I have quoted. To them I can only repeat what Scott says somewhere about Swift's style, perhaps the purest and strongest we have in the language. " Swift's style," said Scott, " seems so simple that one would think any child might write like him, and yet if we try we find to our despair that it is impossible."

Such, then, were the qualities which in their perfect combination put Webster among the very few who stand forth as the world's greatest orators. In this age of ours when the tendency is to overpraise commonplace work, to mistake notoriety for fame, and advertisement for reputation, it is of inestimable worth to a people to have as one of their own possessions such a master of speech, such a standard of distinction and of real excellence as we find in Webster. Such an orator deserves a statue.

But there is yet another ground, deeper and more serious than this. Webster deserves a statue for what he represented, for the message he delivered, and for that for which he still stands and will always stand before his countrymen and in the cold, clear light of history.

He was born just at the end of the war of the Revolution, when the country was entering upon the period of disintegration and impotence known as that of the Confederation. He was too young to understand and to feel those bitter years of struggle and decline which culminated in the adoption of the constitution. But the first impressions of his boyhood must have been of the prosperity, strength, and honor which came from the new instrument of government and from the better union of the States. His father followed his old chief in politics as he had in the field, and Webster grew up a Federalist, a supporter of Washington, Hamilton, and Adams and of the leaders of their party.

As he came to manhood he saw the first assault upon the national principle in the Virginia and Kentucky resolutions. He had entered public life when the second attack came in the movement which ended with the Hartford Convention, and with which, New England Federalist as he was, he could feel no sympathy. Again fifteen years passed and the third assault was delivered in the Nullification doctrines of South Carolina.

Webster was then at the zenith of his powers, and he came

forward as the defender of the constitution. In the reply to Hayne he reached the highest point in parliamentary oratory and left all rivals far behind. He argued his case with consummate skill, both legally and historically. But he did far more than this. He was not merely the great orator defending the constitution, he was the champion of the national principle. Whether the constitution was at the outset an experiment or not, whether it was a contract from which each or all of the signatories could withdraw at will, was secondary. The great fact was that the constitution had done its work. It had made a nation. Webster stood forth in the Senate and before the country as the exponent of that fact and as the defender of the nation's life against the attacks of separatism. This was his message to his time. This was his true mission. In that cause he spoke as none had ever spoken before and with a splendor of eloquence and a force of argument to which no one else could attain.

It is not to be supposed for an instant that Webster discovered the fact that the constitution had made a nation or that he first and alone proclaimed a new creed to an unthinking generation. His service was equally great, but widely different from this. The great mass of the American people felt dumbly, dimly perhaps, but none the less deeply and surely, that they had made a nation some day to be a great nation, and they meant to remain such and not sink into divided and petty republics.

This profound feeling of the popular heart Webster not only represented, but put into words. No slight service this, if rightly considered; no little marvel this capacity to change thought into speech, to give expression to the feelings and hopes of a people and crystallize them forever in words fit for such a use. To this power, indeed, we owe a large part of the world's greatest literature. The myths and legends of Greece were of no one man's invention. They were children of the popular imaginings—vague, varying—floating hither and thither, like the mists of the mountains. But Homer touched them, and they started up into a beautiful, immortal life, to delight and charm untold generations. Æschylus and Sophocles put them upon the stage, and they became types of the sorrows of humanity and of the struggle of man with fate. The Sagas of the far north, confused and diffuse, but full of poetry and imagination, slumbered until the Minnesingers wove them into the Niebelungen Lied and again until a great composer set them before our eyes, so that all men could see their beauty and pathos and read their deeper meanings. Sir Thomas Mallory rescued the Arthurian legends from chaos, and in our own day a great poet has turned them into forms which make their beauty clear to the world. Thus popular imaginings, dumb for the most part, finding at best only a rude expression, have been touched by the hand of genius and live forever.

So in politics Jefferson embodied in the Declaration of Independence the feelings of the American people and sounded to the world the first note in the great march of Democracy, which then began. The "Marseillaise," in words and music, burned with the spirit of the French Revolution and inspired the armies which swept over Europe.

Thus Webster gave form and expression, at once noble and moving, to the national sentiment of his people. In what he said men saw clearly what they themselves thought, but which they could not express. That sentiment grew and strengthened with every hour, when men had only to repeat his words, in order to proclaim the creed in which they believed; and after he was dead Webster was heard again in the deep roar of the Union guns from Sumter to Appomattox.

His message, delivered as he alone could deliver it, was potent in inspiring the American people to the terrible sacrifices by which they saved the nation when he slept silent in his grave at Marshfield. Belief in the Union and the constitution, because they meant national greatness and national life, was the great dominant conviction of Webster's life. It was part of his temperament. He loved the outer world, the vast expanses of sea and sky, all that was large and unfettered in nature. So he admired great States and empires and had little faith in small ones or in the happiness or worth of a nation which has no history and which fears its fate too much to put its fortune to the touch when the accepted time has come.

It was not merely that as a statesman he saw the misery and degradation which would come from the breaking of the Union as well as the progressive disintegration which was sure to follow, but the very thought of it came home to him with the sharpness of a personal grief which was almost agonizing. When, in the 7th of March speech, he cried out, "What States are to secede? What is to remain American? What am I to be?" a political opponent said the tone of the last question made him shudder as if some dire calamity was at hand. The greatness of the United States filled his mind. He had not the length of days accorded to Lord Bathurst, but the angel of dreams had unrolled to him the future, and the vision was ever before his eyes.

This passionate love of his country, this dream of her future, inspired his greatest efforts, were even the chief cause at the end of his life of his readiness to make sacrifices of principle which would only have helped forward what he dreaded most, but which he believed would save that for which he cared most deeply. In a period when great forces were at work which in their inevitable conflict threatened the existence of the Union of States, Webster stands out above all others as the champion, as the very embodiment of the national life and the national faith. More than any other man of that time he called forth the sentiment more potent than all reasonings which saved the nation. It was a great work, greatly done, with all the resources of a powerful intellect and with an eloquence rarely heard among men. We may put aside all his other achievements, all his other claims to remembrance, and inscribe alone upon the base of his statue the words uttered in the Senate, "Liberty and Union, now and forever, one and inseparable." That single sentence recalls all the noble speeches which breathed only the greatness of the country and the prophetic vision which looked with undazzled gaze into a still greater future. No other words are wanted for a man who so represented and so expressed the faith and hopes of a nation. His statue needs no other explanation so long as the nation he served and the Union he loved shall last.

SPEECH AT REPUBLICAN CONVENTION

DELIVERED AT PHILADELPHIA, JUNE 20, 1900

ONE of the greatest honors that can fall to any American in public life is to be called to preside over a Republican National Convention. How great that honor is you know, but you cannot realize, nor can I express the gratitude which I feel to you for having conferred it upon me. I can only say to you in the simplest phrase, that I thank you from the bottom of my heart. " Beggar that I am, I am even poor in thanks, and yet I thank you."

We meet again to nominate the next President of the United States. Four years have passed since we nominated the soldier and statesman who is now President, and who is soon to enter upon his second term. Since the Civil War no Presidential term has been so crowded with great events as that which is now drawing to a close. They have been four memorable years.

To Republicans they show a record of promises kept, of work done, of unforeseen questions met and answered. To the Democrats they have been generous in the exhibition of unfulfilled predictions, in the ruin of their hopes of calamity and in futile opposition to the forces of the times, and the aspirations of the American people. I wish I could add that they had been equally instructive to our opponents, but while it is true that the Democrats, like the Bourbons, learn nothing, it is only too evident that the familiar comparison cannot be completed, for they forget a great deal which it would be well for them to remember.

In 1897 we took the Government and the country from the hands of President Cleveland. His party had abandoned him and were joined to their idols, of which he was no longer one. During the last years of his term we had presented to us the melancholy spectacle of a President trying to govern without a party.

The result was that his policies were in ruin, legislation was at a standstill, and public affairs were in a perilous and incoherent condition. Party responsibility had vanished, and with it all possibility of intelligent action, demanded by the country at home and abroad. It was an interesting, but by no means singular, display of Democratic unfitness for the practical work of government. To the political student it was instructive, to the country it was extremely painful, to business disastrous.

We replaced this political chaos with a President in thorough accord with his party, and the machinery of government began again to move smoothly and effectively. Thus we kept at once our promise of better and more efficient administration. In four months after the inauguration of President McKinley we had passed a tariff bill. For ten years the artificial agitation, in behalf of what was humorously called tariff reform, and of what was really free trade, had kept business in a ferment, and had brought a Treasury deficit, paralyzed industries, depression, panic, and, finally, continuous bad times to a degree never before imagined.

Would you know the result of our tariff legislation, look about you. Would you measure its success, recollect that it is no longer an issue, that our opponents, free traders as they are, do not dare to make it an issue, that there is not a State in the Union to-day which could be carried for free trade against protection. Never was a policy more fully justified by its works, never was a promise made by any party more absolutely fulfilled.

Dominant among the issues of four years ago was that of our monetary and financial system. The Republican Party promised to uphold our credit, to protect our currency from revolution, and to maintain the gold standard. We have done so. We have done more. We have been better than our promise.

Failing to secure, after honest effort, any encouragement for international bimetallism, we have passed a law strengthening the gold standard and planting it more firmly than ever in our financial system, improving our banking laws, buttressing our credit, and refunding the public debt at 2 per cent interest, the lowest rate in the world.

It was a great work well done. The only argument the Democrats can advance to-day in their own behalf on the money question is that a Republican Senate, in the event of Democratic success, would not permit the repeal of a Republican law. This is a specious argument when looked at with considerate eyes, and quite worthy of the intellects which produced it. Apply it generally. Upon this theory, because we have defeated the soldiers of Spain and sunk her ships we can with safety dispense with the army and navy which did the work.

Take another example. There has been a fire in a great city; it has been checked and extinguished, therefore let us abolish the fire department and cease to insure our homes. Distrust in our currency, the dread of change, the deadly fear of a debased standard were raging four years ago, and business lay prostrate before them. Republican supremacy and Republican legislation have extinguished the fires of doubt and fear, and business has risen triumphant from the ashes. Therefore abolish your fire department, turn out the Republicans and put in power the incendiaries who lighted the flames and trust to what remains of Republican control to avert fresh disaster.

The proposition is its own refutation. The supremacy of the party that has saved the standard of sound money and guarded it by law is as necessary for its security and for the existence of honest wages and of business confidence now as it was in 1896.

The moment the Republican Party passes from power, and the party of free silver and fiat paper comes in, stable currency and the gold standard, the standard of the civilized world, are in imminent and deadly peril. Sound currency and a steady standard of value are to-day safe only in Republican hands.

But there were still other questions in 1896. We had already thwarted the efforts of the Cleveland Administration to throw the Hawaiian Islands back to their dethroned Queen and to give England a foothold for her cables in the group. We then said that we would settle finally the Hawaiian question. We have done so. The traditional American policy has been carried out. The flag of the Union floats to-day over the crossroads of the Pacific.

We promised to deal with the Cuban question. Again comes the reply, we have done so. The long agony of the island is over. Cuba is free. But this great work brought with it events and issues which no man had foreseen, for which no party creed had provided a policy. The crisis came, bringing war in its train.

The Republican President and the Republican Congress met the new trial in the old spirit. We fought the war with Spain. The result is history known of all men. We have the perspective now of only a short two years, and yet how clear and bright the great facts stand out, like mountain peaks against the sky, while the gathering darkness of a just oblivion is creeping fast over the low grounds, where lie forgotten the trivial and unimportant things, the criticisms and the fault findings which seemed too huge when we still lingered among them.

Here they are, these great facts: A war of a hundred days, with many victories and no defeats, with no prisoners taken from us and no advance stayed, with a triumphant outcome startling in its completeness and in its worldwide meaning. Was ever a war more justly entered upon, more quickly fought, more fully won, more thorough in its results? Cuba is free. Spain has been driven from the Western Hemisphere. Fresh glory has come to our arms and crowned our flag.

It was the work of the American people, but the Republican Party was their instrument. Have we not the right to say that here, too, even as in the days of Abraham Lincoln, we have fought a good fight, we have kept the faith, we have finished the work?

War, however, is ever like the sword of Alexander. It cuts the knots. It is a great solvent and brings many results not to be foreseen. The world forces unchained in war perform in hours the work of years of quiet.

Spain sued for peace. How was that peace to be made? The answer to this great question had to be given by the President of the United States. We were victorious in Cuba, in Porto Rico, in the Philippines. Should we give those islands back to Spain? "Never!" was the President's reply. Would any American wish that he had answered otherwise? Should we hand them over to some other Power? "Never!" was again the answer.

Would our pride and self-respect as a nation have submitted to any other reply? Should we turn the islands, where we had destroyed all existing sovereignty, loose upon the world to be a prey to domestic anarchy and the helpless spoil of some other nation? Again the inevitable negative. Again the President answered as the nation he represented would have had him answer.

He boldly took the islands, took them knowing well the burden and responsibility, took them from a deep sense of duty to ourselves and others, guided by a just foresight as to our future in the East, and with an entire faith in the ability of the American people to grapple with the new task. When future conventions point to the deeds by which the Republican Party has made history, they will proclaim with especial pride that under a Republican Administration the War of 1898 was fought, and that the peace with Spain was the work of William McKinley.

So much for the past. We are proud of it, but we do not expect to live upon it, for the Republican Party is pre-eminently the party of action, and its march is ever forward. We are not so made that we can be content to retreat or to mark time. The traditions of the early days of our party are sacred to us, and are hostages given to the American people that we will not be unworthy of the great leaders who have gone.

The deeds of yesterday are in their turn a pledge and a proof that what we promise we perform, and that the people who put faith in our declarations in 1896 were not deceived, and may place the same trust in us in 1900. But our pathway has never lain among dead issues, nor have we won our victories and made history by delving in political graveyards.

We are the party of to-day, with cheerful yesterdays and confident to-morrows. The living present is ours, the present of prosperity and activity in business, of good wages and quick payments, of labor employed and capital invested, of sunshine in the market place, and the stir of abounding life in the workshop and on the farm. It is with this that we have replaced the depression, the doubts, the low wages, the idle labor, the frightened capital, the dark clouds which overhung industry and agriculture in 1896. This is what we would preserve, so far as sound government and wise legislation can do it. This is what we brought to the country four years ago. This is what we offer now.

Again we promise that the protective system shall be maintained, and that our great industrial interests shall go on their way unshaken by the dire fear of tariff agitation and of changing duties. Again we declare that we will guard the national credit, uphold a sound currency, based upon gold, and keep the wages of the workingman and the enterprise of the man of business free from that most deadly of all evils, a flucutating standard of value.

The deficit which made this great country in a time of profound peace a borrower of money to meet its current expenditures has been replaced by abundant revenue, bringing a surplus, due alike to prosperity and to wise legislation, so ample that we can now safely promise a large reduction of taxation without imperilling our credit or risking a resort to loans.

We are prepared to take steps to revive and build up our merchant marine, and thus put into American pockets the money paid for carrying American freights. Out of the abundant resources which our financial legislation has brought us we will build the Isthmian Canal, and lay the cables which will help to turn the current of eastern trade to the Golden Gate. We are on good terms with all nations, and mean to remain so, while we promise to insure our peace and safety by maintaining the Monroe Doctrine, by ample coast defences, and by building up a navy which no one can challenge with impunity.

The new problems brought by the war we face with confidence in ourselves, and a still deeper confidence in the American people, who will deal justly and rightly with the islands which have come into their charge. The outcry against our new possessions is as empty as the cant about " militarism," and " imperialism " is devoid of sense and meaning.

Regard for a moment those who are loudest in shrieking that the American people are about to enter upon a career of oppression, and that the republic is in danger. Have they been in the past the guardians of freedom? Is safety for liberty now to be found most surely in the party which was the defender of domestic slavery?

Is true freedom to be secured by the ascendancy of the party which beneath our very eyes seeks to establish through infamous laws the despotic rule of a small and unscrupulous band of usurpers in Kentucky, who trample there not upon the rights of the black men only, but of the whites, and which seeks to extend the same system to North Carolina and Missouri?

Has it suddenly come to pass that the Democratic Party which to-day aims whenever it acquires power to continue in office by crushing out honest elections and popular rule; has it indeed come to pass, I say, that that party is the chosen protector of liberty? If it were so the outlook would be black indeed.

No. The party of Lincoln may best be trusted now, as in the past, to be true, even as he was true, to the rights of man to human freedom, whether within the borders of the United States or in the islands which have come beneath our flag. The liberators may be trusted to watch over the liberated. We who freed Cuba will keep the pledge we made to her and will guide her along the road to independence and stable government until she is ready to settle her own future by the free expression of her people's will. We will be faithful to the trust imposed upon us, and if among those to whom this great work is confided in Cuba, or elsewhere, wrongdoers shall be found, men not only bad in morals, but dead to their duty as Americans and false to the honor of our name, we will punish these basest of criminals to the extent of the law.

For the islands of Hawaii and Porto Rico the political problem has been solved, and by Republican legislation they have been given self-government, and are peaceful and prosperous under the rule of the United States.

In the Philippines we were met by rebellion, fomented by a self-seeking adventurer and usurper. The duty of the President was to repress that rebellion, to see to it that the authority of the United States, as rightfully and as righteous in Manila as in Philadelphia, was acknowledged and obeyed. That harsh and painful duty President McKinley has performed firmly and justly, eager to resort to gentle measures wherever possible, unyielding when treachery and violence made force necessary. Unlike the opponents of expansion, we do not regard the soldiers of Otis and Lawton and McArthur as " an enemy's camp."

In our eyes they are the soldiers of the United States, they are our army, and we believe in them and will sustain them. Even now the Democrats are planning, if they get control of the House, to cut off appropriations for the army and thus compel the withdrawal of our troops from the Philippines. The result would be to force the retirement of such soldiers as would remain in Manila, and their retreat would be the signal for the massacre and plunder of the great body of the peaceful inhabitants of the islands who have trusted to us to protect and guard them.

Such an event would be an infamy. Is the government, is the House, to be given over to a party capable of such a policy? Shall they not rather be intrusted to the party which will sustain the army and suppress the brigands and guerrillas who, under pretence of war, are now adding so freely to the list of crimes committed in the name of liberty by usurpers and pretenders, and who, buoyed up by the Democratic promises, keep up a highwayman warfare in hope of Democratic success in November? It is for the American people to decide this question.

Our position is plain. The restoration of peace and order now so nearly reached in the Philippines shall be completed. Civil government shall be established, and the people advanced as rapidly as possible along the road to entire freedom and to self-government under our flag. We will not abandon our task. We will neither surrender nor retreat. We will not write failure across this page of our history. We will do our duty, our full duty, to the people of the Philippines, and strive by every means to give them freedom, contentment and prosperity.

We have no belief in the old slaveholders' doctrine that the constitution of its own force marches into every newly acquired territory, and this doctrine, which we cast out in 1860, we still reject. We do not mean that the Philippines shall come within our tariff system or become part of our body politic. We do mean that they shall under our teaching learn to govern themselves and remain under our flag, with the largest possible measure of home rule. We make no hypocritical pretence of being interested in the Philippines solely on account of others. While we regard the welfare of those people as a sacred trust, we regard the welfare of the American people first. We see our duty to ourselves as well as to others. We believe in trade expansion.

By every legitimate means within the province of government and legislation we mean to stimulate the expansion of our trade and to open new markets. Greatest of all markets is China. Our trade there is growing by leaps and bounds.

Manila, the prize of war, gives us inestimable advantages in developing that trade. It is the corner-stone of our Eastern policy, and the brilliant diplomacy of John Hay in securing from all nations a guarantee of our treaty rights and of the open door in China rests upon it.

We ask the American people whether they will throw away these new markets and widening opportunities for trade and commerce by putting in power the Democratic Party, who seek under cover of a newly-discovered affection for the rights of man to give up these islands of the East and make Dewey's victory fruitless?

The choice lies between this Democratic policy of retreat and the Republican policy which would hold the islands, give them freedom and prosperity and enlarge those great opportunities for ourselves and our posterity.

The Democratic attitude toward the Philippines rests wholly upon the proposition that the American people have neither the capacity nor the honesty to deal rightly with these islands. They assume that we shall fail.

They fall down and worship a Chinese half-breed whose name they had never heard three years ago, and they slander and cry down and doubt the honor of American soldiers and sailors, of admirals and generals, and public men who have gone in and out before us during an entire lifetime.

We are true to our own. We have no distrust of the honor, the humanity, the capacity of the American people. To feel or do otherwise is to doubt ourselves, our government and our civilization.

We take issue with the Democrats who would cast off the Philippines because the American people cannot be trusted with them, and we declare that the American people can be trusted to deal justly, wisely, and generously with these distant islands and will lift them up to a higher prosperity, a broader freedom, and a nobler civilization than they have ever known. We have not failed elsewhere. We shall not fail here.

Those are the questions we present to the American people in regard to the Philippines. Do they want such a humiliating change there as Democratic victory would bring? Do they want an even more radical change at home? Suppose the candidate of the Democrats, the Populists, the foes of expansion, the dissatisfied, and the envious should come into power, what kind of an administration would he give us? What would his cabinet be?

Think what an electric spark of confidence would run through every business interest in the country when such a cabinet was announced as we can readily imagine he would make. More important still, we ask the American people whether they will put in the White House the hero of uncounted platforms, the prodigal spendthrift of words, the champion of free silver, the opponent of expansion, the assailant of the courts; or whether they will retain in the Presidency the Union soldier, the leader of the House of Representatives, the trained statesman who has borne victoriously the heavy burdens of the last four years; the champion of protection and sound money, the fearless supporter of law and order wherever the flag floats? But there is one question we will put to the American people in this campaign which includes and outweighs all others.

We will say to them: You were in the depths of adversity under the last Democratic Administration; you are on the heights of prosperity to-day. Will that prosperity continue if you make a change in your President and in the party which administers your government? How long will your good times last if you turn out the Republicans and give political power to those who cry nothing but " Woe! woe!"

The lovers of calamity and foes of prosperity who hold success in business to be a crime and regard thrift as a misdemeanor? If the Democrats should win do you think business would improve? Do you think that prices would remain steady, that wages would rise and employment increase when that result of the election was known? Business confidence rests largely upon sentiment. Do you think that sentiment would be a hopeful one the day after Bryan's election?

Business confidence is a delicate plant. Do you think it would flourish with the Democratic Party? . . .

Do you not know from recent and bitter experience what that arrest of movement, that fear of the future, means? It means the contraction of business, the reduction of employment, the increase of the unemployed, lower wages, hard times, distress, unhappiness.

We do not say that we have panaceas for every ill. We do not claim that any policy we, or any one else, can offer will drive from the world sorrow and suffering and poverty, but we say that so far as government and legislation can secure the prosperity and well being of the American people, our administration and our policies will do it. We point to the adversity of the Cleveland years lying dark behind us. It has been replaced by the prosperity of the McKinley years. Let them make whatever explanation they will, the facts are with us.

It is on these facts that we shall ask for the support of the American people. What we have done is known, and about what we intend to do there is neither secrecy nor deception.

What we promise we will perform. Our old policies are here, alive, successful and full of vigor. Our new policies have been begun, and for them we ask support. While the clouds of impending civil war hung dark over the country in 1861 we took up the great task then laid upon us and never flinched until we had carried it through to victory.

Now, at the dawn of a new century, with new policies and new opportunities opening before us in the bright sunshine of prosperity, we again ask the American people to entrust us with their future. We have profound faith in the people. We do not distrust their capacity of meeting the new responsibilities even as they met the old, and we shall await with confidence, under the leadership of William McKinley, the verdict of November.

GRADY

HENRY WOODFEN GRADY, an American orator and journalist, was born at Athens, Georgia, May 24, 1850, and received his education at the State universities of Georgia and Virginia. Engaging in journalism, he was for a time editor successively of the " Courier " and " Commerical " at Rome, Georgia, and, after removing to Atlanta in 1871, was for some six years editorially connected with the Atlanta " Herald." In 1880 he became editor and part-owner of the Atlanta " Constitution," and was its editor at the time of his death, which occurred at Atlanta, December 23, 1889. In the latter part of his career Grady's remarkable eloquence as an orator gave him a national reputation. Among his best-known speeches are his address before the New England Club of New York city, December 21, 1886, a famous prohibition speech at Atlanta in 1887, an address at the Texas State Fair in 1888, and the speech delivered at Boston a few days before his death, on "The Future of the Negro." Grady was an enthusiastic supporter of the prohibition movement, and his speeches on the political situation helped to foster good feeling between North and South.

THE NEW SOUTH

SPEECH DELIVERED BEFORE THE NEW ENGLAND CLUB, NEW YORK, DECEMBER 21, 1886

THERE was a South of slavery and secession—that South is dead. There is a South of union and freedom—that South, thank God, is living, breathing, growing every hour.

These words, delivered from the immortal lips of Benjamin H. Hill, at Tammany Hall in 1866, true then and truer now, I shall make my text to-night.

Mr. President and Gentlemen—Let me express to you my appreciation of the kindness by which I am permitted to address you. I make this abrupt acknowledgment advisedly, for I feel that if, when I raise my provincial voice in this ancient and august presence, I could find courage for no more than the opening sentence, it would be well if in that sentence

I had met in a rough sense my obligation as a guest, and had perished, so to speak, with courtesy on my lips and grace in my heart. Permitted, through your kindness, to catch my second wind, let me say that I appreciate the significance of being the first Southerner to speak at this board, which bears the substance, if it surpasses the semblance, of original New England hospitality, and honors the sentiment that in turn honors you, but in which my personality is lost and the compliment to my people made plain.

I bespeak the utmost stretch of your courtesy to-night. I am not troubled about those from whom I come. You remember the man whose wife sent him to a neighbor with a pitcher of milk, and who, tripping on the top step, fell with such casual interruptions as the landings afforded into the basement, and, while picking himself up, had the pleasure of hearing his wife call out: "John, did you break the pitcher?" "No, I didn't," said John, "but I'll be dinged if I don't."

So, while those who call me from behind may inspire me with energy if not with courage, I ask an indulgent hearing from you. I beg that you will bring your full faith in American fairness and frankness to judgment upon what I shall say. There was an old preacher once who told some boys of the Bible lesson he was going to read in the morning. The boys, finding the place, glued together the connecting pages. The next morning he read at the bottom of one page, " When Noah was one hundred and twenty years old he took unto himself a wife who was "—then turning the page—" 140 cubits long, 40 cubits wide, built of gopher wood, and covered with pitch inside and out." He was naturally puzzled at this. He read it again, verified it, and then said: " My friends, this is the first time I ever met this in the Bible, but I accept this as an evidence of the assertion that we are fearfully and wonderfully made." If I could get you to hold such faith to-night I could proceed cheerfully to the task I otherwise approach with a sense of consecration.

Pardon me one word, Mr. President, spoken for the sole purpose of getting into the volumes that go out annually freighted with the rich eloquence of your speakers, the fact that the Cavalier as well as the Puritan was on the continent in its early days, and that he was " up and able to be about." I have read your books carefully and I find no mention of that fact, which seems an important one to me for preserving a sort of historical equilibrium if for nothing else.

Let me remind you that the Virginia Cavalier first challenged France on the continent; that Cavalier John Smith gave New England its very name, and was so pleased with the job that he has been handing his own name around ever since; and that while Myles Standish was cutting off men's ears for courting a girl without her parents' consent, and forbade men to kiss their wives on Sunday, the Cavalier was courting everything in sight, and that the Almighty had vouchsafed great increase to the Cavalier colonies, the huts in the wilderness being as full as the nests in the woods.

But having incorporated the Cavalier as a fact in your charming little books, I shall let him work out his own salvation, as he has always done, with engaging gallantry, and we will hold no controversy as to his merits. Why should we? Neither Puritan nor Cavalier long survived as such. The virtues and good traditions of both happily still live for the inspiration of their sons and the saving of the old fashion. But both Puritan and Cavalier were lost in the storm of the first Revolution, and the American citizen, supplanting both and stronger than either, took possession of the republic bought by their common blood and fashioned to wisdom, and charged himself with teaching men government and establishing the voice of the people as the voice of God.

My friends, Dr. Talmage has told you that the typical American has yet to come. Let me tell you that he has already come. Great types, like valuable plants, are slow to flower and fruit. But from the union of these colonies, Puritans and Cavaliers, from the straightening of their purposes and the crossing of their blood, slow perfecting through a century, came he who stands as the first typical American, the first who comprehended within himself all the strength and gentleness, all the majesty and grace of this republic—Abraham Lincoln.

He was the sum of Puritan and Cavalier, for in his ardent nature were fused the virtues of both, and in the depths of his great soul the faults of both were lost. He was greater than Puritan, greater than Cavalier, in that he was American, and that in his honest form were first gathered the vast and thrilling forces of his ideal government—charging it with such tremendous meaning and elevating it above human suffering that martyrdom, though infamously aimed, came as a fitting crown to a life consecrated from the cradle to human liberty. Let us, each cherishing the traditions and honoring his fathers, build with reverend hands to the type of this simple but sublime life, in which all types are honored, and in our common glory as Americans there will be plenty and to spare for your forefathers and for mine.

Dr. Talmage has drawn for you, with a master's hand, the picture of your returning armies. He has told you how, in the pomp and circumstance of war, they came back to you, marching with proud and victorious tread, reading their glory in a nation's eyes! Will you bear with me while I tell you of another army that sought its home at the close of the late war—an army that marched home in defeat and not in victory—in pathos and not in splendor, but in glory that equalled yours, and to hearts as loving as ever welcomed heroes home! Let me picture to you the footsore Confederate soldier, as, buttoning up in his faded gray jacket the parole which was to bear testimony to his children of his fidelity and faith, he turned his face southward from Appomattox in April, 1865.

Think of him as ragged, half-starved, heavy-hearted, enfeebled by want and wounds, having fought to exhaustion, he surrenders his gun, wrings the hands of his comrades in silence, and lifting his tear-stained and pallid face for the last time to the graves that dot old Virginia hills, pulls his gray cap over his brow and begins the slow and painful journey. What does he find—let me ask you who went to your homes eager to find, in the welcome you had justly earned, full payment for four years' sacrifice—what does he find when, having followed the battle-stained cross against overwhelming odds, dreading death not half so much as surrender, he reaches the home he left so prosperous and beautiful?

He finds his house in ruins, his farm devastated, his slaves free, his stock killed, his barns empty, his trade destroyed, his money worthless, his social system, feudal in its magnificence, swept away; his people without law or legal status, his comrades slain, and the burdens of others heavy on his shoulders. Crushed by defeat, his very traditions are gone. Without money, credit, employment, material, or training, and, besides all this, confronted with the gravest problem that ever met human intelligence,—the establishing of a status for the vast body of his liberated slaves.

What does he do—this hero in gray with a heart of gold?
Does he sit down in sullenness and despair? Not for a day.
Surely God, who had stripped him of his prosperity, inspired him in his adversity. As ruin was never before so
overwhelming, never was restoration swifter. The soldier
stepped from the trenches into the furrow; horses that had
charged Federal guns marched before the plow, and fields
that ran red with human blood in April were green with the
harvest in June; women reared in luxury cut up their dresses
and made breeches for their husbands, and, with a patience
and heroism that fit women always as a garment, gave their
hands to work. There was little bitterness in all this.
Cheerfulness and frankness prevailed.

"Bill Arp" struck the key-note when he said: "Well, I
killed as many of them as they did of me, and now I'm going
to work." Of the soldier returning home after defeat and
roasting some corn on the roadside, who made the remark to
his comrades: "You may leave the South if you want to,
but I'm going to Sandersville, kiss my wife, and raise a crop,
and if the Yankees fool with me any more I'll whip 'em
again."

I want to say to General Sherman, who is considered an
able man in our parts, though some people think he is a kind
of careless man about fire, that from the ashes he left us in
1864 we have raised a brave and beautiful city; that somehow or other we have caught the sunshine in the bricks and
mortar of our homes, and have builded therein not one
ignoble prejudice or memory.

But what is the sum of our work? We have found out
that in the summing up the free negro counts more than he
did as a slave. We have planted the schoolhouse on the hill-
top and made it free to white and black. We have sowed

towns and cities in the place of theories, and put business above politics. We have challenged your spinners in Massachusetts and your iron-makers in Pennsylvania. We have learned that the $400,000,000 annually received from our cotton crop will make us rich when the supplies that make it are home-raised. We have reduced the commercial rate of interest from twenty-four to six per cent, and are floating four per cent bonds.

We have learned that one northern immigrant is worth fifty foreigners; and have smoothed the path to southward, wiped out the place where Mason and Dixon's line used to be, and hung out our latch-string to you and yours. We have reached the point that marks perfect harmony in every household, when the husband confesses that the pies which his wife cooks are as good as those his mother used to bake; and we admit that the sun shines as brightly and the moon as softly as it did before the war. We have established thrift in city and country. We have fallen in love with our work. We have restored comfort to homes from which culture and elegance never departed. We have let economy take root and spread among us as rank as the crabgrass which sprung from Sherman's cavalry camps, until we are ready to lay odds on the Georgia Yankee as he manufactures relics of the battlefield in a one-story shanty and squeezes pure olive oil out of his cotton seed, against any Down-Easter that ever swappped wooden nutmegs for flannel sausage in the valleys of Vermont. Above all, we know that we have achieved in these "piping times of peace" a fuller independence for the South than that which our fathers sought to win in the forum by their eloquence or compel in the field by their swords.

It is a rare privilege, sir, to have had part, however

humble, in this work. Never was nobler duty confided to human hands than the uplifting and upbuilding of the prostrate and bleeding South—misguided, perhaps, but beautiful in her suffering, and honest, brave, and generous always. In the record of her social, industrial, and political illustration we await with confidence the verdict of the world.

But what of the negro? Have we solved the problem he presents or progressed in honor and equity toward solution? Let the record speak to the point. No section shows a more prosperous laboring population than the negroes of the South, none in fuller sympathy with the employing and land-owning class. He shares our school fund, has the fullest protection of our laws and the friendship of our people. Self-interest as well as honor demand that he should have this. Our future, our very existence, depend upon working out this problem in full and exact justice.

We understand that when Lincoln signed the Emancipation Proclamation, your victory was assured, for he then committed you to the cause of human liberty, against which the arms of man cannot prevail—while those of our statesmen who trusted to make slavery the corner-stone of the Confederacy doomed us to defeat as far as they could, committing us to a cause that reason could not defend or the sword maintain in sight of advancing civilization.

Had Mr. Toombs said, which he did not say, "that he would call the roll of his slaves at the foot of Bunker Hill," he would have been foolish, for he might have known that whenever slavery became entangled in war it must perish, and that the chattel in human flesh ended forever in New England when your fathers—not to be blamed for parting with what didn't pay—sold their slaves to our fathers—not to be praised for knowing a paying thing when they saw it.

The relations of the southern people with the negro are close and cordial. We remember with what fidelity for four years he guarded our defenceless women and children, whose husbands and fathers were fighting against his freedom. To his eternal credit be it said that whenever he struck a blow for his own liberty he fought in open battle, and when at last he raised his black and humble hands that the shackles might be struck off, those hands were innocent of wrong against his helpless charges, and worthy to be taken in loving grasp by every man who honors loyalty and devotion.

Ruffians have maltreated him, rascals have misled him, philanthropists established a bank for him, but the South, with the North, protests against injustice to this simple and sincere people. To liberty and enfranchisement is as far as law can carry the negro. The rest must be left to conscience and common sense. It must be left to those among whom his lot is cast, with whom he is indissolubly connected, and whose prosperity depends upon their possessing his intelligent sympathy and confidence. Faith has been kept with him, in spite of calumnious assertions to the contrary by those who assume to speak for us or by frank opponents. Faith will be kept with him in the future, if the South holds her reason and integrity.

But have we kept faith with you? In the fullest sense, yes. When Lee surrendered—I don't say when Johnston surrendered, because I understand he still alludes to the time when he met General Sherman last as the time when he determined to abandon any further prosecution of the struggle—when Lee surrendered, I say, and Johnston quit, the South became, and has since been, loyal to this Union.

We fought hard enough to know that we were whipped, and in perfect frankness accept as final the arbitrament of the

sword to which we had appealed. The South found her
jewel in the toad's head of defeat. The shackles that had
held her in narrow limitations fell forever when the shackles
of the negro slave were broken. Under the old régime the
negroes were slaves to the South; the South was a slave to
the system. The old plantation, with its simple police regulations and feudal habit, was the only type possible under
slavery. Thus was gathered in the hands of a splendid and
chivalric oligarchy the substance that should have been diffused among the people, as the rich blood, under certain
artificial conditions, is gathered at the heart, filling that with
affluent rapture, but leaving the body chill and colorless.

The old South rested everything on slavery and agriculture, unconscious that these could neither give nor maintain
healthy growth. The new South presents a perfect democracy, the oligarchs leading in the popular movement—a
social system compact and closely knitted, less splendid on the
surface, but stronger at the core—a hundred farms for every
plantation, fifty homes for every palace—and a diversified
industry that meets the complex need of this complex age.

The new South is enamored of her new work. Her soul
is stirred with the breath of a new life. The light of a
grander day is falling fair on her face. She is thrilling with
the consciousness of growing power and prosperity. As she
stands upright, full statured and equal among the people of
the earth, breathing the keen air and looking out upon the
expanded horizon, she understands that her emancipation
came because through the inscrutable wisdom of God her
honest purpose was crossed, and her brave armies were
beaten.

This is ε   ι no spirit of time-serving or apology. The
South has nothing for which to apologize. She believes that

the late struggle between the States was war and not rebellion; revolution and not conspiracy, and that her convictions were as honest as yours. I should be unjust to the dauntless spirit of the South and to my own convictions if I did not make this plain in this presence. The South has nothing to take back. In my native town of Athens is a monument that crowns its central hill—a plain, white shaft. Deep cut into its shining side is a name dear to me above the names of men—that of a brave and simple man who died in a brave and simple faith. Not for all the glories of New England, from Plymouth Rock all the way, would I exchange the heritage he left me in his soldier's death. To the foot of that I shall send my children's children to reverence him who ennobled their name with his heroic blood. But, sir, speaking from the shadow of that memory which I honor as I do nothing else on earth, I say that the cause in which he suffered and for which he gave his life was adjudged by higher and fuller wisdom than his or mine, and I am glad that the omniscient God held the balance of battle in his Almighty hand and that human slavery was swept forever from American soil, the American Union was saved from the wreck of war.

This message, Mr. President, comes to you from consecrated ground. Every foot of soil about the city in which I live is as sacred as a battle-ground of the republic. Every hill that invests it is hallowed to you by the blood of your brothers who died for your victory, and doubly hallowed to us by the blood of those who died hopeless, but undaunted in defeat—sacred soil to all of us—rich with memories that make us purer and stronger and better—silent but staunch witnesses, in its red desolation, of the matchless valor of American hearts and the deathless glory of American arms— speaking an eloquent witness in its white peace and prosperity to the indissoluble union of American States and the imperishable brotherhood of the American people.

Now, what answer has New England to this message? Will she permit the prejudice of war to remain in the hearts of the conquerors when it has died in the hearts of the conquered? Will she transmit this prejudice to the next generation, that in their hearts which never felt the generous ardor of conflict it may perpetuate itself? Will she withhold, save in strained courtesy, the hand which, straight from his soldier's heart, Grant offered to Lee at Appomattox? Will she make the vision of a restored and happy people, which gathered above the couch of your dying captain, filling his heart with grace; touching his lips with praise, and glorifying his path to the grave—will she make this vision on which the last sigh of his expiring soul breathed a benediction, a cheat and delusion? If she does, the South, never abject in asking for comradeship, must accept with dignity its refusal; but if she does not refuse to accept in frankness and sincerity this message of good will and friendship, then will the prophecy of Webster, delivered in this very Society forty years ago amid tremendous applause, become true, be verified in its fullest sense, when he said: " Standing hand to hand and clasping hands, we should remain united as we have been for sixty years, citizens of the same country, members of the same government, united, all united now and united forever." There have been difficulties, contentions, and controversies, but I tell you that in my judgment—

> ——" those opened eyes,
> Which, like the meteors of a troubled heaven,
> All of one nature, of one substance bred,
> Did lately meet in th' intestine shock,
> Shall now, in mutual well-beseeming ranks,
> March all one way."

G

McCALL

SAMUEL WALKER McCALL, an American Congressman, was born at East Providence, Pennsylvania, February 28, 1851, and was educated at Dartmouth College. He studied law at Worcester, Massachusetts, and, after being admitted to the bar, began practice in Boston. For some months of 1888 he was editor of the Boston " Daily Advertiser," and for the session of 1888-89 was a member of the Massachusetts legislature. In 1892 he was elected a Republican Representative to Congress and was re-elected at each subsequent election. During the spring of 1900 he was conspicuous in his minority opposition to the Porto Rico Tariff Bill.

THE PORTO RICO TARIFF

DELIVERED IN THE HOUSE OF REPRESENTATIVES, THURSDAY, FEBRUARY 22, 1900

MR. CHAIRMAN,—The distinguished chairman of the Committee on Ways and Means, who is the able leader of this House, and brings to all economic questions a sound judgment and a wide range of information, has, in my opinion, clearly shown that the pending bill will produce a sufficient revenue. But the question of revenue is, I believe, of slight importance compared with another question involved, upon which I regret to say that I am compelled to dissent from the views entertained by my Republican colleagues on the committee, many of whom I have so often followed in the past with pleasure.

The main question put in issue by the substitute bill reported by the chairman of the committee involves nothing less than the proposition that Congress, in dealing with the Territories of the United States, has absolute power, unfettered by any of the limitations of the constitution. That it is, in short, a power acting outside of the constitution with the capacity to deal with all persons and property in our Territories as it may see fit. The issue raised by the committee is not, Does the constitution govern Porto Rico, but does it govern us? Believing that absolute power was never intended to be given by the framers of the constitution; that it is contrary to the whole spirit of that instrument; that it is contrary, also, to its specific terms, and that a long and unbroken line of decisions of our supreme court are directly against this assertion of power, I feel myelf constrained to oppose this bill.

A great deal has been said about the meaning of the term "United States" in the constitution, and it seems to me much irrelevant learning has been expended in the discussion of that question. It is evident that the term could have been employed in any one of three different senses according to the context—one as expressing simple sovereignty and the national name, another as referring to the individual States composing the Union, and the third referring to the empire or territory over which the new sovereignty was to have sway.

It will require no very ample learning, it seems to me, in our history before the formation of the constitution to enable one to see that the term might have been used in any of these three senses. There is another and broader sense in which the term is used since the great war of the rebellion. Some of the old views of the constitution were totally overthrown by that great convulsion. The close-corporation theory, the idea that our government rested simply upon the States as units, and that the term "United States," in the political sense, meant simply the States composing the Union, it seems to me, gave way then to the broader doctrine that the government of the United States rests not in the States but in the people as a whole, a new body politic created by the constitution.

But, sir, this is no question of mere syntax. What are the vital points? The Revolution was started and fought to a successful conclusion upon the broad principle that one community had no right permanently to levy taxes upon another community. That was the underlying idea which led to the establishment of this government. The power to tax is the very essence of the power to enslave. The right to take a portion of the proceeds of a man's toil by an unlimited power of taxation necessarily involves the right to take them all. This idea, I say, underlies the foundation of our government.

And what more than any other motive led to the abandonment of the old Articles of Confederation and the adoption of our constitution? Was it not the desire to do away with the local toll-gates that had been set up upon the frontiers of each State and to break down the local barriers upon commerce, so that trade might be carried on unfettered throughout the dominion of the United States? The two things, then, that we should expect to find guarded in the constitution, and the two things with reference to which we should most strictly construe all its terms, are, first, the right to tax, and, second, the right to set up again local barriers against trade within our dominion which the constitution was erected to throw down.

Now, I do not propose to consume the time of the House with any elaborate review of the condition of our public lands, or of any other portions of our history prior to the adoption of the constitution than those to which I have alluded, but I come to the direct issue involved by this bill. Section 8 of the first article of the constitution is as follows:

" The Congress shall have power to lay and collect taxes, duties, imposts, and excises to pay the debts, and provide for the common defence and general welfare of the United States; but all duties, imposts, and excises shall be uniform throughout the United States."

Here is the power of taxation specifically given, and in the very section which gives the power the method of its exercise is as distinctly marked out. The power and the method granted in the same breath are coextensive, and wherever Congress has the power to lay and collect duties, imposts, and excises it must lay and collect them uniformly. This would seem to be in accordance with the most natural and simple meaning of the words. Certainly the term " United States " in the uniformity clause does not mean mere sovereignty. It undoubtedly refers to territory, to the places over which this dominion or power is to be exercised.

If we were in any doubt as to the meaning of the words, then I submit that we should solve those doubts in the light of those two great ideas to which I have referred, the one of which caused the Revolution and the other of which led to the adoption of the constitution. We should give that clause the strictest construction and interpret it in case of doubt against the power to tax and against the power to set up local barriers.

But we are not without further light. This very clause has been construed by the great arbiter set up by the constitution for the final settlement of all constitutional and other legal questions. I shall quote now from the case of Loughborough vs. Blake, in which John Marshall, as great a jurist as ever sat upon any bench, rendered the decision of the court:

" The power to lay and collect duties, imposts, and excises may be exercised and must be exercised throughout the United States. Does this term designate the whole or any part of the American empire? Certainly this question can admit of but one answer. It is the name given to our great Republic, which is composed of States and Territories. The District of Columbia or the territory west of the Missouri is not less within the United States than Maryland or Pennsylvania, and it is not less necessary, on the principles of our constitution, that uniformity in the imposition of imposts, duties, and excises shall be observed in the one than the other."

There could not be a more explicit construction placed upon the meaning of any words. This opinion unequivocally holds that the expression " United States " in the clause providing for uniformity of duties, excises, and imposts means the whole American empire and includes the Territories as well as the States. But it is discovered that this expression of opinion is *obiter dictum,* and a good deal of ingenuity has been expended in support of the proposition that the principle which John Marshall put in the forefront of that decision was not the principle upon which the case should have been decided. A reading of the case, however, will convince anyone that it might well have been put upon that principle, and the fact that it was put upon it is some evidence that the court considered the question and thought that it was material to the decision.

A modern school of jurists—so modern that they have only appeared within our body politic during the last eighteen months—have discovered that the District of Columbia, the constitutional status of which was involved in the case of Loughborough *vs.* Blake, was under the constitution while it was a part of a State, and by its subsequent cession it did not lose that status. In other words, although the constitution itself provided for the carving out and cession of just such a district somewhere, in some way when the specific cession of the territory actually occurred the constitution which had been adopted by the State from which it was separated ran with this territory like a covenant running with the land.

All I have to say, Mr. Chairman, upon this proposition is that so far as I can discover it never has occurred to the mind of any justice of our supreme court in the long line of decisions that have been rendered upon the constitutional status of the District of Columbia. The utmost that can be shown by it is the obtuseness of the men who have adorned that bench, although it is barely possible that the point was so small and trivial and insignificant as to be beneath the attention of those great minds.

If the opinion which John Marshall expressed for himself and his associates upon that bench were a mere *obiter dictum*, it would still be entitled to great weight and respect in any tribunal in the world, but it was not *obiter dictum*. It is clear that the principle was from the view the court took of the case involved in the decision. John Marshall enunciated principles. His mind had a wider range than that of the modern police court justice whose intellectual processes it is now sought to impose upon that great man.

This is one unequivocal opinion by the supreme court that the principle involved in the bill presented by the majority of the Committee on Ways and Means is in violation of the constitution which every member here has taken an oath to observe, protect, and defend. But this specific clause of the constitution has again been considered by the Supreme Court of the United States, and the meaning of the term "United States" in the uniformity clause has again been construed. I refer now to the case of Cross *vs.* Harrison (16 Howard,

191). That was a case where, among other issues, the question was raised of the legality of certain duties imposed in the Territory of California after it had been ceded to the United States and before it was admitted as a State. In that case the court declared that "after the ratification of the treaty California became a part of the United States."

More than once in the consideration of that case it treated California, with reference to the clause of the constitution in question, as a part of the United States, and finally it declared that—

"The right claimed to land foreign goods within the United States at any place out of a collection district, if allowed, would be a violation of that provision of the constitution which enjoins that all duties, imposts, and excises shall be uniform throughout the United States.

"Indeed, it must be very clear that no such right exists and that there was nothing in the condition of California to exempt importers of foreign goods into it from the payment of the same duties which were chargeable in the other ports of the United States."

Here, then, are two decisions of our supreme court, made without any dissent, separated from each other by a third of a century, with the court composed in each case of entirely different justices, which hold that the clause requiring duties, imposts, and excises to be uniform throughout the United States applied to Territories. It may be possible that some fine-spun theory may some day point to the conclusion that this second opinion was also a dictum; but in a law case involving a man's life the authority of these cases would be regarded as conclusive, especially as they have been in no decision overruled or even questioned. So much for the specific interpretation by the supreme court of the clause of the constitution in question.

I will now refer briefly—and there is a long line of decisions—to the cases dealing with the same proposition in a more general form, namely, whether Congress, in legislating for the Territories of the United States, has unlimited authority, and acts as an absolute, primitive sort of despotism outside of the constitution, or whether it is controlled by the limitations of the instrument which created it; whether the great doctrine of constitutional liberty is only applicable to the residents of this very narrow and close corporation of States, or whether those principles restrain all our agencies of government wherever they are exercised and wherever our laws have sway. . . .

Reference has been made to the Dred Scott case, and I have on account of the discredited character of that case in another particular refrained from quoting the opinion of the chief justice upon the question here involved. But this can be said, that never was any judicial opinion subjected to a more fiery test than was the opinion of the majority of the court in that case by Mr. Justice Curtis in his masterly dissenting opinion, in which he so nobly vindicated the rights of manhood, and yet almost the one point of the opinion of the majority of the court which was accepted by Mr. Justice Curtis was upon this very point. After a full consideration of the question of the power of Congress over Territories he said:

" If, then, this clause does contain a power to legislate respecting the territory, what are the limits of that power ?

" To this I answer, that, in common with all the other legislative powers of Congress, it finds limits in the express prohibitions on Congress not to do certain things; that, in the exercise of the legislative power, Congress can not pass an ex post facto law or bill of attainder; and so in respect to each of the other prohibitions contained in the constitution."

The Slaughter House cases (16 Wallace) plainly held that the fourteenth amendment, relating to citizenship, extends to the Territories. And in United States *vs.* Wom Kim Ark (169 U. S.) there can be no question whatever that the court considered the term " United States " in the citizenship clause of the fourteenth amendment, as including the Territories. See especially the expressions " born within the dominion," " born within the jurisdiction and allegiance," " born within the sovereignty," " the same right in every State and Territory," " born within the territorial limits of the United States," " born in this country; " finally, " the amendment in clear words and in manifest intent includes children born within the territory of the United States."

In the Morman Church *vs.* United States (136 U. S.) the court cites the case of Murphy *vs.* Ramsey approvingly and says:

" Doubtless Congress in legislating for the Territories would be subject to those fundamental limitations in favor of personal rights which are formulated in the constitution and its amendments. But its limitations would exist rather by inference and the general spirit of the constitution, from which Congress derives all its powers, than by any express or direct application of its provisions."

This is one of the cases which are cited by those who claim despotic power in Congress over the Territories; but it is entirely beyond question that the court holds that Congress in legislating for the Territories is subject to the limitations formulated in the constitution and its amendments. That the court put this restriction upon a ground that is somewhat rhetorical, and more in the nature of exhortation than a reason, does not change the fact that it holds that Congress is subject to these limitations. But three of the justices who sat in that case would not accept these shadowy sources of authority, so similar to the divine origin of the rights of kings, and they dissented through Mr. Chief Justice Fuller, who says:

" In my opinion Congress is restrained not merely by the limitations expressed in the constitution, but also by the absence of any grant of power expressed or implied in that instrument. . . . I regard it of vital consequence that absolute power should never be conceded as belonging under our system of government to any of its departments."

But in the more recent case of Thomson *vs.* Utah (170 U. S.), Mr. Justice Harlan, in delivering the opinion of the court, said " that the provisions of the constitution of the United States relating to the right of trial by jury in suits at common law apply to the Territories of the United States is no longer an open question," and again: " It is equally beyond question that the provisions of the national constitution relating to trial by jury for crimes and to criminal prosecutions apply to the Territories of the United States."

For the first time in our history Congress is attempting to tax goods going into an American territory. The fact that in the mutations of a century Congress has not attempted to exercise that power, although we always had large areas of territory, is some evidence that the power was not believed to exist.

The weakness of the case of those who contend for the despotic power of Congress is well illustrated by the authorities which they quote. They refer to the case of Fleming *vs.* Page, where our armies had taken possession of a Mexican port. The port had not been formerly ceded or annexed to the United States. The court simply held that military occupation did not make American territory, and the clear intimation was that if the port in question had been ceded by a treaty duly ratified or annexed by act of Congress it would become American territory. The case is not in point at all, but if it is to be considered there is not only nothing in it inconsistent with the proposition I am supporting, but its clear implication is entirely in its favor.

Then there are the cases with reference to the judicial department. In no one of those cases is it held or assumed that Congress has unlimited power over the Territories. The absence of a local government in the Territories, such as the States have, must have occurred to the framers of the constitution, and these cases all hold in effect that Congress possesses over the Territories, in addition to its national powers, the powers ordinarily exercised by a local State government. As a matter of rational construction it is unreasonable to hold that the framers of the constitution intended a judiciary with a life tenure to be created for Territories which might be admitted as States in the Union in the course of a few years.

Congress doubtless has, under a fair construction of the constitution, all those powers necessary to give the people of a Territory that full measure of government which the people of a State enjoy, but that it can play the despot, that it has the power to pass a law taking away the life of a citizen, that it can pass an ex post facto law, that it can under the guise of taxation take from an American citizen in a Territory his property in defiance of the provisions of the constitution, are propositions for which there can be found no basis in judicial authority whatever.

I have said the strength of this view is shown by the weakness of the authorities cited in support of the proposition that Congress has unlimited power. I have referred to the decisions in regard to the Federal judiciary. There is no line in the case of Hepburn *vs.* Ellzey (2 Cranch) or New Orleans *vs.* Winter (1 Wheaton) which is in the slightest degree inconsistent with the position of the court as set forth in Loughborough *vs.* Blake and again in subsequent cases. Take the case of Ross (140 U. S.), which is relied upon by the advocates of this bill as strong authority. That was a case where a crime had been committed on board an American ship while at anchor in a Japanese harbor.

It was clearly a case where there was a divided jurisdiction, where probably more could justly be said for the jurisdiction of Japan than for our own. It was such a case as would necessarily call for the exercise of the treaty-making power. A treaty had been made and a statute passed in pursuance of its terms under which Ross was tried by a consular court. It is beyond question that the court did not consider the crime as committed upon American territory, but outside of American territory. The report of the majority of the committee quotes from that case. It might well have quoted further. The court says:

" By the constitution the government is ordained and established ' for the United States of America,' and not for countries outside of their limits."

Would the court have used this language in speaking of a Territory of the United States? And again:

" The constitution cannot have any operation in another country. When, therefore, the representatives or officers of our government are permitted to exercise authority of any kind in any country, it must be on such conditions as the two countries may agree."

Does the national government make treaties with its Territories? Is it not clear that the court is discriminating between places where the United States has sovereignty and places where it has not? But this is made clear beyond a question. The court says:

" The deck of a private American vessel, it is true, is considered for many purposes constructively as territory of the United States, yet persons on board of such vessels, whether officers, sailors, or passengers, can not invoke protection of the provisions referred to until brought within the actual territorial boundaries of the United States."

The court thus in each instance makes a distinction between that which is American territory and that which is not. Its reasoning clearly implies that if the crime had been committed within the territorial limits of the American empire, the constitutional guaranties would apply.

The terms of the treaty by which Porto Rico was ceded to the United States do not affect the question. The status of the inhabitants at the time of the cession is left to be determined hereafter, but the status of the territory is fixed. The sovereignty and dominion over it reside in the government of the United States, and it is, from the constitutional aspect and the aspect of the law of nations, territory of the United States.

A treaty cannot enlarge the powers of Congress under the constitution, for a treaty can have no other force than law; and so far as its effect in this country is concerned, it can be repealed by act of Congress. The utmost that could be claimed, it seems to me, is that a treaty might stipulate with effect against the exercise of a part of the constitutional power of Congress; but I think it very doubtful if even that proposition could be maintained, and it is not material in the present discussion.

When we regard, then, the circumstances out of which our government and the constitution sprang, the words themselves of the taxing power, the direct adjudication of their meaning by the supreme court, the long line of authorities which deny the existence of absolute power in Congress, it seems to me it is clear that the theory of despotic power is absolutely repugnant to our institutions, and that if our supreme court should hold that such a power existed, it would have to reverse itself as no court has ever reversed itself since time began.

The discussion of the question of political rights only befogs the issue, for it has been held that suffrage is not a constitutional right. Congress, under the constitution, has full political power over the Territories.

If the majority view of the constitutional status of Porto Rico be correct, the bill violates another clause of the constitution which is also in favor of freedom of trade within our dominion. I refer to the provision that " no tax or duty shall be laid on articles exported from any State." Either Porto Rico is a part of the United States within the meaning of the constitution or it is not. If it is a part of the United States the uniformity clause clearly applies. If it is not a part of the United States within the meaning of the constitution, then in order for the productions of the United States to reach it they must be exported from the States. In that case our goods would be exported from a State, and after a short sea voyage agents of the United States, at a port over which the United States has control, would levy a duty upon them, which when paid would become subject to an appropriation by the national government as much as any money in the Treasury. The indirection of the transaction in no wise changes its character. In the view of the constitution taken by the majority it becomes clearly an export duty, and is therefore prohibited.

But it is said with a fine emphasis that since our right to tax these people precisely as we please is called in question, we should pass this bill, however unjust it may be, to vindicate our power. But if you are going to assert your power, which was questioned by John Marshall three quarters of a century ago, why not assert it in a bolder way? Why not show your strength by shearing your wolves—New Mexico, Oklahoma, and Alaska—instead of this poor little pet lamb of Porto Rico? Again, we are asked to pass this bill, that this great constitutional question can come before the supreme court.

Sir, that question, precisely as it exists, can now come before the court; but if you pass this bill it will go there with the added weight that attaches to the action of the great political department of the government. I believe the court will stand firmly by its decisions; but we have a duty imposed upon us of construing the constitution in the first instance for ourselves. We have had one decision of the court rendered in times of great political stress that a black man had no rights which a white man was bound to respect, and this country was deluged with blood to wash that decision from our laws. Now, we are asked to lay the foundation for a moot case with the weight of Congress behind it and ask for another decision that the white men and the brown men of Porto Rico are merely our chattels, and that the commonest constitutional right secured to the meanest black man that treads American soil does not belong to them, although they are under the flag. Let no act of Congress impart sanction to that idea.

But it is said grandly that if this view of the constitution prevails we can not afford to keep the Philippines. How often might our ancestors have likewise become alarmed over the cession of vast expanses of territory many times in the aggregate in excess of our original area and have been fearful of the result upon their industries and their institutions? And yet the rights secured by the constitution have been recognized over those broad annexations and nobody will say to-day that the whole country was not better for it.

You may be unduly alarmed about the effect of extending the principle of constitutional liberty wherever our sovereignty goes, but so far as we are concerned the blessings of that liberty have been preserved to us at a price in blood and treasure greater than the value of a thousand archipelagoes, and we will not throw away what we have bought so dearly. But the ultimate solution of the Philippine problem has been reserved for us, and I have no doubt we shall solve it wisely if we call into play our sober judgment and do not obscure it with the noisy rant and the fustian of declamation.

But we are now considering the case of a territory which is a part of this continent, admitted to be within the natural radius of our political action, and of great importance to our defence. Our victory over it was a bloodless victory. Instead of resisting our approaches it turned to this great power as a child turns to its mother. I do not view without concern the prospect of this nation forever taxing the people of that island, but if we are to tax them at all there is some safety in the fact that we ourselves are willing to submit to the taxes which we impose and remember that whatever modern methods of interpretation you may employ upon the constitution you will find that the right of one nation to appropriate the earnings of another is no less hateful to-day than at the time of the Revolution. I have said that there is some safety in the fact that the taxing state is willing to pay the taxes which it imposes.

It requires little discernment to see the danger into which a different practice would lead. We impose by this bill a certain per cent of duties upon goods passing between that island and this country. How long will it be before some powerful interests will demand that they be recognized The representatives of these interests vote and elect members of Congress. The Porto Ricans do not vote. Can there be any doubt that the taxes will be levied more and more for the benefit of great interests in this country, and that this hapless people who were told by our generals that they were to receive the glorious blessings of American liberty, who crowned our soldiers with wreaths, will become the victims of our extortion rather than the sharers in our freedom?

How was Spain treating them—selfish, heartless, cruel Spain? At the time of their deliverance they had sixteen representatives and four senators in the Spanish Cortes and helped to make the laws for the whole Spanish empire. They had a ten per cent duty upon goods passing between the two countries, and it was decreed that at the end of the year 1898 these duties were to disappear. They had almost complete autonomy for their own local affairs and a million and a half in the treasury.

Consider, too, for a moment how this differential tariff will operate. Upon a territory smaller than Connecticut there are crowded a million people. The great question with them is the food question. Upon many articles of food our duties are high, but as we are large exporters the price is not increased to our people. But for every bag of flour and every barrel of pork that goes to Porto Rico one fourth of these high duties must be paid, and either the cost of necessary articles of food is increased to them or the American producer gets so much less for his product. The cost to them will almost certainly be increased. Upon the importations of rice I am told the duties will amount to nearly $400,000 a year. Is this the feast of liberty to which you have invited those trusting people?

Remember that if the race from which our institutions sprang has great virtues it has great faults as well. It may not be cruel like the Spanish race; but is it free from cupidity? Do you want an instance from its history which may show you whither you are drifting? To the west of England there rises from the sea an island larger but not more beautiful than Porto Rico—Ireland. English statesmen thought their country needed protection against her products, and the linen and other great industries of Ireland were taxed and legislated almost out of existence for the benefit of the taxing country, and the people of Ireland were beggared. That system has been abandoned, and to-day a British citizen in Ireland has equal rights with a British citizen in any other part of the empire, even in England itself; but generations will not obliterate the bitter memories of the oppression and wrong which rankle in the hearts of the Irish people.

Do you want to make Porto Rico our Ireland? I say far wiser will it be if, instead of entering upon a policy which will make her happy, sunny-hearted children the mere chattels of this government, we follow the humane recommendation of the President and lay the foundations of our empire deep in the hearts of those people. If you will not regard the question from the standpoint of their interests, look at it somewhat broadly from the standpoint of your own. Our injustice will react upon ourselves.

Our nation was founded and has prospered upon the doctrine of constitutional liberty. Do you not see that you are degrading that liberty from a high principle? If so, how long can you expect it to survive at home? We restrain our own power when it may be exerted upon ourselves. You demand now that it shall be absolute and despotic when it may be exerted upon others. If restraint is to be removed, it can more safely be dispensed with when they who wield the power are likely to suffer.

I do not care to see our flag emblazon the principle of liberty at home and tyranny abroad. Sir, I brand with all my energy this hateful notion, bred somewhere in the heathenish recesses of Asia, that one man may exercise absolute dominion over another man or one nation over another nation. That notion comports very little with my idea of American liberty. It was resisted to the last extremity by the heroes who fought at Bunker Hill and starved at Valley Forge. It fell before the gleaming sabres of our troopers at Five Forks and Winchester. It was shot to death by our guns at Gettysburg and Appomattox. A half-million men gave up their lives that their country might stand forth clothed in the resplendent robes of constitutional liberty and that we might have a government of laws and not of men for every man beneath the shining folds of the flag. All the sweet voices of our history plead with us for that great cause to-day. And I do not believe, sir, that this nation will tolerate any abandonment of that principle which has made her morally, as she is physically, without a peer among nations.

LITTLEFIELD

C HARLES E. LITTLEFIELD, an American politician, was born at
Lebanon, York county, Maine, June 21, 1851. He was educated in the
common schools, and, after pursuing the study of law, was admitted to the
bar in 1876. He entered the lower house of the Maine legislature in 1885,
and was Speaker of the House in 1887, and from 1889-93 filled the post of
Attorney General of Maine. In 1899 he was elected to the Fifty-sixth
Congress to fill the vacancy in the House of Representatives caused by the
death of the Republican representative, Nelson Dingley.

THE PEARL OF THE ANTILLES, THE EVER-FAITHFUL ISLE

SPEECH DELIVERED IN THE HOUSE OF REPRESENTATIVES,
FEBRUARY 23, 1900

M R. CHAIRMAN AND GENTLEMEN OF THE
COMMITTEE,—I believe that the pending bill is
un-Republican, un-American, unwarranted, unpre-
decented, and unconstitutional. Inasmuch as I am in the
painful position of differing with a large majority of my political brethren, and as I believe this measure is one of vast importance, of far reaching consequence, involving results
that perhaps none of us can now anticipate, I feel that I
should, perhaps, render the reasons for my position.

I concede, and I gladly concede, the right of leadership to
the distinguished men who, by their long experience and
great abilities, have the responsibility and the honor of leading the Republicans in this House. The leaders of the Republican party will find me, upon all measures that involve
Republican policy, following loyally in their footsteps. When
an issue, however, arises that involves, in my judgment,
grave questions of right and wrong, great questions of prin-

(10755)

ciple, I feel, and I have no doubt they feel, that every individual member of the Republican party must be allowed to think, speak, and act for himself.

Upon such questions I believe it to be the duty of every Republican, and every Democrat, to do the right, as God gives him to see the right.

Profoundly impressed with this view of the case, I shall submit to the House some of the reasons why I believe the pending measure should not receive the approval of the Republican party.

Before I enter at any length upon the discussion of the questions involved in this bill—and I shall discuss the bill somewhat in detail—I invite the attention of the House to the condition of the people, for whom, we are about to legislate. . . .

But I ask attention to a few other suggestions and considerations in relation to this island, in order that we may intelligently appreciate its condition, and situation, and that of the people living thereon.

It is inhabited by about 1,000,000 people. Of these 70,-000 are dark-skinned people; 100,000 of them are of mixed blood; 830,000 of those living upon that island are white, Caucasian people, made up of Spanish, French, Italian, Portugese, English, American, Scotch, and Irish. Its area is about 3,650 square miles, giving, say, 273 persons to the square mile.

The intelligence of these people is not measured (as was suggested, I have no doubt, with honest intent as to accuracy) by the assumption that only ten per cent are able to read or write. The result of the last census, taken under the authority of the United States by Colonel Dingman, who returned to this country within three weeks, shows that about twenty-five per cent can read and write. The island has a property valuation of $160,000,000 to $180,000,000. Before our flag was raised upon its soil it was under Spanish domination. It had an autonomous local government, with universal suffrage.

The people of Porto Rico had the same pro rata representation in the Spanish Cortes as the citizens of the Empire, in Spain itself. They had sixteen members in the lower house, and four members in the upper house. Every citizen of Porto Rico had the same legal rights as a citizen of Spain. With reference to tariff conditions, for several years preceding the advent of Miles upon their soil, they had a ten per cent preferential tariff between themselves and Spain. By virtue of a budget which had been adopted and accepted, and by a statute which had been enacted by the Spanish Cortes, this tariff of ten per cent was to expire on the first of July, 1898, so that on, and after that date, there would have been perfect free trade between Porto Rico, and the parent State, Spain.

The suggestions which have been made by the gentleman who immediately preceded me—the gentleman from Connecticut—in relation to the revenues collected in Porto Rico are, I submit, somewhat misleading. I shall not undertake here, because I have not the time according to the plan which I have marked out for my address, to discuss such matters in detail. I only call attention to the operation of the tariff between Porto Rico and Spain. The license fees that were collected, the taxes that were collected upon incomes, the internal revenue taxes, should not properly be reckoned as any part of the taxation by way of a tariff imposed on products going from Porto Rico to Spain, or upon the products of Spain, going into Porto Rico.

Such a statement is an unfair presentation of the fiscal

condition of this island. The gentleman from Connecticut ingeniously, and confusingly combined them all in his description of fiscal conditions on the island, when nothing but the tariff has any proper place in the consideration of the pending measure. For years, has this island been populated by this white, Caucasian population. It never has had a dollar of public indebtedness. Time, and time again, the island from its own taxation has loaned to Spain money with which to carry on its various wars; and it has loaned to Santo Domingo and Cuba money for their public purposes. When the American flag was raised over this island, it had a surplus of $1,500,000 in its treasury.

The people who inhabit this island are a self-respecting, valorous, and heroic people.

Four times, during the eighteenth century, unaided and alone, the citizens of Porto Rico repelled the atacks of the English navy, once under the command of Drake, and once under the command of Abercrombie, and preserved Porto Rican soil for Porto Rico, against the most powerful of foreign invaders, although it was then a dependency of Spain.

In 1873 there existed upon the island of Porto Rico 39,000 slaves. In 1860 there existed in the Republic 3,000,000 slaves. The Republic freed its slaves at a cost that staggers humanity. It did not free the slaves " until all the wealth piled by the bondsman's two hundred and fifty years of unrequited toil " had been sunk and " until every drop of blood drawn by the lash had been paid by another drawn with the sword."

Porto Rico, in 1873, manumitted its slaves without tumult, without disturbance, without convulsion, without bloodshed, without murder, without outrage, and without revolution. With the consent of the Spanish Cortes, upon motion of a representative of Porto Rico, in one moment 39,000 persons who before that time had been held in human bondage, became freemen.

One day found them slaves; the next day they continued in their employment for the same masters, but working for hire—their own masters. On one day they bent down, bondmen. The next day they stood erect, freemen. This great change was wrought as quietly, and silently, as the dawn precedes the rising of the sun. The little island of Porto Rico paid for those slaves, by its own revenue, from its own prosperity, $7,800,000 in 1873, with a loan that required only fourteen years to pay, and, adding the interest and principal, aggregating the magnificent sum of $12,000,000—paid by whom?

By the people that live to-day in Porto Rico.

For what?

To emancipate 39,000 human bondmen. This nation of "illiterates," this people to whom we now propose to act the part of a "good Samaritan!" That was a deed worthy of the highest triumph of Christian civilization anywhere. The mechanics of Porto Rico, consisting of masons, blacksmiths, leather-workers, and silversmiths, are superior in their various branches to similar mechanics in nearly every part of the civilized world. The carpenters and cabinetmakers do not rank so high.

This is the condition of the island; this is the character of the people for whom the American Congress is about to legislate. They are an intelligent people, not barbarians, not slaves, but a free people, and I submit, as I shall submit later to the Republican party—for I do not stand here to address gentlemen upon the other side of this House—I submit, as I shall submit later to the Republican party, that they are a people who, by their history, by their character, by their intelligence, their endeavor, and inheritance, are entitled to fair treatment at the hands of the Republic, and to the maintenance of its plighted faith.

Thus stood the Pearl of the Antilles, " The Ever Faithful Isle," when, a rich and willing prize, it fell into our hands. I devote a moment to the question of raising revenue in Porto Rico for their own purposes, and then I pass from this branch of the question, to a discussion of the provisions of this bill.

It is estimated that $3,000,000 annually is necessary for the wants of this island, $1,000,000 to be devoted to public administration, $1,000,000 to be devoted to schools, and $1,000,000 to be devoted to public works. This is a large estimate, a liberal and a generous estimate. The amount that was used for schools in Porto Rico last year, and the preceding years, was only $345,000; and no wise and economical administration can properly expend in Porto Rico in the next two or three years three times the sum that is now being used, because it is a practical impossibility, under what they have there as a common-school system, to make such an expenditure economically.

It was conceded by the gentleman from Ohio [Mr. Grosvenor] in his speech yesterday, that $1,500,000 will be raised from the internal revenue tax upon rum. It is also conceded that under ordinary methods of local taxation they will raise about $500,000 besides, taking the island in its present prostrated condition, in all $2,000,000 of the $3,000,000 necessary to be raised.

Just a word as to their condition and situation. This estimate which I have given you of $500,000 is based upon the present condition of Porto Rico. And what is that? As was very handsomely and accurately described by the able chairman of the Ways and Means Committee, it is one of utter and awful devastation and ruin, with the absolute prostration of every industry in the island of Porto Rico. . . .

The estimate is, that even in that condition, with agriculture paralyzed, the amount which I have stated can be raised. And I should say here, perhaps, for the information of gentlemen that while this island is fertile, and its soil only needs to be tickled with a hoe to laugh with a harvest, that its fields when once allowed to pass out from under cultivation, go back in less than a year's time into a state of natural wildness, so that they have to be reclaimed again, before any profit can be made from them in agriculture. A large portion of the island is in that condition to-day. Yet, in that condition, it is conceded that by the ordinary methods of taxation this amount can be raised. The ordinary method of taxation there is simply this: It is in the nature of an income tax— a percentage on the income of the planter of sugar, tobacco, or coffee, or the man who is engaged in business, professional or otherwise—a reasonably fair method of taxation.

It is estimated by men capable of judging upon this question that when this island once gets back to its pristine condition (which will, perhaps, require two years' time), with the improved conditions of agriculture and methods of manufacture, that it is expected will be carried into this island by American industry, energy, enterprise, and intelligence, that the tax, upon the same basis, would aggregate from $5,000,000 to $10,000,000. This island, this Pearl of the Antilles, is no pauper or mendicant, standing begging at the doors of the American Congress for alms, or for the work of a " good Samaritan." All that the island of Porto Rico asks is to have the American Congress give it a stable government, an opportunity to take care of itself, and then take off its

hands and let it take care of itself, a thing that it can well
do. . . .

We had better listen, and think now, than to listen later.
A word here as to the assertion of the President of the
United States as to " the plain duty " of the Republican party
and of the American Congress. It is as much the duty of
the Democrats as the Republicans, because later, when I
reach that stage in this discussion, I shall base it upon the
broad proposition that, to my mind, appeals to every patriot,
and every man who believes in the good faith of the Republic,
its honor, and its integrity. Every Democrat who sits on
this floor is interested in that proposition as well as my Republican friends, with whom I just now can not act upon this
bill.

As to the suggestion of the gentleman from Ohio that
there had been a change in conditions I would like any gentlemen here to suggest what change there has been. He
suggested—and I want to call your attention to this particularly—he suggested that there had been a change in conditions. The report of General Davis was made September 5,
1899. In the middle of the preceding August that awful
tornado, that terrific cyclone, swept over this fateful island
and carried these coffee plantations from the mountain sides,
an indistinguishable mass of ruin, into the valleys below.
That awful ruin had visited the Pearl of the Antilles, before
this report was made by General Davis to the President of
the United States. No calamity has visited the island since.
No calamity is now impending over it, except what may be
involved in this measure now pending.

There has been no change in conditions, there has been
nothing that can be suggested. When William McKinley—
and, by the way, I shall spend no time in this discussion in

referring to Andrew Jackson, or Thomas Jefferson, or Tom Benton, or any of that great galaxy of men—for me it is sufficient if William McKinley, the honored President of this Republic, the distinguished representative of the Republican party, who is enthroned in the hearts and affections of all our people, will follow in the footsteps of Washington and Lincoln. A great many things have been done by the other distinguished gentlemen that I would not like to have any Republican President undertake to do, or even think of.

What does President McKinley say? He said when he sent his message to the House—and I have received no communication from the President of the United States since—mark that—he communicated to me through the constitutional channel; I say since then, neither directly nor indirectly, have I received any communication from the President of the United States that would tend to indicate that when he said—not that it was his opinion, not that he thought, nor that he would advise or suggest, but that it was "the plain duty"—stop and listen to that a minute—"the plain duty" of the Republican Congress to give free trade between Porto Rico and the United States, he did not mean it. That is an assertion of fact. It was either true or false.

If conditions have changed, let some gentleman suggest it while I am speaking. If there has been any change of conditions that could be mentioned by any gentleman since the President of the United States said it was our "plain duty," let him assert it now. That statement was either true or false when he made it, and if it was true or false when he made it, it is true or false now. I believe it was absolutely true.

I say to my friends that I am not ready, upon the question of policy even, to cast a vote in this House against what the

President of the United States has truthfully said was my "plain duty." I stand upon that proposition. I stand by the President of the United States, and a little later I will call your attention to some significant reasons why.

What is this bill? I take it in detail. The second provision in it imposes what they call an import duty on the manufactures and products of the United States "coming into Porto Rico." The bill imposes a duty on all goods "coming from Porto Rico" into the United States and on goods "coming into Porto Rico" from the United States. "Coming" both ways. I suppose the language of the bill is so couched, in the futile effort to get rid of a provision of the constitution which provides that "no tax or duty shall be laid on articles exported from any State." (Constitution, Article I, section 9, paragraph 5.) I submitted to two members of the Ways and Means Committee the question, as to whether they could give me any legal distinction between these propositions: First, a vessel is loaded with lumber, say in Portland, and starts for Porto Rico. Under this bill we will assume the tariff to be one thousand dollars.

Under this bill they collect the duty when she arrives, and who collects it? The United States government. Into whose pocket does it go? Into the United States government's. Second, what legal distinction is there between collecting the duty when she clears from Portland for Porto Rico, before she leaves the State, or collecting it afterwards in Porto Rico? The same hand collects it either in Portland, or in San Juan. It goes into the same pocket in either case, into the same Treasury, and is to be disbursed, under the provisions of this bill, without any appropriation from the public Treasury, which the constitution provides. But I do not suppose the constitution is anything between friends

I suggested that question to the chairman of the Ways and Means Committee, and asked him if the tax was collected in the city of Portland on the products of the United States going into Porto Rico, whether it would not be a tax on "articles exported from any State," and he could not tell me. I asked him what the legal distinction was, when the same duty, on the same cargo, was collected by the same hand, for the same Treasury, in Porto Rico. He could not tell me what the distinction was, or whether there was any. I heard his speech after I had put the question to him; he occupied an hour and a half about other things, and he did not tell me then. I put the same question to another member of the Ways and Means Committee, who gave me no answer. He has not yet made a speech. I suppose when he gets round to it he may answer it. But I have not had the pleasure of hearing that question answered, much as I have desired to have it answered in order to bring me to the support of this branch of the measure, by reason of its harmony with the constitution. I sought from two members of the Ways and Means Committee an answer to this question more than four days ago—yes, last week. It is not answered yet.

What did they do? I imagine they suggested the question to the distinguished gentleman from New York [Mr. Ray], the chairman of the Judiciary Committee—a man of eminence, ability, and character, a man whose suggestion ought to have weight with this House, and does. How did he answer it? I did not hear his speech, but I have read a part of it in the "Record." He states that he spent a whole day looking up the lexicographers and dictionaries, for the purpose of finding a definition of "export." I have an idea that the gentleman rather looked for a definition that would help his case; because, being on that committee, I know that if he had whirled round in his revolving chair in that committee room, and reached his hand out to the revolving bookcase, he could have put it upon Bouvier's " Law Dictionary," where he would have found in one minute's time a very good definition. After his exhaustive research he discovered that " export " meant the exporting of goods " to a foreign country; " but Bouvier would have shown him this:

" Export: The act of sending goods and merchandise from one country to another."

Now, in the name of all the gods at once, is it possible that by virtue of a treaty, or by virtue of conquest, we have eliminated Porto Rico from the map of the earth and it is no longer even a " country? "

Let me read another definition. I think the gentleman ought not to have spent so much time on this question. " Much study is a weariness of the flesh." The gentleman referred to the " Standard Dictionary," which is not yet old enough in its present form to have been cited by the courts as an authority.

I understand the gentleman from New York to admit that if " export " as used in the constitution does not mean going into a " foreign country," then the act is unconstitutional as providing for an export duty. I am not going to weary myself very much on this point as it is not the important feature. I am simply suggesting this as one of the inconsistencies of the bill.

I read the definition as given in the " American and English Encyclopedia of Law: "

" To export an article of commerce is to carry such article out of a country or place."

When an article passes from the United States to Porto

Rico does it, or does it not, go out of " a country or place ? " It seems to me it does; and it seems to me that when it goes out of the country, then, according to this legal authority—I do not refer to the literary authority quoted by the gentleman, but according to this legal authority—it becomes an export, and does not necessarily involve the idea of going to a " foreign country."

Let us turn to the " Century Dictionary," which has been quoted quite frequently by the courts. Its definition is:

" Export: That which is exported; a commodity carried from one place or country to another, for sale; generally in the plural."

That unfortunate island is, it seems, for some purposes foreign, and for other purposes domestic, corresponding with the condition of certain gentlemen in this House some years ago who undertook to be present and absent at one and the same time, according as one or another purpose was to be accomplished. In order to sustain the validity of the tariff upon goods coming into the United States from Porto Rico, Porto Rico is held to be a foreign country. In order to sustain the validity of the tariff upon goods exported from the United States to Porto Rico, under this discovery of the chairman of the Judiciary Committee, Porto Rico is a domestic country. I think I understand the argument, but I do not feel impressed or oppressed with its weight.

The gentleman from New York, who made his speech under some degree of excitement, said that he would like to look in the face of any lawyer who would undertake to dissent from some of the propositions which he laid down. I do not see the gentleman in his seat, but if he wants to see me he can look into my face, for I have never turned my
H back on any man. That is one of the things I do not do.

One of his propositions, as I understand, is that because the constitution says that under some circumstances a State can lay an export duty, with the consent of Congress, and because Congress has the powers of the general government and the States (which they have discovered in connection with some of these cases which they undertake to discuss), therefore—what?

Under the constitution, Congress can suspend the operation of that clause of the constitution which provides that no export duty shall be imposed on articles sent out of a State; that is, the State could act with the consent of the Congress; but as it has been held in general terms, in discussing a clause of the constitution that has no connection whatever with this, that Congress has the powers of the State as to a possession, it can give its consent, and then act for the State, and when it acts for the State it is supposed to give its own consent, and hence you have the absolute repeal, by the mere operation of logic, of an express prohibition of the constitution. I think this proposition may be fairly designated as metaphysical, and while it is as well founded undoubtedly as many of the propositions upon which the Committee rely, little is hazarded when it is asserted that if the court ever sustain this clause of the bill it will not be upon this attenuated ground.

I have another objection to this branch of the bill. I submit that it is un-Republican. When—and I asked this question of the chairman of the Committee on Ways and Means, and if I misrepresent or misquote him I will thank him to correct me at once—I asked the chairman of the Committee on Ways and Means when in the history of the Republican party, that party ever voted to impose a tariff upon American capital and American labor? Ever before? He did not answer. He did not answer in his speech. Will any man on this floor answer? Where is the warrant in the history, or the platforms, of the Republican party, the party of protection to what? To American labor and American capital, against foreign labor and foreign capital. Where is the warrant in the platforms of the Republican party, or in the history of the Republican party, or in the assertion of any man who undertook to belong to the Republican party, for imposing a tariff upon American labor and American capital?

The necessaries of life—flour, rice, codfish, pork, bacon, corn meal, fresh beef, and mutton—to-day go into Porto Rico free. Bags for sugar, shooks, rough lumber, agricultural implements, machinery, trees, shrubs, seeds, and school furniture are all free under an Executive order. They have been going in free since October 21, 1899. This bill makes them all subject to twenty-five per cent of the Dingley tariff.

The people of Porto Rico, partly as the result of our disturbance of their affairs, are starving. They have scarcely anything with which to buy food, if the food was there. In the exercise of our enlightened philanthropy, and from a desire to play the part of the "good Samaritan," our first act is to increase the cost to them of the necessaries of life by a tariff, and to that extent place it beyond their power to sustain life. An allopathic dose of that brand of philanthropy would tend to depopulate the island.

Let me illustrate this for just a moment. Let us see where we are. Let us understand what we have got to meet in the coming campaign. The tariff upon coarse lumber coming from any foreign country into any part of the United States, and into Porto Rico—because that is enough a part of the United States to have the tariff apply—is two dollars a thousand. What does this bill do? Our lumbermen have the protection of two dollars a thousand, as against the Canadian lumbermen, and I see a man sitting in this hall who lives within a mile of the territory over which floats the Cross of St. George. To discriminate against its industries the Dingley bill, the work of my distinguished and lamented predecessor, with the co-operation of the great men in this House, was passed. That gave to the lumber industry a protection of two dollars on a thousand. What does this bill do? It takes off twenty-five per cent of it and leaves it with a protection of one dollar and fifty cents on a thousand. On codfish it is precisely the same in proportion.

I only use this as an illustration. Where is the warrant in Republican history, where is the warrant in a Republican platform, for discriminating against these industries and these products that happen to be exported to Porto Rico by the amount of twenty-five per cent of the Dingley tariff, and putting no duties whatever upon other products or manufactures going to other countries or other places in this country? Where is that proposition? I submit it as a Republican proposition. I make no complaint for this reason, but it illustrates the operation of the bill.

I now take the provision in this bill in which the great fundamental proposition is involved. The amount at stake I shall not take time to discuss. I do not undertake to weigh in the scales of an apothecary the integrity of the Republic or human rights of people anywhere. If they are infringed so far as I am concerned, by so much as a hair, I will not approve or adopt the proposition.

This provision does what? It imposes a tariff of one quarter of the Dingley tariff upon the products of Porto Rico coming into the United States, and upon what products? Upon sugar and upon tobacco. There is none upon coffee.

The value of the coffee produced before this awful cyclone struck this devoted island was $4,200,000 a year. The value of the sugar was $2,700,000 a year. The value of the tobacco was $300,000 a year. This imposes a tax for the revenue of Porto Rico upon two industries, sugar and tobacco, and leaves coffee entirely free, and coffee represents as much as both of them—yes, more than both of them put together. And so far as this tax is concerned, conceived in the " good Samaritan " habit, in the " good Samaritan " theory, of the gentleman from Connecticut [Mr. Russell], out of great philanthropy and benevolence—this philanthropy that takes out of a man's pocket with the right hand, and shifts it over to the left hand, and carries it back to his left-hand pocket, less expense of collection—magnificent philanthropy and benevolence, without a copper's expense to the magnificent people who exercise the philanthropy and benevolence!— upon whom does it rest? It rests solely upon the producers of sugar and tobacco.

Of course there are other industries, but these are the principal ones. It leaves the producers of sugar and tobacco paying all that tax, the coffee planters and all other property and business paying none of it. That is the practical proposition. Why is this suggested here now? What is its purpose? What is its object? It is said that it is not to protect any American industry; it is said that it does not bear grievously upon Porto Rico; but what else is said? It is said that we are here and now—and that is the great objection which I have to this bill—it is said that we are, here and now, as the representatives of the Republican party, to announce to the world our policy in connection with Porto Rico and the Philippine Archipelago.

And what is that policy? That policy is to protect the in-

dustries of the United States, against the industries of Porto
Rico and the Philippine Archipelago. That means what?
That we are going to develop those territories? That we are
going to give them an opportunity to blossom like the rose?
It means this, and you may as well meet it here as meet it
hereafter: It means that when they can raise sugar in Porto
Rico, that does not interfere with us, they can raise it and
send it here.

It means that when they raise it, so that it does interfere
with us, we will put our foot upon their necks, with a tariff, ·
and stop it from coming here in competition with our sugar.

It means that anywhere and everywhere, in Porto Rico
or the Philippine Archipelago, any industry or any occupation, however much it may be developed under the flag, with
our energy, and our enterprise, and our industry, the moment
it comes into competition with anything raised or manufactured in the Republic, meaning the forty-five States, according to the new theory of sublimated selfishness, just that
moment the Republic will put its hand upon it and keep it
down, so that it will not compete. How much will you develop Porto Rico and the Philippine Archipelago on that
policy?

I say here frankly, I say here coolly, and I am not excited
about this, that I do not believe that proposition will appeal
to the good sense, the fair mind, honest judgment, of the
people who have been in the habit of voting loyally the Republican ticket. I care nothing about the other side. So
far as we are concerned, I do not believe it will appeal to
them. That is the proposition—that Porto Rico and the
Philippine Archipelago are an orange for us to squeeze. The
twelve millions subject people in these islands are simply,
under this proposition, " hewers of wood and drawers of

water " for seventy-five millions free people. How much American capital will go into Porto Rico or into the Philippine Archipelago, if this proposition is to be sustained, when they know that any development they may make there is subject to the repressing hand of an American Congress? They are our own people in more senses than one, according to the theory of those who propose this bill—peculiarly our own, because they are a good deal more our own, if they have no constitutional rights, than they would be if they came in as a part of this body politic, with the political rights of American citizens, so that they could protect their own interests.

This is from the standpoint of policy and fair dealing.

The breach of good faith is another reason why I am opposed to this measure.

In 1898 the army of the United States, in a war declared in the interest of humanity, and upon the proposition that the old flag would carry with it liberty and freedom and equal opportunity and all the blessings of a Christian civilization, went where? It went to the island of Porto Rico, and Major-General Miles held the standard. I will read to the House, the proclamation with which General Miles signalized his advent upon Porto Rican soil. It is dated Ponce, Porto Rico, July 28, 1898.

In it he said, among other things, referring to the soldiers of the Union:

" They come bearing the banner of freedom, inspired by a noble purpose, to seek the enemies of our country and yours, and to destroy or capture all who are in armed resistance. They bring you the fostering arm of a nation of free people, whose greatest power is in its justice and humanity to all those living within its folds."

This is not the conversation of any Secretary of War itinerating over this magnificent island. He said further:

" We have not come to make war upon the people of a country that for centuries has been oppressed, but, on the contrary, to bring you protection, not only to yourselves but to your property, to promote your prosperity "—

And now mark the language—

—" and to bestow upon you the immunities and blessings of the liberal institutions of our government."

Now, if the gentlemen of the Ways and Means Committee, instead of spending so much time in trying to ascertain that the United States meant the United States, and that a State meant a State, and that forty-five States constitute the United States, and that the United States, meaning forty-five States, is described by the boundary line of the forty-five States— if they had taken their dictionaries and looked just for a moment at Webster, for his definition of immunity, they would have ascertained what the promise was that General Miles made to this devoted people. What does " immunity " mean?

" Freedom or exemption from any charge "—

—and it did not take me a day to hunt this up—

" Freedom or exemption from any charge, duty, obligation, office, tax, imposition, penalty, or service."

Was there any tax, in the nature of a tariff, in any part of the Republic, between the States and the Territories, when General Miles made that promise to these people? The word " immunity " in his proclamation could have referred to nothing by any decent construction of the English language except what? Immunity from charges, taxes, and service. The same immunity that the citizens of the United States enjoyed, and in no State or Territory was there then, nor will there ever be, any duty or tax upon exports and imports between States or Territories, or States and Territories. That is one of "the immunities and blessings of the liberal institutions of our government." Relying upon this proclamation these people did what?

They prostrated themselves before him; they covered him with wreaths and garlands of flowers; they kissed the flag that was carried there under that promise, and the delegates from Porto Rico stand here, asking the Republican party to make good the promise made by General Miles for the Republic, when they eagerly delivered "The Ever-Faithful Isle" into his all-conquering hands. Miles, the magnificent representative of our institutions, the typical American citizen, who won his way by sheer force of merit, ability, and valor, from the position of a common soldier, step by step, to the position of leader of the Armies of the Republic.

I never will vote to violate the promise he made or to repudiate the pledge. The Republican party can not afford, in this or any other campaign, to violate that sacred promise. It is written in the blood of our heroes that fought at El Caney, San Juan, and Santiago. It was made in the presence of all Christendom, and it is sealed by the God of battles. The Republic can not violate that promise made to this weak and helpless people without sullying its honor and tarnishing its fame. It is not written in the history of the Republican party that at any time, or anywhere, from the hour of its birth agony, when it sprang into existence, full panoplied as the unconquerable champion of liberty and freedom, under the valiant leadership of the great Pathfinder, it ever violated its plighted faith, or swerved from the path of rectitude and honor. . . .

It is suggested by the gentleman from Kansas [Mr. Long], and well suggested, in a speech which it was not my pleasure to hear, but which undoubtedly has increased his reputation and demonstrates his ability, that the treaty contains a provision that Spain can have the same tariff with these possessions that we give to them, and if we give the open door to Porto Rico we give the open door to Spain. We do it unless— what? Unless we violate the agreement we made with Spain; and it is entirely competent, if the Republic sees fit to do so, to violate that agreement.

But here stand two agreements—one made with Spain, and one made with the prostrate, helpless, long-suffering, starving Porto Rico. Which shall be violated? If I had my choice, and were I compelled to determine between them, I would violate our faith with a power which, until we brushed it off the earth as a military and naval power during the last two years, had some ability to protect and defend itself. I would not go before the civilized world upon the proposition that we would break faith with the downtrodden and the oppressed.

I would go further than that. I would not break faith with either. I stand behind the eminent gentlemen who negotiated that treaty. I believe they acted in the interest of the Republic, and as faithful representatives of the American people. We cannot repudiate the promise made by General Miles on the shores of Porto Rico. I believe the Republic can afford to keep all of its promises, no matter what the consequences be. It should not violate or repudiate either.

I read now a speech made by General Henry to the alcalde and citizens of Porto Rico at the close of hostilities and the celebration of peace in Porto Rico:

"Alcalde and Citizens: To-day the flag of the United States floats as an emblem of undisputed authority over the island of Porto Rico, giving promise of protection to life, of liberty, prosperity, and the right to worship God in accordance with the dictates of conscience. The forty-five States represented by the stars emblazoned on the blue field of that flag unite in vouchsafing to you prosperity and protection as citizens of the American Union. . . . I congratulate you all on beginning your public life under new auspices, free from governmental oppression, and with liberty to advance your own country's interests by your united efforts."

Now they are learning that " protection as citizens of the American Union " was " a delusion and a snare; " that they are not " citizens of the American Union," and it was never intended that they should be; that the " protection " referred to was the protection of the citizens of the United States, in " the American Union," against the people of Porto Rico. This is reading between the lines with a vengeance. The alcalde, in his innocence and simplicity, replied, in part:

. . . "Porto Rico has not accepted American domination on account of force. She has suffered for many years the evils of error, neglect, and persecution, but she had men who studied the question of government, and who saw in America her redemption, and a guaranty of life, liberty, and justice. There we came willingly and freely, hoping, hand and hand with the greatest of all republics, to advance in civilization and progress, and to become part of the Republic, to which we pledge our faith forever."

I can not dwell longer upon this painful proposition. I must call your attention to what Secretary Elihu Root, the great lawyer, the honest man, the representative Republican, upon these facts, said. He says:

" But the highest considerations of justice and good faith demand that we should not disappoint the confident expectation of sharing in our prosperity with which the people of

Porto Rico so gladly transferred their allegiance to the United States, and that we should treat the interests of this people as our own, and I wish most strongly to urge that the customs duties between Porto Rico and the United States be removed."

Here you have the solemn promise made by General Miles when he conquered these islands, the promise relied upon by them, its construction by Mr. Root, Secretary of War, and the statement of that eminent Republican, that true patriot, William McKinley, when he said it is our " plain duty " to give these people free trade; and yet it is proposed that we shall act contrary to the advice of Davis, contrary to the advice of the delegates, contrary to the advice of Root, contrary to the advice of the President of the United States, in violation of our faith, and that by gentlemen who undertake to know more here than the men know there, about their condition and what ought in justice to be done.

There are two sides to this as a political proposition. I do not want to defend upon the stump—I hope there will be no occasion to do so—I do not want to defend upon the stump the proposition that the Republican party with its eyes open, with its attention, called to the fact, persisted in violating the good faith of the Republic. Why, gentlemen here say that we are about to inaugurate a policy of colonial government. I want to ask the gentlemen in this House if they desire to signalize their entry upon a colonial government, in their very first act, by a breach of good faith. Do you remember the history of proud Spain? What is it? What is it that has characterized Spain ever since the sixteenth century, ever since Pizarro rode ruthless and roughshod over Mexico, and the Duke of Alva filled the Netherlands with carnage, blood, butcheries, and indescribable horrors, in his infamous attempt to crush out the very beginning of civil and religious liberty? What is it that has characterized her and made her contemptible before every honorable nation upon the earth? It is her duplicity and her breaches of good faith.

Will the Republican party, in the teeth of the declaration of the Secretary of War and the President of the United States, signalize its embarkation upon that policy with its first act a breach of good faith? That policy upon the part of Spain, has made her for all time a "hissing and a by-word" and a reproach to all Christian peoples. I stand here, if I stand alone, as a member of the Republican party, the party that I love, the party that has done so much for the liberty and welfare and prosperity and development of the Republic, to enter my solemn protest against such an act.

Even under the guise of "good Samaritanism," even under the guise of "philanthropy" or any guise or subterfuge of any sort, I can not and will not agree to it. I leave that for my friends to discuss and reflect upon. It is hardly worth while for a man who sits in the House, and happens to hear coming from persons, unduly and unnecessarily alarmed, a demand for this legislation, to shut his eyes and think that these things do not exist because he does not then see them. They are here; they will be with us; they will be like the Old Man of the Sea; they will cling to our backs throughout the next campaign and, I fear, through many others.

Porto Rico kneels to-day, weak, helpless, starving, with her hands held toward us in supplication. She pleads for the fulfilment of this promise. Her prayers may fall upon deaf ears that will not hear in this House, but there is one tribunal to which I fully believe they may confidently appeal— the enlightened, unselfish, Christian conscience of a great and free people.

DRUMMOND

HENRY DRUMMOND, a distinguished Scotch theologian and biologist, was born at Sterling, August 17, 1851; he was graduated at Edinburgh and in 1887 was appointed lecturer on natural science at the Free Church College, Glasgow, becoming full professor in 1884. He travelled in the Rocky Mountains, Central Africa, Japan, Australia, and elsewhere, and wrote several fascinating books relating his experiences. He also lectured with great success in the United States. The main object of his teaching was to reconcile evangelical Christianity with the doctrine of evolution. His " Natural Law in the Spiritual World," published in 1883, had an enormous sale on both sides of the Atlantic, and his lecture on " The Greatest Thing in the World" secured his fame as a great religious teacher. He died at Tunbridge Wells, after a long illness, March 11, 1897. Among his best-known works are " Tropical Africa " (1888); " Travel Sketches in Our New Protectorate " (1890); " The Ascent of Man " (1894).

ADDRESS ON THE GREATEST THING IN THE WORLD

EVERY one has asked himself the great question of antiquity as of the modern world: what is the *summum bonum*—the supreme good? You have life before you. Once only you can live it. What is the noblest object of desire, the supreme gift to covet?

We have been accustomed to be told that the greatest thing in the religious world is Faith. That great word has been the key-note for centuries of the popular religion; and we have easily learned to look upon it as the greatest thing in the world. Well, we are wrong. If we have been told that, we may miss the mark. I have taken you, in the chapter which I have just read, to Christianity at its source; and there we have seen, " The greatest of these is love."

It is not an oversight. Paul was speaking of faith just a moment before. He says, " If I have all faith, so that I

can remove mountains, and have not love, I am nothing."
So far from forgetting he deliberately contrasts them, " Now
abideth Faith, Hope, Love," and without a moment's
hesitation the decision falls, " The greatest of these is
Love."

And it is not prejudice. A man is apt to recommend to
others his own strong point—Love was not Paul's strong
point. The observing student can detect a beautiful tenderness growing and ripening all through his character as Paul
gets old; but the hand that wrote, " The greatest of these is
love," when we meet it first, is stained with blood.

Nor is this letter to the Corinthians peculiar in singling
out love as the *summum bonum*. The masterpieces of
Christianity are agreed about it. Peter says, " Above all
things have fervent love among yourselves." *Above all
things*. And John goes further, " God is love." And you
remember the profound remark which Paul makes elsewhere,
" Love is the fulfilling of the law." Did you ever think what
he meant by that? In those days men were working their
passage to Heaven by keeping the Ten Commandments, and
the hundred and ten other commandments which they had
manufactured out of them.

Christ said, I will show you a more simple way. If you
do one thing, you will do these hundred and ten things, without ever thinking about them. If you love, you will uncon-
sciously fulfil the whole law.

And you can readily see for yourselves how that must be
so. Take any of the commandments. " Thou shalt have no
other gods before me." If a man love God, you will not
require to tell him that. Love is the fulfilling of that law.
" Take not his name in vain." Would he ever dream of taking his name in vain if he loved him? " Remember the Sab-

bath day to keep it holy." Would he not be too glad to have one day in seven to dedicate more exclusively to the object of his affection?

Love would fulfil all these laws regarding God. And so, if he loved Man, you would never think of telling him to honor his father and mother. He could not do anything else. It would be preposterous to tell him not to kill. You could only insult him if you suggested that he should not steal— how could he steal from those he loved? It would be superfluous to beg him not to bear false witness against his neighbor. If he loved him it would be the last thing he would do. And you would never dream of urging him not to covet what his neighbors had. He would rather they possessed it than himself. In this way "Love is the fulfilling of the law." It is the rule for fulfilling all rules, the new commandment for keeping all the old commandments, Christ's one secret of the Christian life.

Now Paul had learned that; and in this noble eulogy he has given us the most wonderful and original account extant of the *summum bonum*. We may divide it into three parts. In the beginning of the short chapter, we have Love contrasted; in the heart of it, we have Love analyzed, toward the end, we have Love defended as the supreme gift.

Paul begins by contrasting Love with other things that men in those days though much of. I shall not attempt to go over those things in detail. Their inferiority is already obvious.

He contrasts it with eloquence. And what a noble gift it is, the power of playing upon the souls and wills of men, and rousing them to lofty purposes and holy deeds. Paul says, "If I speak with the tongues of men and of angels, and have not love, I am become as sounding brass, or a tinkling cymbal." And we all know why. We have all felt the brazenness of words without emotion, the hollowness, the unaccountable unpersuasiveness, of eloquence behind which lies no Love.

He contrasts it with prophecy. He contrasts it with mysteries. He contrasts it with faith. He contrasts it with charity. Why is Love greater than faith? Because the end is greater than the means. And why is it greater than charity? Because the whole is greater than the part. Love is greater than faith, because the end is greater than the means. What is the use of having faith? It is to connect the soul with God. And what is the object of connecting man with God? That he may become like God. But God is Love. Hence Faith, the means, is in order to Love, the end. Love, therefore, obviously is greater than faith. It is greater than charity, again, because the whole is greater than a part. Charity is only a little bit of Love, one of the innumerable avenues of Love, and there may even be, and there is, a great deal of charity without Love.

It is a very easy thing to toss a copper to a beggar on the street; it is generally an easier thing than not to do it. Yet Love is just as often in the withholding. We purchase relief from the sympathetic feelings roused by the spectacle of misery, at the copper's cost. It is too cheap—too cheap for us, and often too dear for the beggar. If we really loved him we would either do more for him, or less.

Then Paul contrasts it with sacrifice and martyrdom. And I beg the little band of would-be missionaries—and I have the honor to call some of you by this name for the first time—to remember that though you give your bodies to be burned, and have not Love, it profits nothing—nothing! You can take nothing greater to the heathen world than the impress and reflection of the Love of God upon your own character. That is the universal language.

It will take you years to speak in Chinese, or in the dialects of India. From the day you land, the language of Love, understood by all, will be pouring forth its unconscious eloquence. It is the man who is the missionary, it is not his words. His character is his message. In the heart of Africa, among the great Lakes, I have come across black men and women who remembered the only white man they ever saw before—David Livingstone; and as you cross his footsteps in that dark continent, men's faces light up as they speak of the kind Doctor who passed there years ago. They could not understand him; but they felt the Love that beat in his heart. Take into your new sphere of labor, where you also mean to lay down your life, that simple charm, and your lifework must succeed. You can take nothing greater, you need take nothing less. It is not worth while going if you take anything less. You may take every accomplishment; you may be braced for every sacrifice; but if you give your body to be burned, and have not Love, it will profit you and the cause of Christ nothing.

After contrasting Love with these things, Paul, in three verses, very short, gives us an amazing analysis of what this supreme thing is. I ask you to look at it. It is a compound thing, he tells us. It is like light. As you have seen a man of science take a beam of light and pass it through a crystal prism, as you have seen it come out on the other side of the prism broken up into its component colors—red, and blue, and yellow, and violet, and orange, and all the colors of the rainbow—so Paul passes this thing, Love, through the magnificent prism of his inspired intellect, and it comes out on the other side broken up into its elements.

And in these few words we have what one might call the Spectrum of Love, the analysis of Love. Will you observe what its elements are? Will you notice that they have common names; that they are virtues which we hear about every day, that they are things which can be practised by every man in every place in life; and how, by a multitude of small things and ordinary virtues, the supreme thing, the *summum bonum*, is made up?

The Spectrum of Love has nine ingredients:

Patience . . .	"Love suffereth long."
Kindness . . .	"And is kind."
Generosity . . .	"Love envieth not."
Humility . . .	"Love vaunteth not itself, is not puffed up."
Courtesy . . .	"Doth not behave itself unseemly."
Unselfishness . .	"Seeketh not her own."
Good Temper . .	"Is not easily provoked."
Guilelessness . .	"Thinketh no evil."
Sincerity . . .	"Rejoiceth not in iniquity, but rejoiceth in the truth."

Patience; kindness; generosity; humility; courtesy; unselfishness; good temper; guilelessness; sincerity—these make up the supreme gift, the stature of the perfect man. You will observe that all are in relation to men, in relation to life, in relation to the known to-day and the near to-morrow, and not to the unknown eternity. We hear much of love to God; Christ spoke much of love to man. We make a great deal of peace with heaven; Christ made much of peace on earth. Religion is not a strange or added thing, but the inspiration of the secular life, the breathing of an eternal spirit through this temporal world. The supreme thing, in short, is not a thing at all, but the giving of a further finish to the multitudinous words and acts which make up the sum of every common day.

There is no time to do more than make a passing note upon each of these ingredients. Love is *Patience*. This is the normal attitude of Love; Love passive, Love waiting to begin; not in a hurry; calm; ready to do its work when the summons comes, but meantime wearing the ornament of a meek and quiet spirit. Love suffers long; beareth all things; believeth all things; hopeth all things. For Love understands, and therefore waits.

Kindness. Love active. Have you ever noticed how much of Christ's life was spent in doing kind things—in *merely* doing kind things? Run over it with that in view, and you will find that he spent a great proportion of his time simply in making people happy, in doing good turns to people. There is only one thing greater than happiness in the world, and that is holiness; and it is not in our keeping; but what God *has* put in our power is the happiness of those about us, and that is largely to be secured by our being kind to them.

"The greatest thing," says some one, "a man can do for his Heavenly Father is to be kind to some of His other children."

I wonder why it is that we are not all kinder than we are? How much the world needs it. How easily it is done. How instantaneously it acts. How infallibly it is remembered. How superabundantly it pays itself back—for there is no debtor in the world so honorable, so superbly honorable, as Love. "Love never faileth." Love is success, Love is happiness, Love is life. "Love, I say," with Browning, "is energy of Life."

> "For life, with all it yields of joy or woe
> And hope and fear,
> Is just our chance o' the prize of learning love,—
> How love might be, hath been indeed, and is."

Where Love is, God is. He that dwelleth in Love dwelleth in God. God is Love. Therefore *love*. Without distinction, without calculation, without procrastination, love. Lavish it upon the poor, where it is very easy; especially upon the rich, who often need it most; most of all upon our equals, where it is very difficult, and for whom perhaps we each do least of all. There is a difference between trying to please and giving pleasure.

Give pleasure. Lose no chance of giving pleasure. For that is the ceaseless and anonymous triumph of a truly loving spirit. " I shall pass through this world but once. Any good thing therefore that I can do, or any kindness that I can show to any human being, let me do it now. Let me not defer it or neglect it, for I shall not pass this way again."

Generosity. " Love envieth not." This is love in competition with others. Whenever you attempt a good work you will find other men doing the same kind of work, and probably doing it better. Envy them not. Envy is a feeling of ill will to those who are in the same line as ourselves, a spirit of covetousness and detraction. How little Christian work even is a protection against un-Christian feeling. That most despicable of all the unworthy moods which cloud a Christian's soul assuredly waits for us on the threshold of every work, unless we are fortified with this grace of magnanimity. Only one thing truly need the Christian envy, the large, rich, generous soul which " envieth not."

And then, after having learned all that, you have to learn this further thing, *Humility*—to put a seal upon your lips and forget what you have done. After you have been kind, after Love has stolen forth into the world and done its beautiful work, go back into the shade again and say nothing about it. Love hides even from itself. Love waives even self-satisfaction. " Love vaunteth not itself, is not puffed up."

The fifth ingredient is a somewhat strange one to find in this *summum bonum: Courtesy.* This is Love in society,

Love in relation to etiquette. "Love doth not behave itself unseemly." Politeness has been defined as love in trifles. Courtesy is said to be love in little things. And the one secret of politeness is to love. Love cannot behave itself unseemly. You can put the most untutored persons into the highest society, and if they have a reservoir of Love in their heart, they will not behave themselves unseemly. They simply cannot do it.

Carlyle said of Robert Burns that there was no truer gentleman in Europe than the ploughman poet. It was because he loved everything—the mouse, and the daisy, and all the things, great and small, that God had made. So with this simple passport he could mingle with any society, and enter courts and palaces from his little cottage on the banks of the Ayr. You know the meaning of the word " gentleman." It means a gentle man—a man who does things gently with love. And that is the whole art and mystery of it. The gentle man cannot in the nature of things do an ungentle, an ungentlemanly thing. The ungentle soul, the inconsiderate, unsympathetic nature cannot do anything else. " Love doth not behave itself unseemly."

Unselfishness. " Love seeketh not her own." Observe: Seeketh not even that which is her own. In Britain the Englishman is devoted, and rightly, to his rights. But there come times when a man may exercise even the higher right of giving up his rights. Yet Paul does not summon us to give up our rights. Love strikes much deeper. It would have us not seek them at all, ignore them, eliminate the personal element altogether from our calculations.

It is not hard to give up our rights. They are often external. The difficult thing is to give up ourselves. The more difficult thing still is not to seek things for ourselves at all.

After we have sought them, bought them, won them, deserved them, we have taken the cream off them for ourselves already. Little cross then perhaps to give them up. But not to seek them, to look every man not on his own things, but on the things of others—*id opus est.* " Seekest thou great things for thyself ?" said the prophet; " *seek them not.*" Why ? Because there is no greatness in *things.* Things cannot be great. The only greatness is unselfish love. Even self-denial in itself is nothing, is almost a mistake. Only a great purpose or a mightier love can justify the waste. It is more difficult, I have said, not to seek our own at all, than, having sought it, to give it up. I must take that back. It is only true of a partly selfish heart. Nothing is a hardship to Love, and nothing is hard.

I believe that Christ's yoke is easy. Christ's " yoke " is just his way of taking life. And I believe it is an easier way than any other. I believe it is a happier way than any other. The most obvious lesson in Christ's teaching is that there is no happiness in having and getting anything, but only in giving. I repeat, there is no happiness in having or in getting, but only in giving. And half the world is on the wrong scent in the pursuit of happiness. They think it consists in having and getting, and in being served by others. It consists in giving, and in serving others. He that would be great among you, said Christ, let him serve. He that would be happy, let him remember that there is but one way—it is more blessed, it is more happy, to give than to receive.

The next ingredient is a very remarkable one: *Good Temper.* " Love is not easily provoked." Nothing could be more striking than to find this here. We are inclined to look upon bad temper as a very harmless weakness. We speak of it as a mere infirmity of nature, a family failing, a matter of temperament, not a thing to take into very serious account in estimating a man's character. And yet here, right in the heart of this analysis of love, it finds a place; and the Bible again and again returns to condemn it as one of the most destructive elements in human nature.

The peculiarity of ill temper is that it is the vice of the virtuous. It is often the one blot on an otherwise noble character. You know men who are all but perfect, and women who would be entirely perfect, but for an easily ruffled, quick-tempered, or " touchy " disposition.

This compatability of ill temper with high moral character is one of the strangest and saddest problems of ethics. The truth is there are two great classes of sins—sins of the Body, and sins of the Disposition. The Prodigal Son may be taken as a type of the first, the Elder Brother of the second. Now society has no doubt whatever as to which of these is the worse. Its brand falls, without a challenge, upon the Prodigal.

But are we right? We have no balance to weigh one another's sins, and coarser and finer are but human words; but faults in the higher nature may be less venial than those in the lower, and to the eye of Him who is Love, a sin against Love may seem a hundred times more base. No form of vice, not worldliness, not greed of gold, not drunkenness itself, does more to un-Christianize society than evil temper.

For embittering life, for breaking up communities, for destroying the most sacred relationships, for devastating homes, for withering up men and women, for taking the bloom off childhood, in short, for sheer gratuitous misery-producing power, this influence stands alone.

Look at the Elder Brother, moral, hard-working, patient,

dutiful—let him get all credit for his virtues—look at this man, this baby, sulking outside his own father's door. " He was angry," we read, " and would not go in." Look at the effect upon the father, upon the servants, upon the happiness of the guests. Judge of the effect upon the Prodigal—and how many prodigals are kept out of the Kingdom of God by the unlovely character of those who profess to be inside? Analyze, as a study in Temper, the thunder-cloud itself as it gathers upon the Elder Brother's brow. What is it made of ?

Jealously, anger, pride, uncharity, cruelty, self-righteousness, touchiness, doggedness, sullenness—these are the ingredients of this dark and loveless soul. In varying proportions, also, these are the ingredients of all ill temper. Judge if such sins of the disposition are not worse to live in, and for others to live with, than sins of the body. Did Christ indeed not answer the question Himself when he said, " I say unto you, that the publicans and the harlots go into the Kingdom of Heaven before you." There is really no place in Heaven for a disposition like this. A man with such a mood could only make Heaven miserable for all the people in it. Except, therefore, such a man be born again, he cannot, he simply cannot, enter the Kingdom of Heaven. For it is perfectly certain—and you will not misunderstand me— that to enter Heaven a man must take it with him.

You will see then why Temper is significant. It is not in what it is alone, but in what it reveals. This is why I take the liberty now of speaking of it with such unusual plainness. It is a test for love, a symptom, a revelation of an unloving nature at bottom. It is the intermittent fever which bespeaks unintermittent disease within; the occasional bubble escaping to the surface which betrays some rottenness underneath; a sample of the most hidden products of the soul dropped involuntarily when off one's guard; in a word, the lightning form of a hundred hideous and un-Christian sins. For a want of patience, a want of kindness, a want of generosity, a want of courtesy, a want of unselfishness, are all instantaneously symbolized in one flash of Temper.

Hence it is not enough to deal with the Temper. We must go to the source, and change the inmost nature, and the angry humors will die away of themselves. Souls are made sweet not by taking the acid fluids out, but by putting something in—a great Love, a new Spirit, the Spirit of Christ. Christ, the Spirit of Christ, interpenetrating ours, sweetens, purifies, transforms all. This only can eradicate what is wrong, work a chemical change, renovate and regenerate, and rehabilitate the inner man. Will-power does not change men. Time does not change men. Christ does.

Therefore, " Let that mind be in you which was also in Christ Jesus." Some of us have not much time to lose. Remember, once more, that this is a matter of life or death. I cannot help speaking urgently, for myself, for yourselves. " Whoso shall offend one of these little ones, which believe in me, it were better for him that a millstone were hanged about his neck, and that he were drowned in the depth of the sea." That is to say, it is the deliberate verdict of the Lord Jesus that it is better not to live than not to love. It is better not to live than not to love.

Guilelessness and *Sincerity* may be dismissed almost with a word. Guilelessness is the grace for suspicious people. And the possession of it is the great secret of personal influence. You will find, if you think for a moment, that the people who influence you are people who believe in you. In an atmosphere of suspicion men shrivel up; but in that atmosphere they expand, and find encouragement and educative fellowship. It is a wonderful thing that here and there in this hard, uncharitable world there should still be left a few rare souls who think no evil. This is the great unworldliness. Love " thinketh no evil," imputes no motive, sees the bright side, puts the best construction on every action. What a delightful state of mind to live in! What a stimulus and benediction even to meet with it for a day! To be trusted is to be saved. And if we try to influence or elevate others, we shall soon see that success is in proportion to their belief of our belief in them. For the respect of another is the first restoration of the self-respect a man has lost; our ideal of what he is becomes to him the hope and pattern of what he may become.

"Love rejoiceth not in iniquity, but rejoiceth in the truth." I have called this Sincerity from the words rendered in the Authorized Version by " rejoiceth in the truth." And, certainly, were this the real translation, nothing could be more just. For he who loves will love Truth not less than men. He will rejoice in the Truth—rejoice not in what he has been taught to believe; not in this Church's doctrine or in that; not in this ism or in that ism; but " in the Truth." He will accept only what is real; he will strive to get at facts; he will search for Truth with a humble and unbiased mind, and cherish whatever he finds at any sacrifice. But the more literal translation of the Revised Version calls for just such a sacrifice for truth's sake here.

For what Paul really meant is, as we there read, " Rejoiceth not in unrighteousness, but rejoiceth with the truth," a quality which probably no one English word—and certainly not Sincerity—adequately defines. It includes, perhaps more strictly, the self-restraint which refuses to make capital

out of others' faults; the charity which delights not in exposing the weakness of others, but " covereth all things;" the
sincerity of purpose which endeavors to see things as they
are, and rejoices to find them better than suspicion feared or
calumny denounced.

So much for the analysis of Love. Now the business of
our lives is to have these things fitted into our characters.
That is the supreme work to which we need not address ourselves in this world, to learn Love. Is life not full of opportunities for learning Love? Every man and woman every
day has a thousand of them. The world is not a playground;
it is a schoolroom. Life is not a holiday, but an education.
And the one eternal lesson for us all is how better we can
love.

What makes a man a good cricketer? Practice. What
makes a man a good artist, a good sculptor, a good musician?
Practice. What makes a man a good linguist, a good stenog-
rapher? Practice. What makes a man a good man?
Practice. Nothing else.

There is nothing capricious about religion. We do not
get the soul in different ways, under different laws, from
those in which we get the body and the mind. If a man
does not exercise his arm he develops no biceps muscle; and
if a man does not exercise his soul, he acquires no muscle
in his soul, no strength of character, no vigor of moral fibre,
nor beauty of spiritual growth. Love is not a thing of enthusiastic emotion. It is a rich, strong, manly, vigorous
expression of the whole round Christian character—the
Christlike nature in its fullest development. And the con-
stituents of this great character are only to be built up by
ceaseless practice.

What was Christ doing in the carpenter's shop? Prac-

tising. Though perfect, we read that he learned obedience,
and grew in wisdom and in favor with God. Do not quarrel,
therefore, with your lot in life. Do not complain of its
never-ceasing cares, its petty environment, the vexations you
have to stand, the small and sordid souls you have to live
and work with. Above all, do not resent temptation; do not
be perplexed because it seems to thicken round you more and
more, and ceases neither for effort nor for agony nor prayer.
That is your practice. That is the practice which God ap-
points you; and it is having its work in making you patient,
and humble, and generous, and unselfish, and kind, and
courteous. Do not grudge the hand that is molding the
still too shapeless image within you. It is growing more
beautiful, though you see it not, and every touch of temptation may add to its perfection. Therefore keep in the midst
of life. Do not isolate yourself. Be among men, and
among things, and among troubles, and difficulties, and ob-
stacles. You remember Goethe's words: *Es bildet ein
Talent sich in der Stille, Doch ein Character in dem Strom
der Welt:* "Talent develops itself in solitude; character in
the stream of life." Talent develops itself in solitude—the
talent of prayer, of faith, of meditation, of seeing the un-
seen; Character grows in the stream of the world's life.
That chiefly is where men are to learn love.

How? Now, how? To make it easier, I have named
a few of the elements of love. But these are only elements.
Love itself can never be defined. Light is a something more
than the sum of its ingredients—a glowing, dazzling, tremu-
lous ether. And love is something more than all its elements—a palpitating, quivering, sensitive, living thing. By
snythesis of all the colors, men can make whiteness, they
cannot make light. By synthesis of all the virtues, men

can make virtue, they cannot make love. How then are we to have this transcendent living whole conveyed into our souls? We brace our wills to secure it. We try to copy those who have it. We lay down rules about it. We watch. We pray. But these things alone will not bring Love into our nature. Love is an effect. And only as we fulfil the right conditions can we have the effect produced. Shall I tell you what the cause is?

If you turn to the Revised Version of the First Epistle of John you will find these words: "We love because he first loved us." "We love," not "We love him." That is the way the old version has it, and it is quite wrong. "We love—because he first loved us." Look at that word "because." It is the cause of which I have spoken. "Because he first loved us," the effect follows that we love, we love him, we love all men.

We cannot help it. Because he loved us, we love, we love everybody. Our heart is slowly changed. Contemplate the love of Christ, and you will love. Stand before that mirror, reflect Christ's character, and you will be changed into the same image from tenderness to tenderness. There is no other way. You cannot love to order. You can only look at the lovely object, and fall in love with it, and grow into likeness to it. And so look at this Perfect Character, this Perfect Life. Look at the great Sacrifice as he laid down himself, all through life, and upon the Cross of Calvary; and you must love him. And loving him, you must become like him.

Love begets love. It is a process of induction. Put a piece of iron in the presence of an electrified body, and that piece of iron for a time becomes electrified. It is changed into a temporary magnet in the mere presence of a permanent magnet, and as long as you leave the two side by side they are both magnets alike.

Remain side by side with him who loved us, and gave himself for us, and you too will become a permanent magnet, a permanently attractive force; and like him you will draw all men unto you, like him you will be drawn unto all men. That is the inevitable effect of Love. Any man who fulfils that cause must have that effect produced in him.

Try to give up the idea that religion comes to us by chance, or by mystery, or by caprice. It comes to us by natural law, or by supernatural law, for all law is Divine. Edward Irving went to see a dying boy once, and when he entered the room he just put his hand on the sufferer's head, and said, " My boy, God loves you," and went away. And the boy started from his bed, and called out to the people in the house, " God loves me! God loves me! "

It changed that boy. The sense that God loved him overpowered him, melted him down, and began the creating of a new heart in him. And that is how the love of God melts down the unlovely heart in man, and begets in him the new creature, who is patient and humble and gentle and unselfish. And there is no other way to get it. There is no mystery about it. We love others, we love everybody, we love our enemies, because he first loved us. Now I have a closing sentence or two to add about Paul's reason for singling out love as the supreme possession. It is a very remarkable reason. In a single word it is this: it lasts.

" Love," urges Paul, " never faileth." Then he begins again one of his marvellous lists of the great things of the day, and exposes them one by one. He runs over the things that men thought were going to last, and shows that they are all fleeting, temporary, passing away.

" Whether there be prophecies, they shall fail." It was the mother's ambition for her boy in those days that he should become a prophet. For hundreds of years God had never spoken by means of any prophet, and at that time the prophet was greater than the King. Men waited wistfully for another messenger to come, and hung upon his lips when he appeared as upon the very voice of God. Paul says, " Whether there be prophecies, they shall fail." This Book is full of prophecies. One by one they have " failed "; that is, having been fulfilled their work is finished; they have nothing more to do now in the world except to feed a devout man's faith.

Then Paul talks about tongues. That was another thing that was greatly coveted. " Whether there be tongues, they shall cease." As we all know, many, many centuries have passed since tongues have been known in this world. They have ceased. Take it in any sense you like. Take it, for illustration merely, as languages in general—a sense which was not in Paul's mind at all, and which though it cannot give us the specific lesson will point the general truth.

Consider the words in which these chapters were written— Greek. It has gone. Take the Latin—the other great tongue of those days. It ceased long ago. Look at the Indian language. It is ceasing. The language of Wales, of Ireland, of the Scottish Highlands is dying before our eyes The most popular book in the English tongue at the present time, except the Bible, is one of Dickens's works, his " Pickwick Papers." It is largely written in the language of London street-life; and experts assure us that in fifty years it will be unintelligible to the average English reader.

Then Paul goes farther, and with even greater boldness adds, " Whether there be knowledge, it shall vanish away."

The wisdom of the ancients, where is it? It is wholly gone. A schoolboy to-day knows more than Sir Isaac Newton knew. His knowledge has vanished away. You put yesterday's newspaper in the fire. Its knowledge has vanished away. You buy the old editions of the great encyclopædias for a few pence. Their knowledge has vanished away.

Look how the coach has been superseded by the use of steam. Look how electricity has superseded that, and swept a hundred almost new inventions into oblivion. One of the greatest living authorities, Sir William Thompson, said the other day, " The steam-engine is passing away."

" Whether there be knowledge, it shall vanish away." At every workshop you will see, in the back yard, a heap of old iron, a few wheels, a few levers, a few cranks, broken and eaten with rust. Twenty years ago that was the pride of the city. Men flocked in from the country to see the great invention; now it is superseded, its day is done.

And all the boasted science and philosophy of this day will soon be old. But yesterday, in the University of Edinburgh, the greatest figure in the faculty was Sir James Simpson, the discoverer of chloroform. The other day his successor and nephew, Professor Simpson, was asked by the librarian of the University to go to the library and pick out the books on his subject that were no longer needed. And his reply to the librarian was this: " Take every text-book that is more than ten years old, and put it down in the cellar." Sir James Simpson was a great authority only a few years ago: men came from all parts of the earth to consult him; and almost the whole teaching of that time is consigned by the science of to-day to oblivion. And in every branch of science it is the same. " Now we know in part. We see through a glass darkly."

Can you tell me anything that is going to last? Many things Paul did not condescend to name. He did not mention money, fortune, fame; but he picked out the great things of his time, the things the best men thought had something in them, and brushed them peremptorily aside. Paul had no charge against these things in themselves. All he said about them was that they would not last.

They were great things, but not supreme things. There were things beyond them. What we are stretches past what we do, beyond what we possess. Many things that men denounce as sins are not sins; but they are temporary. And that is a favorite argument of the New Testament. John says of the world, not that it is wrong, but simply that it "passeth away." There is a great deal in the world that is delightful and beautiful; there is a great deal in it that is great and engrossing; but it will not last. All that is in the world, the lust of the eye, the lust of the flesh, and the pride of life, are but for a little while. Love not the world therefore. Nothing that it contains is worth the life and consecration of an immortal soul. The immortal soul must give itself to something that is immortal. And the only immortal things are these: "Now abideth faith, hope, love, but the greatest of these is love."

Some think the time may come when two of these three things will also pass away—faith into sight, hope into fruition. Paul does not say so. We know but little now about the conditions of the life that is to come.

But what is certain is that Love must last. God, the Eternal God, is Love. Covet therefore that everlasting gift, that one thing which it is certain is going to stand, that one coinage which will be current in the Universe when all the other coinages of all the nations of the world shall be useless and unhonored. You will give yourselves to many things, give yourselves first to Love. Hold things in their proportion. Hold things in their proportion. Let at least the first great object of our lives be to achieve the character defended in these words, the character—and it is the character of Christ—which is built round Love.

I have said this thing is eternal. Did you ever notice how continually John associates love and faith with eternal life? I was not told when I was a boy that " God so loved the world that he gave his only begotten Son, that whosoever believeth in him should have everlasting life." What I was told, I remember, was, that God so loved the world that, if I trusted in him, I was to have a thing called peace, or I was to have rest, or I was to have joy, or I was to have safety. But I had to find out for myself that whosoever trusteth in him—that is, whosoever loveth him, for trust is only the avenue to Love—hath everlasting life. The gospel offers a man life.

Never offer men a thimbleful of Gospel. Do not offer them merely joy, or merely peace, or merely rest, or merely safety; tell them how Christ came to give men a more abundant life than they have, a life abundant in love, and therefore abundant in salvation for themselves, and large in enterprise for the alleviation and redemption of the world. Then only can the Gospel take hold of the whole of a man, body, soul, and spirit, and give to each part of his nature its exercise and reward. Many of the current Gospels are addressed only to a part of man's nature. They offer peace, not life; faith, not Love; justification, not regeneration. And men slip back again from such religion because it has never really held them. Their nature was not all in it. It offered no deeper and gladder life-current than the life that was lived before. Surely it stands to reason that only a fuller love can compete with the love of the world.

To love abundantly is to live abundantly, and to love forever is to live forever. Hence, eternal life is inextricably bound up with love. We want to live forever for the same reason that we want to live to-morrow. Why do you want to live to-morrow? It is because there is some one who loves you, and whom you want to see to-morrow, and be with, and love back. There is no other reason why we should live on than that we love and are beloved. It is when a man has no one to love him that he commits suicide. So long as he has friends, those who love him and whom he loves, he will live; because to live is to love. Be it but the love of a dog, it will keep him in life; but let that go and he has no contact with life, no reason to live. He dies by his own hand.

Eternal life also is to know God, and God is love. This is Christ's own definition. Ponder it. " This is life eternal, that they might know thee the only true God, and Jesus Christ whom thou has sent."

Love must be eternal. It is what God is. On the last analysis, then, love is life. Love never faileth, and life never faileth, so long as there is love. That is the philosophy of what Paul is showing us; the reason why in the nature of things Love should be the supreme thing—because it is going to last; because in the nature of things it is an Eternal Life. It is a thing that we are living now, not that we get when we die; that we shall have a poor chance of getting when we die unless we are living now. No worse fate can befall a man in this world than to live and grow old alone, unloving, and unloved. To be lost is to live in an unregenerate condition, loveless and unloved; and to be saved is to love; and he that dwelleth in love dwelleth already in God.   For God is love.

Now I have all but finished.   How many of you will join me in reading this chapter once a week for the next three months?   A man did that once and it changed his whole life. Will you do it?   It is for the greatest thing in the world. You might begin by reading it every day, especially the verses which describe the perfect character.   " Love suffereth long, and is kind; love envieth not; love vaunteth not itself."

Get these ingredients into your life.   Then everything that you do is eternal.   It is worth doing.   It is worth giving time to.   No man can become a saint in his sleep; and to fulfil the condition required demands a certain amount of prayer and meditation and time, just as improvement in any direction, bodily or mental, requires preparation and care.

Address yourselves to that one thing; at any cost have this transcendent character exchanged for yours.   You will find as you look back upon your life that the moments that stand out, the moments when you have really lived, are the moments when you have done things in a spirit of love.   As memory scans the past, above and beyond all the transitory pleasures of life, there leap forward those supreme hours when you have been enabled to do unnoticed kindnesses to those round about you, things too trifling to speak about, but which you feel have entered into your eternal life.

I have seen almost all the beautiful things God has made; I have enjoyed almost every pleasure that he has planned for man; and yet as I look back I see standing out above all the life that has gone four or five short experiences when the love of God reflected itself in some poor imitation, some small act of love of mine, and these seem to be the things which alone of all one's life abide. Everything else in all our lives is transitory. Every other good is visionary. But the acts of love which no man knows about, or can ever know about— they never fail.

In the Book of Matthew, where the Judgment Day is depicted for us in the imagery of One seated upon a throne and dividing the sheep from the goats, the test of a man then is not, "How have I believed?" but "How have I loved?"

The test of religion, the final test of religion, is not religiousness, but Love. I say the final test of religion at that great Day is not religiousness, but Love; not what I have done, not what I have believed, not what I have achieved, but how I have discharged the common charities of life. Sins of commission in that awful indictment are not even referred to. By what we have not done, by sins of omission, we are judged.

It could not be otherwise. For the withholding of love is the negation of the spirit of Christ, the proof that we never knew him, that for us he lived in vain. It means that he suggested nothing in all our thoughts, that he inspired nothing in all our lives, that we were not once near enough to him to be seized with the spell of his compassion for the world. It means that—

> "I lived for myself, I thought for myself,
> For myself, and none beside—
> Just as if Jesus had never lived,
> As if he had never died."

It is the Son of Man before whom the nations of the world shall be gathered. It is in the presence of *Humanity* that we shall be charged. And the spectacle itself, the mere sight of it, will silently judge each one. Those will be there whom we have met and helped; or there, the unpitied multitude whom we neglected or despised.

No other Witness need be summoned. No other charge than lovelessness shall be preferred. Be not deceived. The words which all of us shall one Day hear sound not of theology but of life, not of churches and saints but of the hungry and the poor, not of creeds and doctrines but of shelter and clothing, not of Bibles and prayer-books but of cups of cold water in the name of Christ.

Thank God the Christianity of to-day is coming nearer the world's need. Live to help that on. Thank God men know better, by a hairsbreadth, what religion is, what God is, who Christ is, where Christ is. Who is Christ? He who fed the hungry, clothed the naked, visited the sick. And where is Christ? Where?—whoso shall receive a little child in My name receiveth Me. And who are Christ's? Every one that loveth is born of God.

THE ALCHEMY OF INFLUENCE

IF events change men, much more persons. No man can meet another on the street without making some mark upon him. We say we exchange words when we meet; what we exchange is souls. And when intercourse is very close and very frequent, so complete is this exchange that recognizable bits of the one soul begin to show in the other's nature, and the second is conscious of a similar and growing debt to the first.

This mysterious approximating of two souls who has not witnessed? Who has not watched some old couple come down life's pilgrimage hand in hand, with such gentle trust

and joy in one another that their very faces wore the self-
same look? These were not two souls; it was a composite
soul. It did not matter to which of the two you spoke, you
would have said the same words to either. It was quite indifferent which replied, each would have said the same. Half
a century's reflecting had told upon them; they were changed
into the same image.

It is the Law of Influence that we become like those whom
we habitually admire: these had become like because they
habitually admired. Through all the range of literature, of
history, and biography this law presides. Men are all
mosaics of other men. There was a savor of David about
Jonathan and a savor of Jonathan about David. Jean Val-
jean, in the masterpiece of Victor Hugo, is Bishop Bienvenu
risen from the dead. Metempsychosis is a fact.

George Eliot's message to the world was that men and
women make men and women. The Family, the cradle of
mankind, has no meaning apart from this. Society itself is
nothing but a rallying point for these omnipotent forces to
do their work. On the doctrine of Influence, in short, the
whole vast pyramid of humanity is built.

But it was reserved for Paul to make the supreme application of the Law of Influence. It was a tremendous inference
to make, but he never hesitated. He himself was a changed
man; he knew exactly what had done it; it was Christ. On
the Damascus road they met, and from that hour his life
was absorbed in his. The effect could not but follow—on
words, on deeds, on career, on creed. The "impressed
forces" did their vital work. He became like him whom he
habitually loved.

"So we all," he writes, "reflecting as a mirror the glory
of Christ, are changed into the same image."

Nothing could be more simple, more intelligible, more natural, more supernatural. It is an analogy from an every-day fact. Since we are what we are by the impacts of those who surround us, those who surround themselves with the highest will be those who change into the highest. There are some men and some women in whose company we are always at our best. While with them we cannot think mean thoughts or speak ungenerous words. Their mere presence is elevation, purification, sanctity.

All the best stops in our nature are drawn out by their intercourse, and we find a music in our souls that was never there before. Suppose even that influence prolonged through a month, a year, a lifetime, and what could not life become?

Here, even on the common plane of life, talking our language, walking our streets, working side by side, are sanctifiers of souls; here, breathing through common clay, is Heaven; here, energies charged even through a temporal medium with the virtue of regeneration. If to live with men, diluted to the millionth degree with the virtue of the Highest, can exalt and purify the nature, what bounds can be set to the influence of Christ?

To live with Socrates—with unveiled face—must have made one wise; with Aristides, just. Francis of Assisi must have made one gentle; Savonarola, strong. But to have lived with Christ? To have lived with Christ must have made one like Christ; that is to say, A Christian.

As a matter of fact, to live with Christ did produce this effect. It produced it in the case of Paul. And during Christ's lifetime the experiment was tried in an even more startling form. A few raw, unspiritual, uninspiring men were admitted to the inner circle of his friendship. The change began at once.

Day by day we can almost see the first disciples grow. First there steals over them the faintest possible adumbration of his character, and occasionally, very occasionally, they do a thing or say a thing that they could not have done or said had they not been living there. Slowly the spell of his Life deepens. Reach after reach of their nature is overtaken, thawed, subjugated, sanctified. Their manners soften, their words become more gentle, their conduct more unselfish.

As swallows who have found a summer, as frozen buds the spring, their starved humanity bursts into a fuller life. They do not know how it is, but they are different men. One day they find themselves like their Master, going about and doing good. To themselves it is unaccountable, but they cannot do otherwise. They were not told to do it, it came to them to do it.

But the people who watch them know well how to account for it—" They have been," they whisper, " with Jesus." Already even, the mark and seal of his character is upon them— " They have been with Jesus."

Unparalleled phenomenon, that these poor fishermen should remind other men of Christ! Stupendous victory and mystery of regeneration that mortal men should suggest to the world, God!

There is something almost melting in the way his contemporaries, and John especially, speak of the influence of Christ. John lived himself in daily wonder at him; he was overpowered, overawed, entranced, transfigured. To his mind it was impossible for any one to come under this influence and ever be the same again. " Whosoever abideth in him sinneth not," he said.

It was inconceivable that he should sin, as inconceivable as that ice should live in a burning sun, or darkness coexist

with noon. If any one did sin, it was to John the simple
proof that he could never have met Christ. "Whosoever
sinneth," he exclaims, "hath not seen him, neither known
him." Sin was abashed in this Presence. Its roots withered. Its sway and victory were forever at an end.

But these were his contemporaries. It was easy for them
to be influenced by him, for they were every day and all the
day together.

But how can we mirror that which we have never seen?
How can all this stupendous result be produced by a Memory,
by the scantiest of all Biographies, by One who lived and left
this earth eighteen hundred years ago? How can modern
men to-day make Christ, the absent Christ, their most constant companion still?

The answer is that Friendship is a spiritual thing. It is
independent of Matter, or Space, or Time. That which I
love in my friend is not that which I see. What influences
me in my friend is not his body but his spirit. It would have
been an ineffable experience truly to have lived at that time—

> "I think when I read the sweet story of old,
>   How when Jesus was here among men
> He took little children like lambs to his fold,
>   I should like to have been with him then.

> "I wish that his hand had been laid on my head,
>   That his arms had been thrown around me,
> And that I had seen his kind look when he said,
>   'Let the little ones come unto me.'"

And yet, if Christ were to come into the world again, few
of us probably would ever have a chance of seeing him.
Millions of her subjects, in this little country, have never seen
their own Queen. And there would be millions of the subjects of Christ who could never get within speaking distance
of him if he were here.

Our companionship with him, like all true companionship,

is a spiritual communion. All friendship, all love, human and divine, is purely spiritual. It was after he was risen that he influenced even the disciples most. Hence in reflecting the character of Christ, it is no real obstacle that we may never have been in visible contact with himself.

There lived once a young girl whose perfect grace of character was the wonder of those who knew her. She wore on her neck a gold locket which no one was ever allowed to open. One day, in a moment of unusual confidence, one of her companions was allowed to touch its spring and learn its secret. She saw written these words—" Whom having not seen, I love." That was the secret of her beautiful life. She had been changed into the Same Image.

Now this is not imitation, but a much deeper thing. Mark this distinction. For the difference in the process, as well as in the result, may be as great as that between a photograph secured by the infallible pencil of the sun, and the rude outline from a school-boy's chalk.

Imitation is mechanical, reflection organic. The one is occasional, the other habitual. In the one case, man comes to God and imitates him; in the other, God comes to man and imprints himself upon him. It is quite true that there is an imitation of Christ which amounts to reflection. But Paul's term includes all that the other holds, and is open to no mistake.

" Make Christ your most constant companion "—this is what it practically means for us. Be more under his influence than under any other influence. Ten minutes spent in his society every day, ay, two minutes if it be face to face, and heart to heart, will make the whole day different. Every character has an inward spring, let Christ be it. Every action has a keynote, let Christ set it.

Yesterday you got a certain letter. You sat down and wrote a reply which almost scorched the paper. You picked the cruelest adjectives you knew and sent it forth, without a pang, to do its ruthless work. You did that because your life was set in the wrong key. You began the day with the mirror placed at the wrong angle. To-morrow, at daybreak, turn it towards him, and even to your enemy the fashion of your countenance will be changed.

Whatever you then do, one thing you will find you could not do—you could not write that letter. Your first impulse may be the same, your judgment may be unchanged, but if you try it the ink will dry on your pen, and you will rise from your desk an unavenged, but a greater and more Christian, man. Throughout the whole day your actions, down to the last detail, will do homage to that early vision. Yesterday you thought mostly about yourself. To-day the poor will meet you, and you will feed them. The helpless, the tempted, the sad, will throng about you, and each you will befriend. Where were all these people yesterday? Where they are to-day, but you did not see them. It is in reflected light that the poor are seen. But your soul to-day is not at the ordinary angle. " Things which are not seen " are visible. For a few short hours you live the Eternal Life. The eternal life, the life of faith, is simply the life of the higher vision. Faith is an attitude—a mirror set at the right angle.

When to-morrow is over, and in the evening you review it, you will wonder how you did it. You will not be conscious that you strove for anything, or imitated anything, or crucified anything. You will be conscious of Christ; that he was with you, that without compulsion you were yet compelled, that without force, or noise, or proclamation, the revolution was accomplished. You do not congratulate yourself as one who has done a mighty deed, or achieved a personal success, or stored up a fund of " Christian experience " to ensure the same result again. What you are conscious of is " the glory of the Lord."

And what the world is conscious of, if the result be a true one, is also " the glory of the Lord." In looking at a mirror one does not see the mirror, or think of it, but only of what it reflects. For a mirror never calls attention to itself—except when there are flaws in it.

That this is a real experience and not a vision, that this life is possible to men, is being lived by men to-day, is simple biographical fact. From a thousand witnesses I cannot forbear to summon one. The following are the words of one of the highest intellects this age has known, a man who shared the burdens of his country as few have done, and who, not in the shadows of old age, but in the high noon of his success, gave this confession—I quote it with only a few abridgments—to the world:

" I want to speak to-night only a little, but that little I desire to speak of the sacred name of Christ, who is my life, my inspiration, my hope, and my surety. I cannot help stopping and looking back upon the past. And I wish, as if I had never done it before, to bear witness, not only that it is by the grace of God, but that it is by the grace of God as manifested in Christ Jesus, that I am what I am. I recognize the sublimity and grandeur of the revelation of God in his eternal fatherhood as one that made the heavens, that founded the earth, and that regards all the tribes of the earth, comprehending them in one universal mercy; but it is the God that is manifested in Jesus Christ revealed by his life, made known by the inflections of his feelings, by his discourse, and by his deeds—it is that God that I desire to confess to-night, and of whom I desire to say, ' By the love of God in Christ Jesus I am what I am.'

" If you ask me precisely what I mean by that, I say, frankly, that more than any recognized influence of my father or my mother upon me; more than the social influence of all the members of my father's household; more, so far as I can trace it, or so far as I am made aware of it, than all the social influences of every kind, Christ has had the formation of my mind and my disposition. My hidden ideals of what is beautiful I have drawn from Christ. My thoughts of what is manly, and noble, and pure, have almost all of them arisen from the Lord Jesus Christ. Many men have educated themselves by reading Plutarch's "Lives of the Ancient Worthies," and setting before themselves one and another of these that in different ages have achieved celebrity; and they have recognized the great power of these men on themselves. Now I do not perceive that poet, or philosopher, or reformer, or general, or any other great man, ever has dwelt in my imagination and in my thought as the simple Jesus has.

" For more than twenty-five years I instinctively have gone to Christ to draw a measure and a rule for everything. Whenever there has been a necessity for it, I have sought— and at last almost spontaneously—to throw myself into the companionship of Christ; and early, by my imagination, I could see him standing and looking quietly and lovingly upon me. There seemed almost to drop from his face an influence upon me that suggested what was the right thing in the controlling of passion, in the subduing of pride, in the overcoming of selfishness; and it is from Christ, manifested to my inward eye, that I have consciously derived more ideals, more models, more influences, than from any human character whatever.

"That is not all. I feel conscious that I have derived from the Lord Jesus Christ every thought that makes heaven a reality to me, and every thought that paves the road that lies between me and heaven. All my conceptions of the progress of grace in the soul; all the steps by which divine life is evolved; all the ideals that overhang the blessed sphere which awaits us beyond this world—these are derived from the Saviour. The life that I now live in the flesh I live by the faith of the Son of God.

"That is not all. Much as my future includes all these elements which go to make the blessed fabric of earthly life, yet, after all, what the summer is compared with all its earthly products—flowers, and leaves, and grass—that is Christ compared with all the products of Christ in my mind and in my soul. All the flowers and leaves of sympathy; all the twining joys that come from my heart as a Christian —these I take and hold in the future, but they are to me what the flowers and leaves of summer are compared with the sun that makes the summer. Christ is the Alpha and Omega, the beginning and the end of my better life.

"When I read the Bible, I gather a great deal from the Old Testament, and from the Pauline portions of the New Testament; but after all, I am conscious that the fruit of the Bible is Christ. That is what I read it for, and that is what I find that is worth reading. I have had a hunger to be loved of Christ. You all know, in some relations, what it is to be hungry for love. Your heart seems unsatisfied till you can draw something more toward you from those that are dearest to you. There have been times when I have had an unspeakable heart-hunger for Christ's love. My sense of sin is never strong when I think of the law; my sense of sin is strong when I think of love—if there is any difference between law and love.   It is when drawing near the Lord Jesus Christ, and longing to be loved, that I have the most vivid sense of unsymmetry, of imperfection, of absolute unworthiness, and of my sinfulness.   Character and conduct are never so vividly set before me as when in silence I bend in the presence of Christ, revealed not in wrath, but in love to me.   I never so much long to be lovely, that I may be loved, as when I have this revelation of Christ before my mind.

"In looking back upon my experience, that part of my life which stands out, and which I remember most vividly, is just that part that has had some conscious association with Christ.   All the rest is pale, and thin, and lies like clouds on the horizon.   Doctrines, systems, measures, methods—what may be called the necessary mechanical and external part of worship; the part which the senses would recognize—this seems to have withered and fallen off like leaves of last summer; but that part which has taken hold of Christ abides."

Can any one hear this life-music, with its throbbing refrain of Christ, and remain unmoved by envy or desire?   Yet till we have lived like this we have never lived at all.

ILES

GEORGE ILES, an American literarian, the son of an English soldier, was born in Gibraltar, June 20, 1852. In 1887, after a residence of thirty years in Montreal, he removed to New York. From 1876 to 1896 he was a constant contributor to the "Popular Science Monthly," and one of his articles, "A Class in Geometry," was republished as a little book in 1894. His "Art of Large Giving," which reviewed the most famous American benefactions, appeared in the "Century Magazine" for March, 1897. During 1892, at the request of Mr. Charles A. Dana, he wrote for the New York "Sun" a series of illustrated articles on invention and discovery, which also appeared simultaneously in a number of leading newspapers throughout the Union. This line of work was continued by Mr. Iles in "Flame, Electricity, and the Camera," issued in London and New York in 1900, and commended by the late John Fiske as the most fascinating volume he had read in ten years. In this work Mr. Iles depicts the varied applications of electricity, and proves that its mastery is comparable with that of flame as a leap in human power and interpretation. In critical quarters his book is regarded as the most original and telling American contribution to the philosophy of development.

For some years Mr. Iles took a leading part in bringing trustworthy literary guidance to the service of readers and students. In 1890 he edited, jointly with Mr. R. R. Bowker, "The Reader's Guide to the Literature of Economic and Political Science;" in 1895, with the aid of Mrs. Augusta H. Leypoldt, he brought together 2,100 titles as "A List of Books for Girls and Women and their Clubs," abounding in excellent critical notes. Two years afterward he edited an annotated bibliography of fine art. A work published in 1901, and entitled "A Guide to the Literature of American History," exemplified his methods for the appraisal of literature more fairly and fully than any preceding attempt.

Mr. Iles's address, here presented, was delivered before the American Library Association at Waukesha, Wisconsin, July 9, 1901. As a result of his plea there is some likelihood that a Library Institute, such as he suggested, may soon take form in Washington or New York, to promote the interests of American libraries as a whole, to further in every feasible way the acceptance by all the people of the best and most helpful literature.

Pursuing a plan long entertained, Mr. Iles is now drafting the chapters of a work on invention and discovery, choosing examples from their recent history, and treating his themes with the philosophical breadth of "Flame, Electricity, and the Camera."

(10816)

THE TRUSTEESHIP OF LITERATURE

DELIVERED BEFORE THE AMERICAN LIBRARY ASSOCIATION,
WAUKESHA, WISCONSIN, JULY 9, 1901

SIX months ago the curtain descended upon what is likely to be accounted the most memorable century in the annals of mankind. So salient are three of its characteristics that they challenge the eye of the most casual retrospection.

First of all, we see that knowledge was increased at a pace beyond precedent, to be diffused throughout the world with a new thoroughness and fidelity. Next we must observe how republican government passed from the slender ties spun in the times of Washington, Jefferson, and Adams, to the intimate and pervasive cords of to-day, when, as never before, the good of the bee is bound up with the welfare of the hive.

Parallel with this political union of each and all there was a growth of free organization which, in every phase of life, has secured uncounted benefits which only joined hands may receive. Fresh torches of light fraternally borne from the centers of civilization to its circumference have tended to bring the arts and ideals of life everywhere to the level of the best. These distinctive features of the nineteenth century were in little evidence at its dawn, but they became more and more manifest with each succeeding decade. In American librarianship, as in many another sphere of labor, more was accomplished in the last quarter of the century than in the seventy-five preceding years.

It is as recently as 1852 that Boston opened the doors of the first free public library established in an American city.

Its founders were convinced that what was good for the students at Harvard, the subscribers to the Athenæum, was good for everybody else. Literature, they felt, was a trust to be administered not for a few, but for the many, to be, indeed, hospitably proffered to all. To this hour, by a wise and generous responsiveness to its ever growing duties, the Boston foundation remains a model of what a metropolitan library should be.

As with the capital, so with the State; to-day Massachusetts is better provided with free public libraries than any other commonwealth on the globe; only one in two hundred of her people are unserved by them, while within her borders the civic piety of her sons and daughters has reared more than six score library buildings. The Library Commission of the State is another model in its kind; its powers are in the main advisory, but when a struggling community desires to establish a library, and contributes to that end, the Commission tenders judicious aid. The population of Massachusetts is chiefly urban, an exceptional case, for, taking the Union as a whole, notwithstanding the constant drift to the cities, much more than half the people are still to be found in the country. For their behoof village libraries have appeared in the thousands.

Still more effective, because linked with one another, are the travelling libraries, inaugurated by Mr. Melvil Dewey in New York in 1893, and since adopted in many other States of the Union, and several Provinces of Canada. All this registers how the democracy of letters has come to its own. Schools public and free ensure to the American child its birthright of instruction; libraries, also public and free, are rising to supplement that instruction, to yield the light and lift, the entertainment and stimulus that literature stands ready to bestow. The old-time librarian, who was content to be a mere custodian of books, has passed from the stage forever; in his stead we find an officer anxious that his store shall do all the people the utmost possible good.

To that end he combines the zeal of the missionary with the address of a consummate man of business. Little children are invited to cheery rooms with kind and intelligent hospitality; teachers and pupils from the public schools are welcomed to class-rooms where everything is gathered that the library can offer for their use; helpful bulletins and consecutive reading-lists are issued for the home circle; every book, magazine, and newspaper is bought, as far as feasible, with an eye to the special wants and interests of the community; information desks are set up; and partnerships are formed with expositors of acknowledged merit, with museums of industry, of natural history, of the fine arts. Not the borrowers only, but the buyers of books are remembered. The Standard Library, brought together by Mr. W. E. Foster in Providence, is a shining example in this regard.

The sense of trusteeship thus variously displayed has had a good many sources; let us confine our attention to one of them. During the past hundred years the treasure committed to the keeping of librarians has undergone enrichment without parallel in any preceding age. We have more and better books than ever before; they mean more than in any former time for right living and sound thinking. A rough and ready classification of literature, true enough in substance, divides it into books of power, of information, and of entertainment. Let us look at these three departments a little in detail. Restricting our purview to the English tongue, we find the honor roll of its literature lengthened by the names of Wordsworth, Tennyson, and Matthew Arnold, Carlyle and Ruskin,

Emerson and Lowell. And not only to authors such as these must our debt be acknowledged.

We owe scholarly editors nearly as much. In Spedding's Bacon, the Shakespearian studies of Mr. Furniss, and the Chaucer of Professor Skeat, we have typical examples of services not enjoyed by any former age. To-day the supreme poets, seers, and sages of all time are set before us in the clearest sunshine; their gold, refined from all admixture, is minted for a currency impossible before. In their original, unedited forms, the masterpieces of our language are now cheap enough to find their way to the lowliest cottage of the cross-roads.

It is not, however, in the field of literature pure and simple that the manna fell most abundantly during the past hundred years. Mr. Alfred Russel Wallace, the last of the great students who took all natural history for their province, declares that the advances in discovery, invention and generalization during the nineteenth century outweigh those of all preceding time. Admit this judgment, and at once is explained why the records and the spirit of science dominate the literature of the last ten decades.

And let us note that while books of knowledge have increased beyond measure, they have appeared with a helpfulness and with merits wholly new. For the first time in the history of letters, men and women of successful experience, of practised and skilful pens, write books which, placed in the hands of the people, enlighten their toil, diminish their drudgery, and sweeten their lives. Cross the threshold of the home and there is not a task, from choosing a carpet to rearing a baby, that has not been illuminated by at least one good woman of authority in her theme.

On the heights of the literature of science we have a

quality and distinction unknown before these later days. The modern war on evil and pain displays weapons of an edge and force of which our forefathers never dared to dream; its armies march forward not in ignorant hope, but with the assured expectation of victory. All this inspires leaders like Huxley, Spencer, and Fiske with an eloquence, a power to convince and persuade, new in the annuals of human expression and as characteristic of the nineteenth century as the English poetry of the sixteenth, in the glorious era of Elizabeth. The literature of knowledge is not only fuller and better than of old, it is more wisely employed. In the classroom, and when school days are done, we now understand how the printed page may best direct and piece out the work of the hand, the eye, and the ear; not for a moment deluding ourselves with the notion that we have grasped truth merely because we can spell the word.

To-day we first consider the lilies of the field, not the lilies of the printer; that done it is time enough to take up a formal treatise which will clarify and frame our knowledge. If a boy is by nature a mechanic, a book of the right sort shows him how to construct a simple steam engine or an electric motor. Is he an amateur photographer, other books, excellently illustrated, give him capital hints for work with his camera. It is in thus rounding out the circle which springs from the school desk that the public library justifies its equal claim to support from the public treasury.

In the third and last domain of letters, that of fiction, there is a veritable embarrassment of riches. During the three generations past the art of story-telling culminated in works of all but Shakespearian depth and charm. We have only to recall Scott and Thackeray, Hawthorne, George Eliot, and Thomas Hardy, to be reminded that an age of science

may justly boast of novelists and romancers such as the world
never knew before. No phase of life but has been limned
with photographic fidelity, no realm of imagination but has
been bodied forth as if by experience on fire, so that many a
book which bears the name of fiction might well be
labelled as essential truth. Within the past decade, however,
the old veins have approached their bounds, while new lodes
do not as yet appear. Of this the tokens are the eager sift-
ing of the rubbish heap, the elaborate picturing of the
abnormal and the gross. Pens unable to afford either delight
or cheer have abundant capacity, often with evident malice,
to strike the nerves of horror and of pain. If at the present
hour high achievement in fiction is rare, if we hear more
echoes than ever and fewer voices, quantity abounds to the
point of surfeit. With an output in America alone of 616
works for 1900, all fears of famine may well be allayed.

The main fact of the situation then is that the librarian's
trust has of late years undergone stupendous increase; this
at once broadens his opportunities and adds to his burdens.
Gold and silver, iron and lead, together with much dross,
are commingled in a heap which rises every hour. Before
a trust can be rightly and gainfully administered, its trustees
must know in detail what it is that they guard, what its
several items are worth, what they are good for.

And let us remember that literature consists in but small
part of metals which declare themselves to all men as gold
or lead; much commoner are alloys of every conceivable degree of worth or worthlessness. There is plainly nothing for
it but to have recourse to the crucibles of the professional
assayer, it becomes necessary to add to the titles of our
catalogues some responsible word as to what the books are
and what rank they occupy in an order of just precedence.

This task of a competent and candid appraisal of literature, as a necessity of its trusteeship, has been before the minds of this Association for a good many years. A notable step toward its accomplishment was taken when Mr. Samuel S. Green, in 1879, allied himself with the teachers of Worcester, Massachusetts, that they and he together might select books for the public schools of that city. The work began and has proceeded upon comprehensive lines. Such literature has been chosen as may usefully and acceptably form part of the daily instruction, there is a liberal choice of books of entertainment and inspiration worthily to buttress and relieve the formal lessons. The whole work goes forward with intent to cultivate the taste, to widen the horizons, to elevate the impulses of the young reader. Mr. Green's methods, with the modifications needful in transplanting, have been adopted far and wide throughout the Union. Already they have borne fruit in heightening the standards of free choice when readers have passed from the school bench to the work-a-day world.

Thus thoughtfully to lay the foundation of the reading habit is a task beyond praise; upon a basis so sound it falls to our lot to rear, if we can, a worthy and durable superstructure. It is time that we passed from books for boys and girls to books for the youth, the man and the woman. And how amid the volume and variety of the accumulated literature of the ages shall we proceed? For light and comfort let us go back a little in the history of education, we shall there find a method substantially that of our friend, Mr. Green.

Long before there were any free public libraries at all, we had in America a small band of readers and learners who enjoyed unfailing pilotage in the sea of literature. These readers and learners were in the colleges, where the teachers from examination and comparison in the study, the classroom and the laboratory were able to say that such an author was the best in his field, that such another had useful chapters, and that a third was unreliable or superseded.

While literature has been growing from much to more, this bench of judicature has been so enlarged as to keep steadily abreast of it. At Harvard there are twenty-six sublibraries of astronomy, zoology, political economy, and so on; at hand are the teachers who can tell how the books may be used with most profit. Of the best critics in America of books the larger part are to be found at Harvard, at its sister universities and colleges, at the technological institutes and art schools of our great cities. We see their signed reviews in such periodicals as the " Political Science Quarterly " and the " Physical Review; " or unsigned in journals of the stamp of the " Nation."

Fortunately, we can call upon reinforcements of this vanguard of criticism. It would be difficult to name a branch of learning, an art, a science, an exploration, from folk-lore to forestry, from psychical research to geological surveys, whose votaries are not to-day banded to promote the cause they have at heart. These organizations include not only the foremost teachers in the Union, but also their peers, outside the teaching profession, of equal authority in bringing literature to the balances. And the point for us is that these societies, through their publications and discussions, enable these laymen to be known for what they are. Because the American Historical Association is thus comprehensive, its membership has opened the door for an initial task of appraisal, important in itself and significant for the future.

Drawing his two score contributors almost wholly from

that Association, Mr. J. N. Larned of Buffalo, an honored leader of ours, has, without fee or reward, acted as chief editor of an annotated Bibliography of American History. The work is now passing through the composing-room of Houghton, Mifflin & Co., of Boston; its contributors include professors of history at Bowdoin, Bryn Mawr, Columbia, Harvard, McGill, Toronto, Tulane, and Yale, as well as the Universities of Michigan, Wisconsin, and Chicago; our own Association is worthily represented by Messrs. James Bain, Clarence S. Brigham, V. L. Collins, W. E. Foster, J. K. Hosmer, E. C. Richardson, and R. G. Thwaites. As a rule the notes are signed. Where for any reason a book demanding notice could not be allotted to a contributor, Mr. Larned has quoted the fairest review he could find in print. He has included not only good books, but such other works as have found an acceptance they do not deserve. All told his pages will offer us about 3,100 titles; a syllabus of the sources of American History is prefixed by Mr. Paul Leicester Ford; as an appendix will appear a feature also of great value. In their " Guide to American History," published in 1896, Professors Channing and Hart of Harvard University recommended such collections of books as may be had for five, ten, twenty, fifty, or a hundred dollars. Professor Channing is kind enough to say that he will revise these lists and bring them down to date as a contribution to Mr. Larned's work. Professor Channing may, we trust, name the books in each collection in the order in which they may be most gainfully read.

In times past our bibliographies have begun to need enlargement the moment they left the bindery; in the present case that need is for the first time to be supplied. Mr. Larned's titles come to the close of 1899; beyond that period current literature is to be chosen from and appraised with the editorship of Mr. Philip P. Wells, librarian of the Yale Law Library, who will issue his series in card form. We hope that he may be ready with his cards for 1900 at the time that Mr. Larned's book appears. Thereafter Mr. Wells's series will probably be published quarter by quarter. Beginning with 1897, Mr. W. Dawson Johnston, now of the Library of Congress, has edited for us a series of annotated cards dealing with the contemporary literature of English history.

Both the form and substance of his series are capital. In so far as his cards go directly into catalogue cases, where readers and students must of necessity see them, they render the utmost possible aid. If subscribers in sufficient array come forward, Mr. Larned's book may be remolded for issue in similar card form, with a like opportunity for service in catalogue cases. In the Cleveland Public Library and its branches useful notes are pasted within the lids of a good many volumes. It is well thus to put immediately under the reader's eye the word which points him directly to his goal, or prevents him wasting time in wanderings of little value or no value at all.

With Mr. Larned's achievement a new chapter is opened in American librarianship; he breaks a path which should be followed up with a discernment and patience emulous of his example. If the whole working round of our literature were sifted and labeled after his method, the worth of that literature, because clearly brought into evidence, might well be doubled at least. Every increase in the availability of our books, every removal of fences, every setting up of guideposts, has had a heartening public response. So it will be if we proceed with this effort to bring together the seekers and the knowers, to obtain the best available judgments for the behoof of readers and students everywhere. Economies and politics, so closely interwoven with American history, might well afford the second field for appraisal.

A good many libraries still find aid in the "Reader's Guide" in this department, although it appeared as long ago as 1890. Next might follow the literature of the sciences pure and applied, together with the useful arts. Among useful arts those of the household might well have the lead, for we must not be academic, or ever lose sight of the duties nearest at hand to the great body of the plain people. Mr. Sturgis and Mr. Krehbiel, in 1897, did an excellent piece of work for us in their "Bibliography of the Fine Arts;" their guide might profitably be revised and enlarged in its several divisions, not omitting the introductory paragraphs which make the book unique in its class.

These tasks well in hand, we might come to such accessions of strength and insight as to nerve us for labors of wider range and greater difficulty, where personal equations may baffle even the highest court of appeal, where it is opinion rather than fact that is brought to the scales. I refer to the debatable ground of ethics, philosophy and theology; and, at the other pole of letters, to the vast stretches of fiction and belles-lettres in our own foreign tongues.

With regard to fiction and belles-lettres, one of Mr. Larned's methods has a hint for us. In some cases he has found it best to quote Mr. Francis Parkman, Mr. Justin Winsor, or the pages of the "Nation," the "Dial," the "American Historical Review," and similar trustworthy sources. With respect to novels and romances, essays and literary interpretations, it does not seem feasible to engage a special corps of reviewers. It may be a good plan to ap-

point judicious editors to give us composite photographs of
what the critics best worth heeding have said in the responsible press.

It is in the preponderant circulation of fiction, and fiction
for the most part of poor quality, that the critics of public
libraries find most warrant for attack. They point to the
fact that many readers of this fiction are comparatively well-
to-do, and are exempted by public taxation from supporting
the subscription library and the bookseller. The difficulty
has been met chiefly in two ways; by curtailing the supply
of mediocre and trashy fiction; by exacting a small fee
on issuing the novels brought for a season to a huge demand
by advertising of a new address and prodigality. Appraisal,
just and thorough, may be expected to render aid more important because radical instead of superficial. In the first
place, the best books of recreation, now overlaid by new and
inferior writing, can be brought into prominence; secondly,
an emphasis, as persuasive as it can be made, ought to be
placed upon the more solid stories of our literature.

" Business," said Bagehot long ago, " is really more agree-
able than pleasure; it interests the whole mind, the aggregate
nature of man more continuously and deeply, but it does
not look as if it did." Let it be our purpose to reveal what
admirable substance underlies appearances not always seduc-
tive to the casual glance. Lowell and Matthew Arnold,
Huxley and John Fiske, Lecky and Goldwin Smith are solid
enough, yet with no lack of wit or humor to relieve their
argument and elucidation.

A New York publisher of wide experience estimates that
the average American family, apart from school purchases,
buys less than two books a year. Newspapers and maga-
zines form the staple of the popular literary diet. What

fills the newspapers is mainly news; their other departments of information are often extensive and admirable, but within the limits of the hastily penned paragraph or column they cannot rise to the completeness and quality of a book carefully written and faithfully revised.

The plain fact is, and it behooves us to reckon with it, the average man, to whom we bear our credentials as missionaries, looks upon a book as having something biblical about it. To sit down deliberately and surrender himself to its chapters is a task he waves away with strangely mingled awe and dislike. So he misses the consecutive instruction, as delightful as profitable to an educated taste, which authors, publishers and librarians are ready and even anxious to impart.

We hear a good deal in these days about the need of recreation, and not a word more than is true, but let us remember that the best recreation may consist in a simple change of work. Behold the arduous toil of the city lawyer, or banker, as on a holiday tour he climbs a peak of the Alps or the Adirondacks, or wades the chilly streams of Scotland or Canada, a salmon-rod in his hands. Why does he undergo fatigues so severe? Partly because they are freely chosen, partly because they are fatigues of an unwonted and therefore refreshing kind.

So in the field before us to-day. Truth is not only stranger than fiction, it is more fascinating when once its charms are recognized and entertained. Our public schools throughout the land prove that a true story of exploration, of invention or discovery, of heroism or adventure, has only to be well told to rivet a boy's attention as firmly as ever did " Robinson Crusoe " or " Treasure Island." When readers take up from instinctive appetite, or wise incitement, the best books about flowers or birds, minerals or trees, an art, a science, a research, they come to joys in new knowledge, in judgments informed and corrected, unknown to the tipplers and topers whose staple is the novel, good, bad, and indifferent. And why, if we can help it, should public money ever be spent for aught but the public good?

With a new sense of what is implied in the trusteeship of literature, if we endeavor in the future to ally ourselves with the worthiest critics of books, we must bid good-bye to the temporary expedients which have cramped and burdened our initial labors. The work of the appraisal of literature requires a home, a Central Bureau, with a permanent and adequately paid staff of editors and assistants. The training of such a staff has already begun; in addition to the experience acquired by those enlisted in our present bibliographical tasks, instruction is now given in advanced bibliography at the New York State Library School at Albany, and doubtless also at other library schools. And at the Central Bureau, which we are bold enough to figure to ourselves, much more should be done than to bring books to the balances.

At such a home, in New York, Washington, or elsewhere, every other task should proceed which aims at furthering the good that literature can do all the people. There might be conducted the coöperative cataloguing now fast taking form; there should be extended the series of useful tracts begun by that of Dr. G. E. Wire on "How to Start a Library," by Mr. F. A. Hutchins on "Travelling Libraries." At such a centre should be exhibited everything to inform the founder of a public library; everything to direct the legislator who would create a Library Commission on the soundest lines, or recast library laws in the light of national